Mapping Diaspora

PATRICIA DE SANTANA PINHO

Mapping Diaspora

African American Roots Tourism in Brazil

The University of North Carolina Press *Chapel Hill*

© 2018 The University of North Carolina Press
All rights reserved
Set in Arno by Westchester Publishing Services
Manufactured in the United States of America

The University of North Carolina Press has been a member of the
Green Press Initiative since 2003.

Library of Congress Cataloging-in-Publication Data
Names: Pinho, Patricia de Santana, author.
Title: Mapping diaspora : African American roots tourism in Brazil / Patricia de Santana Pinho.
Other titles: African American roots tourism in Brazil
Description: Chapel Hill : University of North Carolina Press, [2018] | Includes bibliographical
    references and index.
Identifiers: LCCN 2018016247 | ISBN 9781469645315 (cloth : alk. paper) |
    ISBN 9781469645322 (pbk : alk. paper) | ISBN 9781469645339 (ebook)
Subjects: LCSH: African diaspora. | Blacks—Brazil. | Tourism—Brazil. | African Americans—
    Brazil.
Classification: LCC F2659.N4 P55 2018 | DDC 305.896/081—dc23
    LC record available at https://lccn.loc.gov/2018016247

Cover photograph used by permission of the United States Virgin Islands Department of
Tourism (http://visitusvi.com).

An earlier, shorter version of chapter 2 was published as "'Bahia Is a Closer Africa': Brazilian
Slavery and Heritage in African American Roots Tourism," in *African Heritage and Memories of
Slavery in Brazil and the South Atlantic World*, edited by Ana Lucia Araujo (Amherst, NY:
Cambria Press, 2015), 253–84.

Para Gilson e Nanda,

   com quem navego nas águas mornas do amor

Contents

Figures

Acknowledgments

This book is the result of a very long journey, and I am deeply grateful to the many people that supported me along the way. First and foremost, I am thankful to Gilson for his love, patience, generosity, and unwavering companheirismo, and to our beloved daughter Fernanda for coloring our lives with her beauty, dance, astuteness, and a witty sense of humor that always keeps us smiling. Thanks to my loving parents and eternal teachers, Bernadette e Fernando, whose joviality and ability to adapt never cease to amaze me, and to my siblings, Fernandinho, Dido e Mari, for their love and friendship.

I am deeply grateful to the many tourists and travel agents who so graciously allowed me to partake in the intimate moments of their trips, shared so much of their knowledge and insights, and from whom I learned so much over the years. Among them all, my deepest gratitude goes to the lovely Marlene Melton for her warmth and trust. Thanks to all the cultural producers, political activists, tour guides, and tourism professionals who took the time to talk to me. I offer my profound gratitude to all the people who allowed me to interview them. The content of our conversations is what constitutes the soul of this book. My research in Bahia was made possible, above all, by the steadfast support and generosity of Antonio Moraes Ribeiro. Obrigada, Moraes, for opening so many doors into the past and the present. Thanks also to Manoel Passos (Manuca) for his friendly support. I am grateful to the Sisters of the Good Death, without whom Cachoeira simply would not be Cachoeira.

Several great colleagues invited me to present my research in their institutions over the years, and I would like to thank each one of them: Julio Corbea Calzado, Ana Paula Hofling, Nina Banks, John Burdick, Pedro Meira Monteiro, Christopher Dunn, Malcolm McNee, Shirley Tate, Lília Tavolaro, Victoria Langland, Paulina Alberto, Sérgio Costa, and Sean Mitchell.

I am also grateful for events that served as instigating moments of collective critical reflection. Among these gatherings, the panel "Bahia in the Afro-Atlantic World" in the 2014 conference of the Latin American Studies Association in Chicago was truly especial. In addition to the intellectual inspiration of Stefania Capone, Ana Paula Hofling, and Steve Selka, our panel benefited greatly from the generous and thoughtful feedback of our discussant, Paul C. Johnson. Another stimulating gathering that I am grateful to have attended was the conference "Roots/Heritage Tourism in Africa and the African Diaspora: Case Studies for a Comparative Approach," at Florida International University in 2015. Many thanks to Jean Muteba Rahier for putting the conference together and inviting me to contribute. More recently, my participation in the São Paulo Mobilities School, organized by the fabulous Bianca Freire-Medeiros and Thiago Allis in October 2017, was a wonderful opportunity to meet and share my work with inspiring colleagues and graduate students who are researching the various and paradoxical forms of human mobilities, in Brazil and beyond. I am also grateful to many colleagues at the Universidade Federal do Recôncavo, including Luis Claudio Nascimento, Ayrson Heráclito, Osmundo Pinho, Suzana Maia, and Xavier Vatin. May the *golpistas* never put their dirty hands on this remarkable university!

Many thanks to Elaine Maisner at the University of North Carolina Press for believing in my project, providing me with the necessary guidance, and cheering me on at each stage of the transformation of my manuscript into a book. I am happy to have my work published by a press of which I am such a big fan. Big thanks also to my anonymous reviewers for their enthusiastic support and careful feedback. Thank you to *American Legacy* magazine for granting me permission to include some of their images and text in this book, and to Audrey Peterson for making that happen. And thanks to the U.S. Virgin Islands Department of Tourism for allowing me to use the photograph from one of their ads in the cover of this book.

I also appreciate the overall opportunity of carrying out this project. My physical movement back and forth between the United States and Brazil continuously rocked the emotional pendulum between my Brazilian self and my American surroundings, providing me with multiple perspectives from where to think and write. I began to sketch the first, and still faint, traces of this project while I was a postdoc at Yale University and benefited from the wisdom and warmth of Vron Ware and Paul Gilroy. The sketch gained bolder lines during my stay at the State University of New York, in Albany, where I had cherished and like-minded colleagues. Although I do not miss Albany winters one bit, I have fond memories of my colleagues and graduate students in the Department of Latin American, Caribbean, and U.S. Latino Studies. A heartfelt thanks to Pedro Cabán for sustaining this special place that allows faculty and students to flourish, and to our super librarian Jesus Alonso-Regalado for his constant support. A big shout-out to my dear Lacsies Caitlin Janiszewski, Luis Paredes, Gabe Sanchez, and Cory Fischer-Hoffman for keeping me on my toes and lovingly teaching me how to be a better teacher. At SUNY Albany, I was awarded small but very helpful grants from United University Professions

(UUP), a resilient union of which I was very proud to be a member. The UUP Individual Development Awards supported several of my research trips to Brazil.

I could not have found a better home for my personal and professional aspirations than the Department of Latin American and Latino Studies at the University of California, Santa Cruz, where I am surrounded by wonderful, inspiring, and committed colleagues. Many thanks to Fernando Leiva, Gabriela Arredondo, Sylvanna Falcón, Cat Ramirez, and Alessandra Álvares for all their support, and to Pat Zavella for reading and commenting on one of my chapters. Having been born and raised in a southern Atlantic coastal city, I never thought I would find myself living and loving in a northern Pacific beach town, although, deep in my heart, I always hoped that Iemanjá and Oxum would bring me back to the shore. And not only that; I get to share this stunning beauty with the most delightful fellow travelers in the journey of life: Gilson, meu companheiro e melhor amigo, and Nanda, nosso maior presente.

Abbreviations in the Text

ATA	Africa Travel Association
BAHIATURSA	Empresa de Turismo da Bahia/State of Bahia's tourism board
CAHT	Coordenação do Turismo Étnico Afro/Coordination of African Heritage Tourism
EMBRATUR	Empresa Brasileira de Turismo/Brazilian Tourism Board
FESTAC 77	Second World Black and African Festival of Arts and Culture
INNPD	Iniciativa Negra por Uma Nova Política Sobre Drogas/Black Initiative for a New Policy on Drugs
MNU	Movimento Negro Unificado contra a Discriminação Racial/Unified Black Movement against Racial Discrimination
MTUR	Ministério do Turismo/Ministry of Tourism
PATEAB	Programa de Ação do Turismo Étnico Afro da Bahia/Program of Action of African Heritage Tourism
PT	Partido dos Trabalhadores/Workers' Party
SETUR	Secretaria de Turismo do Estado da Bahia/State of Bahia's Secretariat of Tourism
UNWTO	United Nations World Tourism Organization

Mapping Diaspora

Introduction

The first time I encountered a group of African American tourists in Brazil was in August 1996 when I was attending the Festival of the Sisterhood of the Good Death in the historic town of Cachoeira. Because of their Afrocentric dress styles and hairdos, my initial impression was that I was gazing at African visitors. As someone who was born and raised in a tourist destination, and who had become accustomed to the omnipresence of international (read, white European) tourists, I was immediately struck by those black tourists who, like us, I thought, were also from the Global South. Only after talking to some of those tourists on that evening did I realize, however, that they were not Africans, but black Americans who are attracted to Bahia's abundant African culture. And only after interviewing many other African American tourists over the years did I come to appreciate the diversity of their backgrounds and trajectories. Very few of them, in fact, dress in Afrocentric fashion and, most important, their social positions and political leanings vary as well.

African Americans from all walks of life tread the diaspora in search of their heritage. The yearning to experience African culture firsthand and meet other black communities has motivated women and men, of different age groups, and who live in several regions of the United States to travel overseas. While West Africa continues to stand in for the mythical motherland, thus attracting large numbers of African American tourists, other regions of the black diaspora have also become important destinations for those who seek out their African roots. Undoubtedly no other country outside the African continent has been as significant as Brazil for African Americans craving African heritage and aiming to engage with their diasporic counterparts.

The origins of African American roots tourism in Brazil can be traced back to the late 1970s when groups of black artists, intellectuals, and professionals started traveling specifically to Bahia in search of the commonalities they understood they shared with Afro-Brazilians. Brazil became a roots tourism destination at the same time when African Americans were also traveling to the African continent with the purpose of reconnecting with their roots. Therefore, it is important to analyze the specific meanings of Brazil for African American tourists alongside the meanings attributed to the other countries that they visit, within a framework that I call the "map of Africanness."[1] Although

African Americans travel all over the world, the map of Africanness is meant to account for what the roots tourists interpret as places that enhance their Afro-referenced identity, thus it refers mainly to countries located in the African continent and the African diaspora.

In their search for cultural roots, African American tourists have elected Bahia as the major location to visit within Brazil. The tourists spend most of their time, usually ranging between five and ten days, in the Bahian capital city of Salvador, where they visit capoeira schools, Candomblé temples, and the headquarters of *blocos afro*,[2] amid a busy schedule that also includes plenty of sightseeing, shopping, and dining.[3] The visit to an organization devoted to the social and economic empowerment of Afro-Brazilians is also an important part of the itineraries of the roots tourists. A daylong visit to Cachoeira, located approximately 150 kilometers from Salvador, is usually also included in the program, especially in the month of August when the Sisterhood of the Good Death carries out their annual festival. Founded in 1823, the Sisterhood is composed exclusively of older black women, descendants of slaves, and who are at the same time Catholics and Candomblé practitioners. Like most of the syncretic Afro-Brazilian celebrations, the Festival of the Good Death mixes sacred ceremonies with secular rites, including a communal *samba-de-roda* (a traditional form of dancing samba in a circle) and a generous Afro-Brazilian feast prepared by the Sisters and offered to all visitors. The tourism industry's portrayal of the Sisters as living "samples" of Bahia's African heritage contributes to make the festival a major attraction for African American roots tourists. On a more pragmatic level, the fact that the festival happens in August (to celebrate the ascension of the Virgin Mary to heaven, that is, her "good death"), has also contributed for the festival's inclusion in the itineraries of African American tourists since it coincides with the period of summer vacations in the United States.

The African American search for roots in Brazil confirms contemporary understandings that diasporas are as much about the decentered, lateral connections as they are about the teleology of return to an allegedly exclusive center.[4] One of the most important characteristics of African American roots tourism in Brazil is that it strengthens the connections among diaspora communities that are located beyond the African homeland. In other words, it is a type of roots tour that is carried out via a diasporic "detour." A detour is defined as "a long or roundabout route taken to avoid something or to visit somewhere along the way," but it is also "an alternative route when the usual road is temporarily closed."[5] Because many African American tourists have described Bahia as a "more accessible" or "closer Africa," touring Bahia can mean taking a shorter route to Africa, or at least to Africanness, while bypassing the hassles and hurdles that travel to the motherland can entail. The Bahian detour is thus, simultaneously, a "deviation" because it leads to a "circuitous or indirect route," and a "shortcut" that paradoxically expands, instead of limiting, the paths toward Africanness for blacks in the diaspora.[6] This diaspora detour also signals that "diversion," in the sense of fun and recreation, may also be found along the way, in contrast to the feelings of pain and sorrow that frequently mark African American tours to West Africa.

Central Issues

This book examines African American roots tourism in Brazil in light of three deeply intersected, and equally important underlying issues. The first issue is the construction and transformation of diasporic identities through tourism. I am concerned with how national and racial identities mutually construct and contradict one another, especially in a transnational context where multiple identity boundaries are called into place. African Americans interact with Afro-Brazilians simultaneously as coparticipants in the African diaspora and as citizens of the United States. How does international travel remind African Americans that they are members of a superpower? How does being abroad trigger their thoughts and feelings about their own Americanness? How do Afro-Brazilians, in turn, perceive and respond to the presence of African American visitors? In addition to examining how nation and class affect the construction of transnational black identities, I also pay close attention to the gendered dimensions of travel, especially in light of the fact that there are many more women than men carrying out roots tourism in Brazil. Why do female tourists feel that it is their job to "recover" African heritage so as to enhance the black identity of their communities in the United States? I am interested in how individual and collective identities participate in wider, global circuits of power, and how they inform and are informed by asymmetries of gender, race, class, and nation.

The second major issue examined in this book is transnational black solidarity. I look at roots tourism as a realm of dialogue and interaction between two black communities that are challenging the boundaries of nations to emphasize the commonalities of their racial identities. International tourism has often been described as reviving colonialism when it blurs the line that separates service from servitude, for example when the black hands of the descendants of enslaved Africans wait on, clean up after, and provide bodily pleasures for predominantly white European and North American visitors. But what does it mean when the tourists are themselves the descendants of slaves and face forms of discrimination in their home country that are similar to those confronted by their hosts?[7] How much does a shared black ancestry challenge the colonialist aspects of tourist-host relationships, especially when tourism serves as a springboard for projects of racial solidarity? Aware of their power as U.S. citizens and of the clout of their U.S. dollars, African American roots tourists in Brazil have actively deployed their national identity as well as their purchasing power to benefit Afro-Brazilians. The encounters, and disencounters, promoted by roots tourism allow us to study the intricate ways in which difference and inequality permeate the attempts at constructing sameness.

The third major issue addressed in this book is the geopolitics of the black diaspora, which is the backdrop against which African Americans and Afro-Brazilians meet with, and relate to, one another. After all, the transnational dialogue promoted by roots tourism occurs between two black communities that occupy very different positions of power, as one is located in the Global South and the other in the Global North. The novelty of African American roots tourism in Brazil is that, to some extent, it defies the secondary position occupied by Brazil in the black diaspora, where U.S.-centric conceptions of blackness have been hegemonic. At the same time, roots tourism entails several kinds of asymmetries, including the disparity between those who have access to travel and those who do not; the belief of many African American tourists that they can exchange what they view as their "modernity" for the "traditions" of the local black communities with whom they interact; and the much greater access of African Americans to the means through which Africa and the diaspora are represented. *Mapping Diaspora* thus examines the extent to which African American roots tourism in Brazil represents a departure from the paradigm of tourism as a force that deepens global inequalities, and what challenges it offers to the hierarchies of the black Atlantic world.

Despite tourism's intimate connections with exploitation and inequality, unilateral approaches that propose that tourism is evil, or a mere reenactment of colonialism, or just a new form of imperialism, do not suffice to understand tourism's complexities.[8] This book draws on more nuanced studies that highlight the agency of the marginalized and oppressed actors that participate in international tourism.[9] These studies contend that, despite tourism's inherent asymmetries, there is no single outcome of tourism for all in the world's peripheries. Conceiving of tourism as a form of "soft power," Merrill analyzes the uses of tourism by not only U.S. tourists and corporations in Latin American countries, but also by their "hosts" in order to counter U.S. imperialism and negotiate their national identities.[10] Working with the concept of the "tourism encounter," Babb argues that peripheral nations, and the poorest people within these nations, also set the terms of engagement in these interactions.[11] Little challenges the notion that the impact of tourism is necessarily negative for indigenous communities, arguing that it can, in some situations, empower women and transform gender relations in local communities.[12] Freire-Medeiros shows that many residents of Brazilian touristic favelas are favorable to the favela tours, seizing the enthusiastic gringo gaze as a means to counter the stigmatization of their neighborhoods.[13] Inspired by these studies, this book pays attention to how actors who are differently positioned within local and global power hierarchies engage international tourism as a means to strengthen their identities and empower their communities.

As one of the engines that manufacture and structure relationships between centers and peripheries, international tourism is very important for the analysis of geopolitics.[14] Although the notions of "center" and "periphery" are undergoing significant changes under globalization, they continue to be useful to understand inequality, especially in a world that is increasingly controlled by neoliberal capitalism. A location can function simultaneously as a center and as a periphery, depending on what it is being measured against. As one of the emerging economic powers of the early twenty-first century, alongside India, China, and South Africa, Brazil operates as a center for economically weaker countries in Latin America, the African continent, and elsewhere in the so-called developing world. At the same time, Brazil remains an economic periphery in relation to stronger economic centers located in the Global North. Most important for the concerns of this book, Brazil remains peripheral when it comes to the global dissemination of culture and knowledge.

Theoretical Frameworks and Concepts

Cultural studies, postcolonial theory, and the decolonial school of thought similarly establish that although formal colonialism is no longer a reality in most of the world, power imbalances linger on in economic and ideological spheres. One of the characteristics of the coloniality of power is that, despite the end of colonialism, its logic persists within the current social, racial, and political orders.[15] This means not only that the groups that had been ranked as superior, both within and across nations, during colonialism continue to benefit economically from racial hierarchies; they are also at an advantage from having established control over language and text. After all, the conquest and colonization of America were also the conquest and colonization of existing knowledges.[16] This was not, however, a unidirectional process. As argued by

Stam and Shohat, the 1492 "encounter" generated a hybrid intellectual production that was never exclusively European. Indigenous and black modes of
thought triggered epistemological crises among European thinkers and, later
on, significantly shaped the Enlightenment debates. The earth-shattering
twentieth-century events of World War II, the Jewish Holocaust, and Third
World decolonization struggles, further delegitimized the West as the absolute center of knowledge.[17]

I agree with Stam and Shohat that there are multiple geographies of coloniality, and I share their critique that nation-state framing is essentially flawed
because it overlooks the transnational networks of activism and intellectual
dialogues and the multidirectional traffic of ideas. At the same time, I do not
find it possible to dispense with the concepts of center and periphery. The
transnational traffic of ideas does not happen evenly, but is, instead, for the
most part, subjected to geopolitical discrepancies. Not only are Latin American countries peripheral as a consequence of the colonial legacy, but also
because of the weaker means through which their knowledges currently circulate, that is, *not* in English and *not* benefiting from the dominant channels
of distribution of culture, which remain firmly located in the Global North.

There are, nonetheless, other ways of assessing what transforms a location
into a "center." The study of roots or diaspora tourism allows for an alternative understanding of what constitutes centers and peripheries. Akin to Coles
and Timothy and Leite, I define roots tourists in light of Cohen's concept of
"existential tourists," for whom the centers of their societies of origin are
considered to be devoid of deeper meaning.[18] They thus adhere to an elec-
tive center to which they perceive themselves to be deeply connected,
whether spiritually or culturally. In some cases, these are traditional centers
to which their forebears were attached in the past but became alienated from.
"In this case, the desire for a visit to such a center derives from a desire to find
one's spiritual roots. This visit takes on the quality of a home-coming to a
historical home."[19] Because diasporas are intrinsically multicentered configurations, multiple locations can become spiritual and/or cultural "centers" for
roots tourists. This can be seen in the African American search for roots in
Brazil, which should be analyzed alongside their search for roots in the African continent. In that sense, Bahia is a "center" as much as Elmina, Cape
Coast, and Gorée Island.

In *Mama Africa: Reinventing Blackness in Bahia*, I analyzed the Brazilian state
of Bahia as one of the centers of the black Atlantic.[20] In the late colonial
period, Bahia's capital, Salvador, was already a "world city" in the sense defined
by Quijano, that is, as having the capacity to intervene in the global concen-

tration of power and knowledge production.[21] In the present, Bahia's "aura of Africanness" has been further expanded due to the reinventions of its African-isms by a significant number of black cultural organizations, including *blocos afro*, Candomblé temples, and capoeira schools. Bahia's abundant African cul-ture has attracted an increasing number of African American tourists who spend most of the time of their visit in Salvador, but whose itineraries also nec-essarily include participating in the Festival of the Sisterhood of the Good Death in the historic town of Cachoeira, in Bahia's countryside. The con-temporary reinventions of Africa have contributed to solidify Bahia's reputa-tion as "Africa in the Americas" and, thus, as a "closer Africa" for African Americans.

The mapping of the "spiritual" or "heritage centers" that are structured and sustained by the tourism industry should not, however, take precedence over the more conventional world-system map that highlights the core-periphery asymmetries.[22] Both maps coexist, and it is important to explore to what ex-tent and in which ways they do and do not overlap. One of the indications of the overlapping of these maps is that while African American roots tourists experience places as existential tourists, they are at the same time recreational ones in that they are also seeking entertainment, pleasure, relaxation, and a bit of pampering too.[23] As Cohen acknowledges, any traveler might experience several modes of tourism on a single trip.[24] The African American tourists that are the topic of this book are not "off the beaten path." They patronize, along-side conventional and predominantly white, international tourists, luxurious hotels and high-end restaurants, and engage in similar practices of indulgence, waste of natural resources, and conspicuous consumption while abroad. Di-aspora tourism does not necessarily do away with what has been defined in the literature as the "tourist bubble," where tourists are shielded from the po-tential dangers and harassment of international travel.[25] On the contrary, because most diaspora tourists have enough disposable income to carry out international trips, the tourist bubble is more often than not intrinsic to their travel experience. Thus, the relatively new "heritage centers" that their desires produce continue to function, to a great extent, as the same old economic peripheries of the world.

In my research I encountered a diversity of backgrounds that makes it impossible to draw a clear-cut profile of African American tourists in Brazil. African Americans of different age groups, professions, religious affiliations, sexual orientations, and political inclinations, not to mention idiosyncrasies and individual life histories, travel to Brazil, both solo and in the company of others. It would be erroneous to assert that *all* African American tourists imagine and represent the country in the same way or that they have the same motivations to travel. The focus of this book, however, is on organized tour groups that revolve around cultural heritage. The members of these groups share many similarities, including: age, as most of them are in their sixties and seventies, and many are retired; class, since most of them are college-educated, with sufficient disposable income to undertake international travel; and gender, given that most of the tour groups are composed of women. Another major similarity that these tourists share is, obviously, race as they travel in groups formed entirely or almost exclusively of black individuals. Many of the members of these tour groups are also affiliated with black institutions, such as black churches, black professional organizations, black businesses, and black cultural groups.

Another major commonality shared by the tourists that I researched is religious affiliation, as most of them are members of Protestant denominations. However, the extent to which their religion shapes their behavior varies considerably from one person to another, thus differentiating their individual experiences in Brazil. Although a very small number of Protestant or Pentecostal tourists refuse to have any direct interaction with Candomblé because they see this as going against their religious beliefs, most of the tourists consider this Afro-Brazilian religion to be a very important source of "preserved Africanness." In one way or another, Candomblé functions as a central cultural reference for all the tours, and most of the itineraries include a visit to a temple and sometimes a meeting with a Candomblé priest or priestess for shell readings. It may not be necessary to point out that, regardless of one's choosing to establish greater or lesser engagement with Candomblé, the influence of this religion is undeniably present in Afro-Bahian food, music, dance, and arts, and it is thus experienced directly or indirectly by the tourists. It is safe to argue that those tourists who are more open to engage with Candomblé express significantly greater satisfaction with the trip as they feel that their goal of experiencing African heritage in Brazil was fulfilled. It is also important to note that the members of the tour groups that I studied frequently rubbed shoulders with a more specific kind of roots-seekers: U.S. Yoruba revivalists that worship Orishas and who visit Brazil with the explicit intention of connecting with the religion of Candomblé. Because of the specifically religious purpose of their journeys, these groups are beyond the scope of my research.[26]

Another characteristic that is shared by most of the tourists I observed was their little to no engagement with sex tourism. Although once in a while I heard tourists commenting on the sexual attractiveness of specific Brazilian individuals (for example, a seminaked "typical mulata" that was posing for pictures with tourists in Rio de Janeiro's Sambadrome), I never witnessed any romantic or sexual engagement between the members of the groups that I accompanied and the people they met in Brazil. At the same time, it is clear that "heritage tourists" may also be or become "sexual tourists." In some cases, cultural tourists can morph into "incidental sex tourists," as Marcelo Ferreira noted in his master's thesis on African Americans touring Rio de Janeiro for "cultural purposes."[27] In other cases, the intersections between sex and African heritage are apparent from the get-go and inform the practice that Mitchell describes as "sexual pilgrimages" where, for example, African American gay men seek out black spirituality while nostalgically "tapping into alternative, imagined racialized histories in the diaspora."[28]

The African American roots tourists focused on here represent a very specific kind of tourist not just because they are searching for their heritage but because, in contrast to other types of tourists, who are usually interested in the exoticism of the "Other," they crisscross the Atlantic hoping to find the "same," represented by their "black brothers and sisters." In this sense, African American roots tourism allows for the reconnection of the fragmented transnational African affiliation. Thus, I prefer to call this phenomenon "roots" or "heritage tourism" rather than "ethnic tourism," even though this term could also be applied to describe this phenomenon.[29] Roots tourism is certainly a kind of ethnic tourism because it sets in motion people who are searching for elements that can be used to construct their ethnic identities. However, the concept of "ethnic tourism" has been predominantly employed in the literature to describe the process by which people from core countries travel to peripheral areas of the globe to observe the "exotic cultures" of the Other, sometimes even aiming to "go native."[30] Conversely, in roots tourism, the primary goal is to find the same, even though this "same" is usually not quite as similar as many tourists expect. In fact, the frustrations of the roots tourists in Brazil are important outcomes of their visits, even if they do not significantly disrupt the tourists' overall satisfaction with the "Africanness" of the people and the "authenticity" of the culture they encounter.

Another reason why I prefer to call this phenomenon roots tourism is because of the significance of *roots* in African American popular culture in general and in African American tourism specifically. Among the most important motivations for African Americans to visit Brazil is the idea that it is a place where they can have access to their roots, both *cultural roots*—the abundant "African traditions" that many African Americans believe they have lost—and *familial roots*—represented by the diasporic family that was dispersed by slavery and colonialism. Because the understanding of *family* refers here to the larger black diaspora, and not to direct relatives or ancestors, my use of the concept "roots tourism" is different from what some researchers define as "genealogy" or "family history tourism," a type of travel where one searches for traces of one's direct ancestors with the purpose of feeding one's "biographical and narrative construction of self-identity."[31] Finding this information has become ever more important in a world that is becoming increasingly globalized and marked by individual and group mobility.

By contrast, my concept of roots tourism is more closely associated to the use made by Naomi Leite to describe the type of heritage tourism carried out by descendants of the Iberian medieval Jewish population.[32] Employing "roots tourism" and "diaspora tourism" interchangeably, Leite highlights the commonalities of diverse roots tourism experiences. Whether the focus is on African Americans looking for their roots in Ghana, Jewish tourists searching for Medieval Portugal, or Scottish Americans seeking out the birthplace of their ancestors in the Scottish Highlands, all these disparate experiences have in common "the interplay of prior knowledge of the destination (what some call 'diasporic imaginings'), memory, and physical experience of place in the construction and performance of identities that are rooted in the past."[33]

In my view, roots tourism and family history tourism fit under the larger umbrella of "diaspora tourism," a concept that also includes other related tourist practices such as the visits carried out by those who live in the homeland to the places where their original community members have been scattered (for example, Irish tourists visiting Boston or New York City to partake in the celebrations of St. Patrick's day), and the visits of diaspora members to extended communities beyond the homeland (for example, Chinese Americans visiting Chinese communities in Canada), a practice that frequently overlaps with VFR (visiting friends and relatives)-type tourism.[34] African American tourists in Brazil share with the latter the fact that they are searching for their roots not only in the (African) homeland, but also in other sites of the diaspora.

While other trends of tourism, especially ecotourism and sex tourism, have received substantial attention from scholars, roots tourism has only recently begun to be analyzed. Likewise, research on African American tourists is still insufficient, even though in the United States alone tourism carried out by African Americans increased by 16 percent between 2002 and 2004 while the industry itself grew only 1 percent.[35] Coles and Timothy argue that tourism researchers have paid insufficient attention to diaspora experiences of tourism, frequently overlooking the spaces occupied by diaspora tourists and the production of tourism for and by diasporic communities: "Tourism contributes to the construction of contemporary narratives of diasporic heritages which articulate to members of diasporas . . . who they are and how they came to be."[36] Defining diaspora tourism as "tourism primarily produced, consumed, and experienced by diasporic communities," these authors plead for greater theoretical linkages between tourism studies and diaspora studies, especially since diasporic identities necessarily entail roots and routes.[37] Undeniably, all forms of tourism necessarily involve routes, but only some specific types revolve around roots, which is why I conceive of the type of tourism analyzed in this book as roots tourism. While fitting under the wider umbrella-concept of diaspora tourism, which in turn fits under the even wider umbrella of heritage tourism—or what Timothy defines as tourism that revolves around a search for a cultural patrimony that is embedded in the past[38]—roots tourism can also share some of the features of dark tourism (or thanatourism), such as when tourists visit the dungeons where slaves were held in the West African coast before their forced departure to the Americas.

In conceptualizing roots tourism, my goal is not to establish a taxonomic categorization, but rather to assess the ways in which this type of tourism converges with and diverges from other types. I agree with Malcolm Crick that we do not need to develop a field of "tourological studies" nor establish a tourism science where the literature on tourism would be synthesized into a coherent framework, especially because tourism does not occur in isolation but is, rather, "an outcome of the intersection of a number of wider phenomena."[39] Differently from Crick, though, who envisions the continuation of a *multi*disciplinary approach to tourism, where different disciplines pursue their own interests and utilize their own distinctive methodologies, I contend that *trans*disciplinary approaches can allow us to more effectively understand the interconnected structures that produce the complexity of tourism and tourist encounters. My theoretical perspective is, therefore, transdisciplinary in that it does not conform to the artificial boundaries imposed by disciplinary work. More than following the *inter*disciplinary precept of combining fully formed theories and/or methods from different disciplines, a transdisciplinary approach freely *selects* and *adapts* disciplinary elements, such as theoretical categories, concepts, research methods, and so on, to better study a topic.

This book draws on and seeks to contribute to the transdisciplinary approaches of cultural studies, postcolonial theory, and the decolonial project as well as the disciplines of anthropology and sociology. My national origin and academic training in Brazil contribute to locate this book within the tenets of Latin American cultural studies, a transdisciplinary critical-epistemic field inserted in a global scenario but historically anchored in Latin American socio-political materiality.[40] This book thus engages, in different degrees, with some of Latin American cultural studies' major cognitive constellations: neo-colonialism, modernity and postmodernity, identities, and alterities and ethnicities.[41] At the same time, my decade and a half long academic trajectory in the United States, where I have always been affiliated to interdisciplinary departments, have also contributed to shape my perspective, especially because it has exposed me to various transdisciplinary frameworks that equally seek to decolonize knowledge.

Since the late 1990s, scholars have begun to apply the deconstructive frameworks of cultural studies and postcolonial theory to study international tourism.[42] Highlighting the discursive aspect of tourism, these studies have identified the existence of continuities between the colonial images of the Other and contemporary tourism representations of postcolonial peoples. These nostalgic images of the past not only linger on, but they are in fact intrinsic to sustaining the asymmetrical encounters promoted by the tourism industry. In line with these studies, my work is also concerned with how tourism discourses, whether textual or visual, inform and are informed by the representations of peoples and places that become dominant overtime.[43]

Over the last decade, tourism studies have benefited from the publication of several edited volumes that have paid close attention to issues of representation, discourse, and power. Most of these books are multidisciplinary, in that they assemble contributors from a wide array of disciplinary trainings but who, for the most part, work within the boundaries of their respective disciplines.[44] Other volumes, however, have adopted a more transdisciplinary approach.[45] It is clear, in any case, that cultural studies' poststructuralist approaches to tourism discourse and identity construction have become a lot more mainstreamed as they have been increasingly incorporated into disciplinary frameworks, especially in anthropology and cultural geography.

The Research

Despite the mainstreaming of its major tenets, cultural studies has frequently been criticized for not paying much attention to the classical questions of methodology and of being detached from more systematic forms of research.[46] Although a lot of the work carried out under the banner of cultural studies, especially in its British and U.S. variants, has relied more on textual approaches than on "direct" forms of data collection, several cultural studies projects have indeed integrated ethnographic research and other qualitative methods.[47] This has been especially the case in Latin American cultural studies, which has always crossed disciplinary boundaries and amalgamated heterogeneous types of methodologies.[48] Furthermore, given that the products of ethnography are, themselves, texts, ethnography should not necessarily be perceived as endowed with greater authority or authenticity than textual methods.[49]

One of the major goals of my research was to examine the discourses of African American tourists on Brazil and, in turn, the discourses of the Afro-Brazilian actors with whom the tourists interact. The research that generated this book thus combined ethnography, a fundamental although not exclusive method of anthropology, with the poststructuralist analytical tools of cultural studies. The deconstructionist analysis focused on the textual and visual sources that inform the African American gaze on Brazil, thus it included the magazines and books that the tourists read, the films they watch, and the tourism promotional material that they flip through before and while visiting the country. The value of the ethnography was not only in that it allowed me to access the opinions of the interviewees as readers and producers of discourse and actors of change. The "thick descriptions" of the "multiplicity of complex conceptual structures" also made possible the coupling of signification to other practices, habits, and routines, including what is not spoken and what is taken for granted.[50] The combination of these methods was very instructive for understanding how meaning is produced and circulated as it allowed me to contrast the textual sources to the information collected in the ethnography.

The ethnographic work was based on four distinct phases of brief yet in-depth field research (in August 2000, 2004, 2011, and 2012), coupled with several, much less discrete, moments of ethnographic interactions.[51] These interspersed research phases developed over a twelve-year period, and they were almost entirely conducted in Brazil, with only a few interviews carried out in the United States. The first distinct phase of field research was carried out in Bahia in 2000, when I was conducting research for my PhD dissertation on the meanings of Africa for Afro-Bahian cultural organizations. While the original goal of my PhD research was to focus exclusively on Afro-Bahian representations of Africanness, which I referred to as "Bahia's search for Africa," I realized that this same cultural production was simultaneously attracting African American tourists, a phenomenon that I discussed as "the diaspora's search for Bahia."[52] Although that ethnography was originally geared toward a different research project, it serves simultaneously as the first phase of field research for this book too. The reasons are not only because I include some of its findings here, but also because it helped me envision and design the subsequent phases of this book's ethnography.

Because African American tourism had emerged as an incidental topic in my previous project, it did not receive in *Mama Africa* the attention that it deserved. I had no doubt of the topic's importance and that it warranted further study. This explains why, in the following phases of my field research (August 2004, 2011, and 2012), I continued to pursue the same themes that had guided the first phase. Hence, despite the irregular and intermittent ethnographic work, the consistency of the themes researched allowed me analyze the transformations as well as what has remained mostly unchanged in the discourse and practice of African American roots tourists throughout this twelve-year period. Each of the four distinct phases of field research consisted of a combination of participant observation and qualitative, semistructured interviews with tourists, tourist guides, U.S.- and Brazil-based travel agents as well as with the Afro-Brazilian leaders, intellectuals, artists, and activists with whom the tourists interact during their stay in Brazil. In each of these phases, I also asked the tourists to fill out a small questionnaire containing six open-ended questions about their overall experience traveling in Bahia/Brazil, regarding their expectations and their interaction with the local people, and asking them to compare Bahia/Brazil to other places visited. This form was not meant to quantify the tourists' responses, but it intended instead to capture the major ideas and dominant tropes that permeate their discourses on Brazil. I have quoted some of the responses to this questionnaire as well as several sections of the interviews throughout the book.

The interviews that I had the opportunity to carry out in between these distinct phases of field research as well as my participant observation in organizations that work directly with African American tourists make up what I referred to earlier as "the not so discrete phases of ethnographic interactions." In 2009 and 2010 I attended some of the events organized by the Coordination of African Heritage Tourism (CAHT), an office established in 2008 by the state government of Bahia to tend to this ever-growing tourism niche.[53] I also interviewed members of Afro-Brazilian organizations that focus on empowering Afro-Brazilian youth, and which are, for this reason, included in the itineraries of African American tourists.

My last round of field research took place in August 2012 when I accompanied a tour group of fourteen African Americans during their seven-day stay in Bahia and three-day stay in Rio de Janeiro. As usual, there were a lot more women than men in the group: twelve women and two men. One of the men was accompanying his wife and mother-in-law, and the other man did not know anyone in the group before the trip. I had already established a connection with the group's leader, who I will refer to as Sylvia Marie, since 2004, when I accompanied her group throughout their entire stay in Bahia. That had been Sylvia's second visit to Brazil, but it was the first time that she was bringing a group of her own. In 2012 Sylvia was visiting Brazil for the tenth time, and this was then the ninth tour group that she was bringing to the country. In order to respect their privacy and protect their anonymity, all of my informants' names have been replaced with pseudonyms.

In both times that I accompanied Sylvia's groups, I carried out roughly the same activities: I participated in all of the group's city tours as well as the short trips to the town of Cachoeira and to neighboring beaches, and I interviewed most of the tour members. I spent all the days of their stay in Bahia with them, sightseeing, chatting, sharing meals, taking pictures, etc. And although, like most ethnographers, I feared that my presence could be perceived as intruding, or at best annoying, I was always quite welcomed by the groups that I accompanied. Not only were most of the tourists warm and gracious with me; many seemed, in fact, eager to speak about their experience of being in Brazil. They also relied on my "Brazilianness" to ask me all kinds of questions, ranging from seeking solutions to their practical needs (for example, "where can I buy hair rollers?"), to profound questionings about Brazil's social and racial inequalities. The anxiety toward what they tended to see as the country's peculiar definitions of blackness and whiteness was a constant in our conversations. And the question about my own racial identity also came up every now and then. I found that the most honest way of responding to that question was to explain that, despite being "mixed," my light skin allows me to enjoy a lot more privilege than my darker-skinned fellow citizens. Of course, the meanings of my phenotype in the United States, combined with my racialization as Latina and, therefore, nonwhite, position me in a much lower status within the U.S. racial hierarchy.

In addition to being a participant-observer, I played several other roles in the groups that I accompanied: I functioned as an academic lecturer, a cultural broker, and an unofficial translator, taking on tasks that ranged from explaining items on a restaurant menu to translating entire talks offered by Afro-Brazilian activists to the tour groups. As a lecturer, I volunteered my academic expertise to the groups because I felt it was a way of compensating the tour leader and members for the time that they so generously offered me. My role as academic lecturer also produced exciting discussions among us, and it allowed me to further interact intellectually with the tourists.[54] Despite accompanying these groups, however, I cannot say that I was a "full participant" in these package tours. Due to economic constraints, I did not fly with the tour groups from the United States, and instead I met with them right after their arrival in Salvador. For the same reason, I was unable to lodge with them in their upscale hotels, staying instead in the homes of relatives. Most important, my own identity, both as a researcher and a Brazilian, also prevented me from being a full participant in these tours.

The last phase of my field research was very important for my project for two major reasons. First, this was the first time that I accompanied a group of tourists to Rio de Janeiro, which allowed me to substantiate specific arguments that I had made previously regarding the different meanings of Bahia vis-à-vis Rio for how African Americans conceive of their African heritage. Second, it confirmed some of the overall arguments regarding the meanings of Brazil in general that I had developed throughout my several years of intermittent field research. For example, I heard from most of the tourists on this trip that they were in Brazil to find their past, and that they were happy to reconnect with their diaspora brothers and sisters, but they were at the same time disappointed to find so much poverty and racial inequality. Thus, the idea that Afro-Brazilians "lag behind" African Americans was still constantly reiterated. It was especially important to be able to confirm the continuity of these tropes in a new political context where Brazil was undergoing significant progressive transformations. It seems that the country's important programs of wealth redistribution and the wide-scale implementation of racial quotas in university admissions, which have bolstered Afro-Brazilian social mobility, have not yet impacted the overall African American reflection on Brazil.

I began this introduction by describing the first time I gazed at the tourists who later became the subjects of this book. My intention is to emphasize that I am aware of the lessons of reflexivity, and that this book pays attention to the ways in which our gazes are constructed and how they, in turn, construct the subjects of our analysis. As Clifford explains, by acknowledging our own presence and its effects in the field, and by bringing this presence into the texts we write, we are trying to break away from the idea of the omnipresent authorial voice. Instead of attempting to function as an "objective" or "neutral" voice, in my text I show the dialogues that I had with my interviewees, including how, at times, we mutually questioned one another's assumptions. Having adopted a dialogical mode of discourse, I have included in this book not only the sections of the interviews that serve to authenticate my arguments, but also the accounts of those, whether tourists or "locals," who dissent from the dominant discourses. The contrasting of different representations and competing discourses is undoubtedly useful in projects that seek to challenge ethnocentrism, and the inclusion of dialogues in ethnographies have the intent of showing that the interviewee is a speaking subject, who argues, disagrees, and probes back.[55]

At the same time, I do not lose sight of the fact that, ultimately, it is the ethnographer who makes the final decisions regarding which sections of which interviews will survive the many cuts made in the process of writing. As Clifford aptly explains, however monological, dialogical, or polyphonic their form, ethnographies are always, necessarily, "hierarchical arrangements of discourses."[56] It is no longer necessary to explain that ethnographies are systematic and exclusive, and that ethnographers do not tell the whole truth.[57] Like any other author, I cannot intend to account for the "full picture," but only for those bits and pieces of information that I had access to. My research and writing are produced from a specific standpoint, which is shaped by my own political position and constrained by the practical, and even physical, limitations imposed onto a project carried out by an individual researcher.

In order to analyze the specificities of roots tourism, it is important to compare it to other forms of tourism, and to focus on tourists' subjectivities, that is, on the specific meanings that touring particular destinations have for individual tourists.[58] The semistructured interviews with the tourists provided the opportunity of capturing these specific meanings, which are, of course, constructed collectively no matter how idiosyncratic they might appear to be. The collective nature of discourses and the shared meanings that they simultaneously draw on and further disseminate call for a combination of research methods. This explains why, in addition to the ethnographic work, my research is also based on the analysis of visual and textual sources—including documentaries, feature films, tourism brochures and itineraries, magazine articles, and websites—that reveal the dominant tropes of African American discourse on Brazil. As argued by Osagie and Buzinde, "the methodological silences that are often associated with some forms of ethnographic research can be avoided when scholars examine cultural artifacts, such as plays, films, and literary texts that are motivated, if not initiated by the colonized themselves."[59] I would add that this becomes even more interesting when the cultural artifacts are produced by groups that have been "internally colonized" or marginalized (in this case, African Americans) to represent other colonized/marginalized groups abroad.

My interpretation of tourism discourse is grounded on critical discourse analysis, which seeks to identify and highlight the power relations and dynamics that are embedded in representations and in the relationships that they inform. As explained by Albers and James, critical discourse analysis is not so much a formalized research method as a series of methodological perspectives.

One of its major assumptions is that symbolization is always produced and used within a specific context and its associated ideological discourses. Thus, among critical discourse analysis' major purposes are the investigation of how representations are produced and which ones become dominant, and the identification of the multiple and competing discourses and their connections to power asymmetries.[60] In the context of tourism, the articulations between "hosts" and "guests" and the role of tourism agents should be at the center of critical discourse analysis.

In order to detect the major tropes within a discourse, it is necessary to read different sources side by side and in relation to one another. Yet the identification of tropes does not mean that all the sources—whether these are brochures, postcards, itineraries, magazine articles, or the direct interviews with African American tourists—make up a coherent or seamless totality. Discourses are sets of beliefs, values, statements, and categories that are generated within particular historical contexts, and within specific structures of power.[61] And, as Mary Renda and others have pointed out, the focus on discourse should not make us blind to materiality: "The categories of meaning that constitute discourses give shape and form to human bodies, the physical environment, and the material resources and tools wielded by human actors."[62] My focus on discourse and representation does not ignore the embodied experience of traveling, or what Bruner calls "the sheer materiality of being there," that is, the physical and emotional sensations felt while moving from site to site.[63] And although I cannot claim to have partaken in the same sensations felt by the tourists, I acknowledge the interconnectedness between their discourses and their embodied travel experience.

Chapters

Because of the importance to this work of African American discourses on Brazil, all of the chapter titles, with the exception of chapter 3, begin with a phrase uttered by an African American visitor that expresses the meanings of the country for them. In chapter 1, "That's My Face: African American Reflections on Brazil," I contextualize African American roots tourism in Brazil both timewise and space-wise, and I do this in light of the different meanings of the term "reflection." On the one hand, reflection stands in for careful thought about a topic, and on the other hand it indicates the likeness that one finds when looking at a mirror. First, I locate the brief history of African American roots tourism within the longer trajectory of the meanings of Brazil for African Americans, spanning from the late nineteenth century—when, inspired by fantastical imaginings of Brazil as a "racial paradise," groups of African Americans attempted to migrate there—to the present-day, as the country has become an important roots tourism destination. This historical contextualization allows me to draw a profile of the roots tourists and to locate the origin of this practice within the U.S. post–civil rights era. Second, I compare representations of Brazil with those of other countries frequently visited by African American roots tourists, placing them within a wider system of meanings that I call the map of Africanness, a map that is both spatial and temporal. *That's My Face/É Minha Cara* is the title of a documentary by African American filmmaker Thomas Allen Harris that describes how his personal longing for a homeland overlaps with a wider African American quest for a place where a black person can feel comfortable and welcomed. Revealingly, Harris shows that it is Bahia's seemingly preserved Africanness and its atmosphere of historicity that offer these qualities.

The temporal character of the map of Africanness is explored in further detail in chapter 2, "The Way We Were: Brazil in the African American Roots Tourist Gaze." Here I analyze how the particular view of Brazil as a place where African Americans can find their past has been produced. The title comes from an article published in *Essence* magazine that describes Bahia as a place where African Americans can find their cultural roots and that defines Afro-Brazilians as living in a presumed African American past.[64] In this chapter I carry out an "archeology"—in the Foucauldian sense of an intellectual excavation of discursive formations—of the dominant African American tourist gaze on Brazil. By contrasting the discourse of the tourists, or the language they used in the interviews, with narratives found in various textual and audiovisual sources, such as documentary films, books, newspaper articles, and tourism promotional materials, I identified three major intersecting tropes that inform and sustain this gaze: the trope of Bahia as a "closer Africa" for African Americans; the trope of the "happy native," or the perception that because Afro-Brazilians supposedly inhabit the African American past, they are imagined to be essentially more culturally fulfilled than African Americans; and the trope of "black evolution," which defines the Africanness of Afro-Brazilians as an earlier stage in the unidirectional path toward a modern form of blackness, one supposedly already reached by African Americans. In this view, Afro-Brazilians enjoy abundant African tradition, but have yet to achieve black modernity, and should therefore look up to African Americans for guidance.

The notion that African Americans should be leaders of the black world has a much longer history and broader geography, and it is not exclusive to roots tourism discourse. The different iterations of the idea of U.S. black leadership, however, were not developed in order to create hierarchies within the African diaspora, but were instead produced in connection to projects of transnational black solidarity in which more advantaged blacks would take on the role of supporting and liberating their less privileged counterparts. In chapter 3, "Black Gringos in Brazil?: Encounters in Sameness, Difference, Solidarity, and Inequality," I examine how roots tourism has allowed for the construction of black racial solidarity between African Americans and Afro-Brazilians. African American tourists have sought to employ their privilege, knowledge, resources, and even the status of their nationality for the benefit of Afro-Brazilians. In addition to the donations in cash and goods that they frequently make during their visits to Afro-Brazilian organizations, African American tourists have also demanded that more Afro-Brazilians benefit from the tourist dollars that they bring to the country. Afro-Brazilian actors, in general, have responded very positively to such practices and projects of solidarity, even if they are also critical of, and ready to challenge, what they view as the tourists' "Americanness." Most important, Afro-Brazilian activists have also set the terms of engagement in these interactions and, rather than being mere beneficiaries, they have become important agents in these efforts for transnational black solidarity, acting as coproducers in the processes of diaspora-making.

Although both male and female tourists reiterated the binary concept of a traditional African past versus a modern black future, men overwhelmingly expressed the idea of a U.S. black leadership of the African diaspora. Indeed, gender identities further complicate the linear and unidirectional tropes of black evolution. The intersectionality of gender is examined throughout the book; however, chapter 4, "We Bring Home the Roots: African American Women Touring the Diaspora and Bearing the Nation," focuses more closely on the differences and similarities between the male and female roots tourists. It is quite striking that the roots tourism industry in Brazil, as well as elsewhere, seems to be "dominated by women but managed by men."[65] Although the overwhelming majority of the African American roots tourists are female, most of the tour leaders and travel agents are male. Contributing to the studies of the gendered dimensions of travel, this chapter analyzes gender asymmetries not just in terms of ratio, but mostly in regards to discourse since it examines the ways in which African American male and female tourists differently represent Brazil and Afro-Brazilians, as well as how they understand their own roles as members of the African diaspora. Most of the women I interviewed expressed altruistic reasons, besides personal ones, for their roots trips to Brazil. They consider traveling in search of cultural roots a means of recovering African heritage, which they deem essential for the perpetuation of black identities in the United States. I thus argue that there is an expectation that women, at least among a certain generation, play the role of "cultural bearers," where they feel responsible for nourishing the cultural elements of their ethnic group. African American female tourists offered numerous variations of the phrase "We bring home the roots" when explaining the significance of their travels to Brazil and to the African continent. Most of the male tourists, on the other hand, tended to position themselves as well as the United States as occupying a leadership role for the African diaspora at large.

One of the most important aspects analyzed in the studies of diaspora tourism is the role of local governments in attracting roots tourists. Governments of countries as different as China, India, Ghana, Benin, Syria, and Lebanon have actively sought to promote varied forms of roots tourism in order to attract members of their respective diasporas.[66] By contrast, African American roots tourism in Brazil is marked by the almost complete inaction of the government, at both the state and federal levels. This type of tourism was initiated and continues to develop largely as the result of tourist demand, and with very little participation on the part of the state. In chapter 5, "The Awakening Giant: The State's Belated Acknowledgment of Roots Tourism," I look at the response of the Bahian state government to African American tourism, examining how the inertia that dominated since the late 1970s was recently replaced by a more proactive, although still inadequate, position. In 2008, the state tourism board, Bahiatursa, founded the CAHT to cater specifically to the African American roots tourism niche. I am borrowing the phrase "The awakening giant" from an article published in *Ebony* magazine in the late 1990s which discussed the supposedly belated political mobilization of Afro-Brazilians, and depicted the country as finally "awakening to color and identity after a centuries-long sleep."[67] More than a mere reflection of the postmodern proliferation of niches produced by consumer demand, the founding of this office reveals a legitimate, and in fact long overdue, concern on the part of the state with the need to respond specifically to African American roots tourists. I analyze this shift in light of the significant, if insufficient, discursive and practical transformations that occurred in Brazil regarding race and racial equality from 2003 to 2016. This period was marked by the implementation of affirmative action policies and by the two consecutive terms of the left-leaning Workers' Party (PT) in the state government of Bahia and its three consecutive terms in the presidency of the country.[68]

Mapping Diaspora concludes by reflecting on the importance of studying tourism, a form of travel sparked by desire and leisure, in a world where human mobility increasingly takes the shape of forced migration driven by hunger, war, environmental catastrophes, and foreign invasion. As Sheller contends, all kinds of human mobilities are, to a smaller or greater extent, unevenly interconnected. Because of its important geopolitical role, tourism intersects closely with questions of national sovereignty, territoriality, and security, and "is built upon military legacies, colonial histories, and new forms of 'securitization' that have either displaced people in the past or continue to do so today." This is painfully materialized, at its worst, when "tourist islands" become places of refugee landing.[69]

In the Epilogue, I point to two new trends that are developing in the realm of black diaspora travel, assessing whether they may contribute to either destabilize or further strengthen the importance of Brazil as a destination for African Americans. The first trend revolves around a recent increase of African American roots tourism to Cuba, following Barack Obama's and Raul Castro's rapprochement efforts to "thaw" U.S.-Cuban relations. The second type of diaspora travel that seems to be rising slowly but surely is the one carried out by members of black activist organizations that fight racist police profiling and brutality, among which is the Black Lives Matter movement.

The importance of studying human mobility goes beyond its economic magnitude, which should be understood in connection to its equally important qualitative aspects.[70] Because it plays such a powerful role in representing places, peoples, and pasts, tourism constitutes the very world that a region becomes, many times even contributing to the unfolding of concrete material processes.[71] Furthermore, because it may allow agency to be more widely distributed, tourism has also increasingly become a means for oppressed communities to reinvent themselves and construct projects of solidarity across national boundaries. The study of international tourism can therefore pave the way for the understanding of how racial minorities and historically subordinated groups have challenged dominant structures of power.

CHAPTER ONE

That's My Face

African American Reflections on Brazil

People don't realize that the largest number of people of African descent are
here in Brazil. And I think that word needs to get around because it strengthens
our own self-images. We are everywhere, and, hey, more of us are in Brazil than
anywhere, even in America or the Caribbean, and that should have some
strengthening power.

—Sylvia Marie, African American tourism agent, Salvador, August 2012

"Tem certeza que tu é gringo?" (Are you sure you are a gringo?) asks a sweet,
childish voice while the camera zooms in on the smiley faces of little black kids
standing on a sunny beach. This is how African American filmmaker Thomas
Allen Harris portrays the Afro-Brazilian response to his presence in Bahia,
during his visit in 1996. His dark complexion appears to establish an immediate
connection with the black people he encounters way south of the U.S. border.
Fittingly titled *That's My Face/É Minha Cara*, Harris's documentary demonstrates how his personal longing for a black homeland overlaps with a collective
desire for a place where African Americans can feel accepted and see themselves reflected. At the end of the film, the viewer is brought back to that
opening scene, only this time the children no longer question Harris's foreignness, asserting instead his belongingness to Bahia by emphasizing their mutual resemblance: "Ele parece que é baiano!" (He looks like he's baiano!) "Ele
parece comigo!" (He looks like me!).

The construction of Brazil as a potential home place for African Americans
can be traced back to the late nineteenth century when, inspired by the myth
of the Brazilian "racial paradise," several U.S. blacks attempted to migrate to
the country. Although the idea of permanent relocation has since been replaced
with short-term visitation, Brazil continues to hold a special place within
African American representations of the African diaspora. In this chapter, I
contextualize African American roots tourism in Brazil both time-wise and
space-wise. First, I locate the brief trajectory of this type of tourism within the
longer history of the shifting meanings of Brazil in the African American imaginary. This historical contextualization then allows me to draw a profile of the
roots tourists. Because African American roots tourism in Brazil emerged in

the aftermath of the civil rights movement, most roots tourists belong to roughly the same generation and share many of the ideas and ideals of this period. Second, I situate Brazil within what I have called the map of African-ness, or the group of countries visited by roots tourists with the goal of enhancing their cultural identities.[1] I further expand this concept not only by examining the meanings of a greater number of countries contained in the map, but also by explaining the map of Africanness' temporal character.

Whether analyzing African American roots tourism in Brazil through the lens of time or space, or the intersection of both, I examine African American representations of Brazil in light of the multiple meanings of the term "reflection," which includes the careful thought about a topic as well as the resemblance that one finds when looking at a mirror. In roots tourism discourse, the Brazilian mirror reflects the African American face, but in an inverted way: it shows what African Americans and Afro-Brazilians supposedly possess and lack, and that which they could find in one another if absolute sameness were ever to be attained.

Brazil in the African American Imaginary

Black communities in the Americas have frequently imagined one another. The curiosity surrounding how other descendants of enslaved Africans made a life for themselves motivated many members of these communities to seek each other out. Wondering then led to wandering, as in the famous words of Langston Hughes.[2] Since the mid-nineteenth century, and favored by the geopolitical position of the United States, African Americans have been able to carry out the majority of these journeys among the "lateral points" of the diaspora. Allowing them to contrast their own life to that of their diasporic counterparts, these trips often resulted in a good amount of not just comparison but also idealization.

The African American idealization of potential homelands located elsewhere certainly shifted from one historical period to the next as, to a great extent, it reflected what was deemed lacking in the lives of black people in the different conjunctures of the United States. At the same time, it was by traveling abroad that many African Americans became aware of their status as U.S. citizens, which, although not fully realized at home, certainly brought them prestige in foreign lands. In an article published in 1920, for instance, African American physician L. H. Stinton, who had visited Brazil with a group of sixteen African Americans to explore the possibilities of relocation to the country, enthusiastically commented that they were perceived locally as "American from the North" and not once were they referred to as "black." He stated that Brazil would be an ideal place for U.S. blacks to migrate to because, in addition to being a land of opportunities, the Brazilian elite desired their presence: "They look upon the North American Negro as being far advanced in civilization and intelligence; hence they believe that his citizenship would be an asset to their country."[3]

Guridy analyzes how a similar process took place in the Caribbean. Interested in seeing how black people lived in other nations, African Americans, throughout the first half of the twentieth century, traveled to Cuba and Haiti where, due to the U.S. imperial order, passports were not required from U.S. citizens. Challenging the dominant idea that Cuba, during the 1940s and 1950s, was exclusively a playground for white Americans, Guridy examines the then budding tourism of African Americans to the island. Although they shared with white Americans some of the reasons that made Cuba an attractive destination, such as the weather, the beaches, and the exotic culture, they also had very specific motivations, which included the desire to visit their "own people" abroad, to be in a place where they could escape racial segregation, to see Cuban Negroes in high positions of power, and to partake in the African cultural survivals. "The black excursions of the mid-twentieth century made tourism an inextricable part of diaspora-making long before the emergence of contemporary forms of 'heritage tourism.'"[4] Also looking at the 1940s, Gill explains that the National Association for the Advancement of Colored People (NAACP), under the leadership of Walter White, invested in increasing tourism and economic investment in Haiti. Although White's goal was to increase overall American tourism in Haiti, African Americans were among his greatest sphere of influence, and they were therefore the majority of these tourists.[5]

Reports written by African American travelers to Brazil during that same time period reveal that they were motivated to visit the country for very similar reasons, including the desire to see how black people lived and were treated by the dominant sectors of their respective society. One of the reasons why both Brazil and Cuba then became known as versions of a racial paradise for African American travelers is due in part to how they, informed by the U.S. one-drop rule, mistook mulattoes, several of whom were occupying high social and political positions, for blacks. Their standing as foreigners, when not jarred by incidents of racism, further contributed to the inaccurate notion that these countries were a paradise for black people. The search for African cultural survivals, on the other hand, only began to feature as a motivation for African American travel to Brazil a few decades later. Up until the 1950s, the interest in Afro-Brazilian culture had been mostly restricted to academic circles.[6] In any case, the representations made by African Americans of the different countries where black people live have varied across time, and these representations have been, to a great extent, reflections of how African Americans have perceived their own troubled belongingness to the United States.

These shifting depictions were aptly captured in the important book *African-American Reflections on Brazil's Racial Paradise*, David Hellwig's compilation of the writings of several African American intellectuals, writers, activists, and journalists about their impressions of Brazil throughout the better part of the twentieth century. Because all of these fascinating articles engage, in one way or another, with the myth of Brazil as a "racial paradise," Hellwig sorted them out into three distinct phases: The Myth Affirmed (1900–1940); The Myth Debated (1940–1965); and The Myth Rejected (1965–). Although the goal of the book was more to assemble than to analyze these writings, Hellwig provides short yet invaluable commentaries in the book's overall introduction as well as in the brief presentation to each of the book's three sections. In the general introduction, he explains that the absence of legal segregation in Brazil, contrasted to the Jim Crow laws in the United States, contributed to make Brazil appealing to African Americans. During the first four decades of the twentieth century, Brazil was predominantly portrayed as a working model of race relations and a land of opportunity for qualified black Americans since it supposedly had no color line. Some African American leaders even referred to Afro-Brazilian forms of mobilization, such as that of the Frente Negra Brasileira, as possible models for blacks in the United States.[7]

The myth of the Brazilian racial paradise furthered an already existing emigrationist sentiment among African Americans, which had led many to seek homelands in the African continent or in areas of Latin America and the Caribbean.[8] In many of these cases, the role played by state governments in promoting immigration strengthened the desire among many African Americans to flee racism in the United States and enjoy economic opportunities elsewhere. The emigration of black Americans to Liberia in the nineteenth century is the most quintessential example of these combined processes.[9] During the unification of Haiti, a group of black Americans from the Mother Bethel African Methodist Episcopal Church in Philadelphia, accepting the invitation of the Haitian president Jean Pierre Boyer to relocate to the country, settled in Samaná Bay, in the eastern coast of the island of Hispaniola in 1824.[10]

The desire among many African Americans to migrate to Brazil in the early twentieth century was stimulated by advertisements posted by the Brazilian government in U.S. newspapers. Such representations of Brazil as a land of opportunity, devoid of a color line, were quickly disseminated in announcements produced by African American entrepreneurs and placed in African American newspapers. Unbeknownst to these African American leaders was the fact that, despite Brazil's eagerness to attract immigrants, it was white people who the country wanted to import, in tandem with the then dominant notion of white superiority put forward by scientific racism.[11] However, the Brazilian government was not explicit about its decision to prohibit individuals of the "black race" from entering the country, and preferred instead to promote an image of a racially harmonious Brazil.[12] Thus, despite the difficulty in obtaining visas, the myth of the racial Eldorado was so widespread that many African Americans still attempted to relocate to Brazil. In fact, at least for a while, African Americans desiring to settle in Brazil did not realize that the visa denials were the result of Brazil's racist immigration policies, and some even blamed the racism existing in the United States as the reason for such impediment.

In the following years, several African Americans started to legally challenge the visa denials, gradually calling into question the then dominant image of Brazil as racially harmonious. Throughout the 1940s and into the following two decades, African Americans began to reassess the myth of the Brazilian racial paradise. Their writings during this time echo their doubts about whether Brazil would be a better place for blacks than the United States. This is what Hellwig refers to as the second phase, when the myth of the racial paradise was debated. After World War II, African American reflections on Brazil became increasingly influenced by the emerging civil rights movement in the United States, which undermined Jim Crow and fostered racial consciousness among U.S. blacks. A short article published in the very first issue of *Ebony* magazine in 1945, titled "The Truth about Brazil," conveys the perplexity and uncertainty of African American writers concerning Brazilian race relations during this time. While stating that there is no color line in Brazil and that social inequality is the result of class difference and not due to color prejudice, the article criticizes the fact that blacks made up the majority of the Brazilian poor. Furthermore, it argued that poor Brazilian Negroes would gladly prefer the discrimination of America "plus good U.S. food," instead of living with no color line but in such dire poverty.[13]

Since the mid-1960s, black nationalism and the black pride movements in the United States consolidated the African American rejection of the myth of Brazil as a racial paradise. As the ideals of Black Power and Black Is Beautiful became more widespread in the United States, Brazil became less appealing. In face of their increasing racial pride, African Americans began to identify a lack of racial consciousness and mobilization on the part of Afro-Brazilians.

The myth of the racial Eldorado was gradually replaced with the image of Brazil as a runaround for black people.[14] This is then the third phase, when the myth of Brazil as a racial paradise is decidedly rejected. At the same time, Brazil continued to hold an important place in African American understandings of the black diaspora and their own position within it. "The lessons of Brazil are many: that black Americans are not alone; that people of African descent in the New World share a common background and face similar challenges; that it is important to affirm one's biological and cultural heritage and resist pressures toward 'whitening'; and, above all, that racial oppression takes many forms."[15]

What Hellwig does not list as a lesson from Brazil, or from Afro-Brazilians, but which is an element that leaps out of the pages of the articles assembled in the third phase of his book, is the importance of maintaining a cultural connection with Africa. Many of the articles in this section, while emphasizing an alleged political superiority of U.S. blacks over Afro-Brazilians, express enthusiasm for the Africanness found in the daily lives of Brazilian blacks. Gloria Calomee, for instance, although very critical of what she sees as a lack of racial consciousness among Afro-Brazilians, highlights their continued cultural linkage with Africa as a lesson for U.S. blacks: "But what our brothers and sisters in the rest of the Americas have is another kind of unity, based on cultural identity, that unbroken link with Africa which we are still struggling to re-connect. There are important lessons to be learned from each other."[16]

Although Hellwig's classification of African American reflections into three distinct time periods may appear too linear, it does include, in my estimation, an attempt to account for the complexity and transformations of African American social thought. The three phases that organize the book are not portrayed as static or absolute, and they are meant, instead, to indicate which ideas became hegemonic at certain points in time. As Hall reminds us, dominant meanings are not forever fixed, but the pattern of "preferred readings" that provide them with legitimacy do last for a specific amount of time, until they are challenged and to some extent replaced.[17]

In my view, African American roots tourism in Brazil does not constitute a possible "fourth phase" of African American reflections on the country. It is, instead, a phenomenon that emerged within the context of what Hellwig identified as the third phase, and it is therefore profoundly marked by the impact of the civil rights movement. The effects of the civil rights movement were economic, political, and cultural, ranging from the expansion of an African American middle class; a sense of political achievement among African Americans—even if this was later diminished by the persistence of racism and racial inequality; and the increased appreciation of African heritage, which led to, among other things, the strengthening of roots tourism to Africa and the diaspora.

It is important to acknowledge, however, that an embryonic African American tourism to Haiti and Cuba had already emerged in the 1930s and to West Africa in the 1950s. Challenging the commonly held notion that African American tours to the African continent only began after the success of Haley's *Roots*, historian Tiffany Gill argues that African American organized tours to West Africa started, in fact, when African American fashion journalist and travel agent Freddye Henderson took her first tour group to Ghana in 1957 to coincide with the country's independence celebration. In 1955, along with her husband Jacob Henderson, Freddye founded Henderson Travel Services, one of the first African American travel agencies.[18] Not coincidentally, Henderson Travel Services was the travel agency that operated in the First New World Festival of the African Diaspora in Brazil in 1978.

Nonetheless, despite these early individual trips and group tours, African American roots tourism only effectively consolidated into an industry throughout the 1980s, flourishing as part of a wider movement where black racial consciousness in the United States became increasingly grounded on the affirmation of cultural heritage.[19] William, an African American tour leader who was in his mid-seventies when I interviewed him in 2000, also attributed the emergence of roots tourism and the wider interest in African heritage among African Americans to the civil rights movement. This retired public relations professional, with a broad, self-taught, knowledge of Africa and the African diaspora, put together a study/travel group that has, since the mid-1980s, combined the pleasure of tourism with the satisfaction of obtaining knowledge about African heritage:

> As the civil rights movement in the United States and the African liberation movement—the anti-colonial movement—spread, there was a heightened awareness of heritage or at least of origin and then a desire to know more about the cultures that existed in our place of origin, and to determine what effects it had in our present lives and in the lives of people around us. So we wanted to go to the roots and begin to discover the impact of the African experience on our existence in the world. And the term diaspora, of course, was revived in the vocabulary, when originally it had applied to the scattering of the Jews. . . . We make these trips as tourists, for pleasure, for enjoyment, to satisfy curiosity, and finally we

decided that the trips could have a little more meaning than just the superficial enjoyment.[20]

Several authors have analyzed the important roles played by societal institutions as well as the state, the media, and the market in promoting and validating ethnic heritage in the post-civil rights United States, for both black and nonblack communities. As Jacobson shows, the roots craze that began in the 1960s and which was further strengthened in the 1970s, was not an exclusive province of Afrocentrism. The institutionalization of ethnic studies in U.S. universities and the growth of immigration history contributed to disseminate a diverse educational heritage curricula and new approaches to the origins and roots of the different ethnic groups that make up the country's population.[21] At the same time that the culture industries promoted the celebration of ethnic heritage, the state played an analogous role by supporting the restoration of tourism sites of historical importance for immigrants such as Ellis Island and the Statue of Liberty. The search for ethnic origins created a huge heritage market where commodities such as books, clothes, artifacts, and memorabilia, are advertised along with transnational trips to "homelands" located elsewhere. Along with other means such as literature, cinema, and TV, tourism has increasingly become a channel for the fulfillment of the desire to reconnect with a past "land of origin." Thus, increasingly, just as American Jews travel to Israel to visit the ancient land of their ancestors, descendants of Irish, Italian, and Scottish immigrants to the Americas travel to their respective homelands in Europe to get in touch with their "roots."

At the same time, if roots tourism is not exclusively an African American practice and has become widespread in the United States, it is even more important for groups whose histories are marked by migration, separation, and discrimination. Alex Haley's influential book *Roots: The Saga of an American Family*, published in 1976, and its broadcast as a popular TV series just a year later, had a profound effect on U.S. discourses regarding cultural origins.[22] Among African Americans, this more culturally grounded definition of ancestry provoked a shift from the horrors and shame of slavery to an emphasis on the prideful cultural roots of the African ancestors.[23] Journeys to specific African countries became increasingly important among the African American middle class, but other locations in the black diaspora were simultaneously crystallizing into roots tourism destinations. Undoubtedly, no other country outside the African continent has become as significant as Brazil for African Americans craving African heritage and aiming to engage with other members of the diaspora.

Origin of African American Roots Tourism in Brazil: The 1978 New World Festival of the African Diaspora

My research identified a dominant narrative concerning the origin of African American roots tourism in Brazil. The account revolves around the initiative of one particular individual who, having travelled solo to Bahia in the mid-1970s, was so blown away by the Africanness he encountered there, that he decided to return in the following years, bringing with him black intellectuals, educators, artists, activists, and others whom he viewed as potential "multipliers," that is, people who could disseminate the idea of Brazil as a destination for African Americans. Together with an employee of Bahiatursa, whom he befriended, this African American entrepreneur organized the First New World Festival of the African Diaspora, which took place in Salvador and Rio de Janeiro on August 7–17, 1978. Throughout the 1980s and ever since, several of the "multipliers" began to bring their own tour groups to Brazil, gradually transforming what had been informal trips into a structured tourism industry revolving around Afro-Bahian cultural traditions.

This narrative was reiterated by several of my key interviewees, including the Bahiatursa employee who coorganized the festival and who has, since then, been an active supporter of African American tourism in Bahia, Lidia Matos, a Brazilian guide who has been actively involved with African American roots tourism since the early 1980s, Lionel Washington, an African American travel agent who is one of the pioneers in the field, and this African American entrepreneur, who I was finally able to track down and interview in October 2014.[24] In addition to confirming virtually the same account of the origin of African American tourism in Brazil, all of these interviews emphasized a set of common themes, including: the need to strengthen the African diaspora by promoting face-to-face encounters among black people from different countries; the importance of creating a greater awareness among African Americans of the Africanness that is available in Brazil; and the greater identification shared among black communities located outside of the African continent in contrast to the relative estrangement that sets apart diasporic blacks from African blacks.

The African American entrepreneur who coorganized the 1978 festival explained that, around that time, he had been working with development projects in Rio de Janeiro where he repeatedly heard of Bahia and its rich African culture. Upon landing in Salvador, Bahia's capital, for the first time in the mid-1970s, he was surprised and somewhat angry upon realizing that all that overwhelmingly African culture had been kept from him for so long. He was critical of what he viewed as the narrow focus on Africa that was going on in the United States at the time, both in the academic and commercial settings. There was a great interest in Africa among African Americans, and one of the outcomes of the revival of African culture was that many African Americans were then visiting the African continent. Although that was all very positive, he thought that not enough attention was being paid to the 500 years of the shared history of the New World African Diaspora: "People were not really giving any value to the New World experience, which was a tremendous experience, and overlooking all the qualities and benefits and gifts of the New World experience. People were looking past the common origin experience: which was the fact of being brought across the Ocean, against their will. Whether you were brought to Brazil, Peru, Venezuela, Colombia, Trinidad, you were brought against your will."[25]

He emphasized that this "common origin experience," which includes the forceful removal from the African homeland and the exploitation of one's free labor as a slave, contributed greatly to establish a stronger identification among diasporic black communities in the Americas than between diasporic blacks and Africans. The sameness shared among Afro-descendants in the diaspora is, in his view, greater even than what is shared among black groups in the African continent. There has been, however, insufficient awareness of this commonality shared by New World blacks.

> When you looked across the New World, from Canada to Argentina, and you looked at people of African descent in this geographic context, they had more in common with one another than if you looked across Africa, where the language differences, the tribal differences, the religious differences, the political differences were much more diverse than what we held in common as people of African descent in the New World. The languages were fewer, there were fewer religions, and the economic and political experiences were basically identical. I always had that as part of my interest: How could I generate more awareness about this particular New World experience?[26]

The First New World Festival of the African Diaspora would be the answer to this question, and it was therefore envisioned to function as a springboard for the much-needed diasporic dialogues and exchanges among black peoples in the Americas. Inspired by FESTAC 77, the Second World Black and African Festival of Arts and Culture, which had taken place in Nigeria the year before, the festival held in Bahia in 1978 would also include a mix of lectures, meetings, tours, arts exhibitions, and dance and music shows, all with the goal of broadening the awareness of Brazil among the African American community in the United States and creating a forum for knowledge exchange.[27] "The objective of the festival was to open channels and dialogues that did not exist between the African American community and the African-Brazilian community. It was to create contacts, channels, awareness, information, between people of African descent in the New World through which there would be ongoing dialogue and activities."[28] The text of the festival's program confirms that the major goal was to focus on the exchanges between these two diasporic communities: "The specific purpose of the Festival in Brasil [sic] is to bring together Afro-American artists and creativity and parallel elements in Brasil [sic] as illustrations of both cultural continuity and divergence from their African sources."[29]

The other coorganizer of the festival, a native of Cachoeira and longtime Bahiatursa employee, described the event in very similar terms, and he underscored the centrality of this festival in stimulating African American tourism in Brazil. For him, one of the reasons why the festival has had such an enduring effect in the promotion of Brazil as a tourism destination for African Americans is because of the "key people" (pessoas chave) that had been invited to participate in 1978 and who have since then become the so-called multipliers of the festival's goals. Many of these intellectuals, educators, and artists have returned to Brazil, bringing their own groups of friends, colleagues, and acquaintances, thus expanding the network of African Americans interested in Brazil.[30]

Evidence of the multiplying effect of the 1978 festival is that, ten years later, one of the festival's participants brought to Bahia 267 members of the National Conference of Artists, a U.S.-based association of black painters, photographers, sculptors, and art historians. Quoted in a newspaper report that described the event, one of the artists in attendance explained that these international events have an important role in disseminating among African Americans a specifically African image of Bahia: "'That put a lot of artists who had been looking at Africa in touch here, and they began to see how much African retention is here,' said Paul Goodnight, a Boston painter. 'They went back to the United States and began spreading that message.'"[31] In 1999, *Essence* magazine editor-in-chief and well-known writer Susan Taylor led a large group of African American women to experience a one-week spiritual retreat in Bahia.[32] Since then, several congresses of African American professional associations have taken place in Brazil, and with a special focus on Bahia, including the Winter Symposium of the Association of Black Cardiologists (December 27, 2005–January 3, 2006), and the International Education Conference of the

National Association of Black Social Workers (August 4–18, 2006), among other conferences.[33]

Lidia Matos, the Brazilian guide who has worked with African American roots tourism since the early 1980s had told me a very similar version of how African American tourism first started in Bahia. She too emphasized the importance of the 1978 festival and the central role played by both this African American pioneer and the Bahiatursa employee. She explained that the former had very thoughtfully handpicked the people who would be participating in the festival as he was interested in bringing "opinion makers" (*formadores de opinião*), that is, people who would disseminate in the United States a greater awareness of the need to connect with Afro-Brazilian culture and people. He was also, she explained, very concerned with supporting the Sisterhood of the Good Death, who were at the time suffering from lack of funding and from the generalized indifference of the local society and government.

This information was also relayed by the Bahiatursa employee, for whom the lack of appreciation for the Sisterhood is an expression both of racial discrimination and of religious prejudice against Candomblé: "Most people in Cachoeira couldn't care less about the Sisters, and this is because of the Sisterhood's connection to Candomblé. Also, the Sisters are poor black women, so the Cachoeiran elite don't pay them much attention."[34] He then explained that the Sisterhood only began to be recognized locally because of the foreign validation that they have attained due to the presence of the African American tourists who see them as a symbol of African culture. All the members of the Sisterhood of the Good Death that I interviewed expressed a similar view of the African American tourists as not only important benefactors but also as displaying for the Sisters a level of esteem not commonly expressed by local Cachoeirans. Commenting on this, one of the Sisters stated, "The Americans have a very high regard for us, but the people from here don't appreciate us because we are daughters of slaves."[35]

The historical records of the First New World Festival of the African Diaspora significantly corroborate the narrative outlined by my key interviewees. On the Brazilian side, the tourism agency in charge of the logistics was KONTIK, which is credited as one of the first local agencies to take tourists to Candomblé ceremonies and to visit predominantly black neighborhoods in Salvador at a time when these tourism practices were still quite unusual. On the American side, the festival was handled by Henderson Travel Services, Inc., a major African American tourism agency based in Atlanta, in partnership with Atlanta University's Center for African and African American Studies. The flyer that promoted the event describes it as following in the footsteps of previous festivals held in the African continent, such as FESTAC 77, where black communities have sought to communicate with one another across national boundaries. Thus, the goal of the event in Bahia is described as similar to previous "Bi-National Festivals which would bring the boundless creativity of Afro-Americans into direct contact with the achievements of their brethren in the various sectors of the western hemisphere."[36]

The festival's flyer reveals the upscale character of the event. Besides listing the costly expenses of the tour, the flyer contains diagrams of the two five-star Othon Hotels which would accommodate the participants respectively in Salvador—described as the "Legendary City . . . with its deep African accents"—and Rio de Janeiro—depicted as "one of the world's most brilliant and beautiful cities."[37] In addition to Othon, the other hotels that hosted the festival attendants were Meridien and Hotel da Bahia. All of these venues were at the time among Salvador's most expensive and luxurious hotels, and they were certainly very little frequented by Afro-Brazilians. The festival's lectures were held in the conference rooms of these hotels, and the musical performances took place in Salvador's most important theater, the Teatro Castro Alves, also a space that was predominantly off-limits for black Brazilian patrons.

The class identity of the festival participants also indicates the high-end atmosphere of the event. In one of the few published reports on the First New World Festival of the African Diaspora, one of the attendees explains that the participants were highly educated black Americans who came from twenty-six different states of the United States, from the East Coast to the West Coast, north to south: "They represented an important segment of the Black American world: librarians, educators—elementary through university—graphic and performing artists, writers, representatives of such diverse fields as medicine, business, travel, public relations, law, mental health, social and community work. The participants' combined years of education easily totaled hundreds of years."[38] An article published in the *Washington Post* confirmed the class identity of the festival attendees: "Despite a hefty price tag that ranged from $1,000 to $1,400 per person for the two-week package tour, response was strong, especially among black academics and professionals."[39] The lecturers included academic superstars such as historians John Henrik Clarke and Richard A. Long. The renowned Afro-Brazilian intellectuals Abdias do Nascimento and Lélia Gonzalez, although originally invited to be speakers in the festival, were ultimately prevented from lecturing due to the censorship of the military dictatorship. Among the performers were dancers and choreographers Clyde Morgan and Marie Brooks and her Children's Dance Theatre.

The touristic and commercial character of the festival did not go unchallenged and were criticized by some of the African American participants as well as by a number of Afro-Brazilian activists. Tate's article, despite celebrating the festival as "a mini-revolutionary and historical event, a coming together of those two largest concentrations of Black folk in the African diaspora," condemns what she deemed as the event's nonblack profiting.[40] Her article also describes the opposition to the festival in Rio de Janeiro by the then recently founded Movimento Negro Unificado contra a Discriminação Racial (MNU). She explains that the MNU activists picketed during a visit of the African Americans to the Museum of Modern Art in Rio, and they circulated an information sheet explaining the reason for their protest and withdrawal of support for the festival. The handout denounced the profit-making and touristic aspects of the festival as foreshadowing any chance of a real exchange among diasporic blacks: "The Festival of Black Culture . . . would deserve our full support if it were a real interchange between Black Brazilians and Americans, giving us the opportunity to enlarge our relations on an international level. . . . But, in fact, what we have seen as the main axis since its idealization was the clear commercial intention based on a program of tourism."[41]

With a lot less detailing but without any probing, the African American coorganizer of the festival explained that some level of tension took place due to the opposition posed by a group of Afro-Brazilian activists. He did not connect this, however, to the touristic or commercial aspects of the festival, but explained it instead as the result of the lack of understanding on the part of these activists of the festival's purpose and significance. He also underscored the powerful symbolic impact of having hundreds of African Americans occupying spaces that were practically off-limits for black people in Brazil. He views this as having been especially important in the context of the military dictatorship, when the myth of racial democracy and the denial of racism were dominant: "At that time in Brazil, people were really saying that there was no type of Apartheid, there was no type of racism. And one of the reasons why it wasn't apparent is because there was no need to worry. When we were in the Meridien Hotel, the Hotel da Bahia, and the Othon Hotel, which were brand new hotels at that time, most of the black community in Brazil had never been in these places, and would never try to go in these places, so there was no need to try to keep them from going to these places 'cause they weren't trying to go to these places anyhow."[42]

But the festival faced resistance from above as well as from below. In a now declassified document that had been produced just two months before the event, Brazil's minister of foreign relations wrote to the president of the republic to inform him of the preparations being made by African American intellectuals and to warn him of the "dangers" that such a festival could pose to Brazil. In the minister's opinion, among the potential problems that could result from the festival were the "simplistic" or "false vision" of the situation of blacks in Brazil, and the use of the term "diaspora," which he described as "not applicable" to the country. Because he saw the festival as representing a threat to Brazil's "racial democracy," the minister determined that the Brazilian tourism boards should not support the event.[43]

The Brazilian government's opposition to the 1978 festival did not remain a secret and it was, in fact, discussed in both the Brazilian and the American media. An article in the *Washington Post*, for instance, exposed the tensions between Embratur and Itamaraty, and the government's concern over the potential consequences of the African American gaze of the Afro-Brazilian racial situation: "Originally, the Black Diaspora Festival was to be supported by Embratur, the Brazilian national tourist authority, and other Brazilian government cultural agencies; but suddenly less than a month before the festival's scheduled August 7 opening, that official blessing vanished. Officials at Embratur were not available for comment on the matter. But Brazilian press reports have attributed the government withdrawal to fears that the festival activities would include seminar discussions in which the Brazilian racial situation would be analyzed and criticized by Brazilian blacks and visiting Americans."[44]

The African American pioneer's analysis of the government's rationale to obstruct the festival is corroborated by the content of Itamaraty's memo and newspaper reports. On the other hand, his take on the Afro-Brazilian activists' resistance to the festival diverges significantly from the content of the statement of the MNU handout quoted in Tate's article. Perhaps even more important is that his reading of the activists' position is in tandem with a representation that seems to be dominant within contemporary African American reflections on Afro-Brazilian political mobilization as being less developed than their own: "It was a perfect storm: What we had on one side, was Itamaraty and the government pressuring the tourism board to back off, and pressuring everybody they could to keep the event from happening.[45] And what we had on the other side was a very young and sputtering and naïve black revolutionary movement beginning in Brazil that didn't understand the full scope of it and was pressuring us from the other side. And so we were in between the Brazilian government trying to stop us and the black revolutionaries trying to make a revolutionary statement in the context of the event that was going on."[46]

Identifying the Roots Tourists

The analysis of the 1978 First New World Festival of the African Diaspora is of critical importance for the study of the contemporary phenomenon of African American roots tourism in Brazil for several reasons. First, and perhaps most obviously, because the festival contributed to deepen the understanding of the African diaspora for African Americans wherein Brazil, located outside the African continent, would become an increasingly appealing destination. Second, the festival promoted a specific image of Brazil as a highly Africanized country due to Bahia's Africanness, an image that drew on previous notions put forward mostly by academics in the 1940s and 1950s, and which continues to inform the African American tourist gaze.[47] Third, the 1978 festival sheds light on the identity of the present-day roots tourists. This does not mean that the roots tourists who visit Brazil today are the same individuals that came in the late 1970s, although many of them did begin to visit Brazil then and have carried out several return trips over the decades. What it does mean is that there is a significant overlap between the goals of the festival and the pursuits of the roots tourists, which points to how deeply the festival contributed to inform the contemporary African American reflections on Brazil.

As explained in this book's introduction, although there is a good amount of diversity among the African American tourists who visit Brazil, the members of the tour groups that revolve around heritage tourism share several characteristics including: their age, which ranges from the late fifties to the late seventies; their gender, as the majority are women; and their middle-class identities, since most of them are college-educated professionals or retirees who can afford to travel abroad approximately once a year. Many tourists also belong to what several of them have defined as "Afrocentric" institutions, including black churches and black professional associations, and several of them are also members of the Africa Travel Association (ATA).[48]

Roots tourism is an important realm where the ideas and ideals of the civil rights movement have been sustained, even if they have been simultaneously mainstreamed and commodified. This explains the roots tourists' search for Africanness and their desire to deepen their links with the broader African diaspora. As a consequence, the members of these tour groups are, fundamentally, *international* tourists. Most of them have visited a large number of Caribbean, African, and European countries, but they have carried out far less tourism trips within the United States, and even far less so (if any) in search of cultural roots.[49] Evidence of this is that several of the tourists I interviewed were members of organizations such as the Travelers Century Club, which gives awards to people who have visited 100 countries, 150 countries, and so on. According to Lidia Matos, a Brazilian tourist guide who has specialized in this niche since the early 1980s, most of the African American tourists have already visited African countries before traveling to Brazil: "Most of them have visited Africa, including Egypt, Senegal, Ghana, Ivory Coast, and other countries on the West Coast."[50] When I asked her if the profile of the tourists had changed over the years, she said that today there is a greater diversity among the tourists, compared to the early 1980s when they were predominantly activists. However, in her opinion, their interest in Brazil's Africanness is still what unites them all.

The Bahiatursa employee who coorganized the 1978 festival depicted the African American tourists in a very similar way. He too emphasized their interest in Afro-Brazilian culture and how this quest for heritage can be traced back to the festival: "They are very interested in the issue of *ancestralidade* [the heritage of the ancestors] and in the religion of Candomblé. They are very impressed by that. But this has a lot to do with the specific people that came first, in the 1970s, and the networks that developed from that." I asked him about the language barrier since the overwhelming majority of the African American tourists do not speak Portuguese, to which he replied: "The atmosphere of the Festival of the Good Death and the whole mysticism are such that language is not even necessary. It all speaks for it itself really."[51]

The quest for Africanness is the most prominent characteristic of the roots tourists, and it is certainly their major motivation to visit Brazil. Although on rare occasions the religious affiliation of a few of the tourists prevented them from engaging with the Africanness of Candomblé, such as not feeling comfortable enough to visit a *terreiro*, most of the tourists that I met were delighted to plunge into all forms of Afro-Brazilian culture that they encountered, regardless of their religion. In fact, it is safe to state that the majority of the roots tourists profess some form of evangelical creed, but this very rarely hindered their encounters with Brazil's Africanness. This is very different from the dominant attitude among Brazilian Pentecostals, as well as many Catholics, who more often than not shun, and sometimes outright demonize, the religion of Candomblé. Perplexed by the openness of the African American Protestants and Pentecostals toward Candomblé, one of the Sisters of the Good Death stated, "Os crentes de lá não discriminam a gente!" (The evangelicals from over there [the United States] don't discriminate against us!).[52]

Lidia Matos's comment on the diversity of the religious affiliations of the tourists with whom she has worked confirms their overall openness to and interest in learning about Candomblé: "I sometimes work with Baptists and other very observing Protestants, but this has never been a problem. They know that Candomblé is more than a religion. It is a style of life, a whole culture."[53] I asked several tourists about whether they felt comfortable engaging with Candomblé, and the responses were overwhelmingly positive. Maryanne's response illustrates well the respect and appreciation that many of the tourists have for Afro-Brazilian religions, even in the rare occasion in which their religious affiliation might prevent them from a closer interaction. A Baptist, and a retired educator in her late sixties, Maryanne explained that although she would feel somewhat uncomfortable eating the Candomblé food or attending a ceremony, she can watch it without practicing it: "I don't judge them, but because I have this other [Christian] knowledge, I don't participate in it. I don't eat the food. I will listen to it, but I will not be in the presence of a priestess when they have a reading, for instance. I respect them and I allow them to respect me."[54]

Perhaps more representative of the dominant attitude toward Candomblé among the African American tourists was John's explanation of the importance of religion for the lives of black people in the diaspora. John, a college professor of social work in his early fifties, and a nondenominational Christian, placed the Africanness of Candomblé at the center of the roots tourist's search for identity abroad:

> We've been disconnected from our heritage. In America we are in an European culture that rejects us as people. And, oh, just that feeling of being connected again, and establishing that sense of identity! So we're in search of an identity, of an African identity. So we've been going to Africa, going to Cuba, going to Bahia, because there is more African survivalism [sic] here in Bahia than in any other part of the Americas. And that's one of the reasons why we come. A lot of the religion is intact, and religion is at the heart of the black experience. Most of us who come over here are Christians, and we see the syncretism of Catholicism and Candomblé, and this gives us an idea that we can maintain both: our Christianity and our African culture. We are not Yoruba practitioners. Most of us just want to know about it, and to know that we have that kind of connection.[55]

During my fieldwork in 2012, I witnessed the tension that emerges once in a while between the few tourists who refrain from visiting Candomblé *terreiros* and the majority of the tourists who yearn for this kind of experience. When I asked one of the members of the tour group that I was accompanying whether he would be participating in the visit to the Candomblé *terreiro*, planned for later that evening, he responded enthusiastically: "Of course I'm coming! This is one of the reasons I'm here!" And then he added, with a wink and a sarcastic tone: "*I* don't have any religious hang-ups." He was alluding to the three elderly sisters, the only three members in a group of fourteen, who would not be attending the ceremony. Perhaps embarrassed to admit that they would not be comfortable engaging with Candomblé, these ladies justified their decision on the basis that they were not willing to pay the extra 40 reais (approximately US$20) each for the visit. The tour guide, who had made all the arrangements for this visit, and who was a member of the *terreiro*, went out of his way to explain that the money was to cover the transportation cost (since this visit was not part of the original itinerary), and not to "purchase a ticket" to the ceremony. In fact, just the scrumptious meal that was generously offered to us all in the *terreiro* certainly cost more than the charged fee.

And speaking of money, another important characteristic shared by the tourists I observed is the practice of conspicuous consumption. Although most of their consumption revolves around Afro-Bahian heritage, which is certainly welcomed by a wide range of local actors, their excessive purchasing does not go unnoticed. On one occasion when I was accompanying a tour group in 2004, we visited an artisan's store in Ribeira, a historical neighborhood of Salvador. The store sold mainly painted tiles, most of which depicted "typical" Afro-Brazilian scenes and icons, such as *baianas* selling *acarajés*, black men playing capoeira, and images of the Orixás. When we arrived at the store, the walls were totally covered with tiles for sale. By the time we left the store, about forty minutes later, the walls were practically bare, as the tourists had bought virtually all the tiles. David, the tour guide that accompanied this group, and who, at the time of our extensive interview, had worked in this tourism niche for fifteen years, highlighted that consumerism was a distinguishing feature of African American tourists. Although he was very careful so as to not oversimplify his description of the tourists, he could not overlook their intense consumption habits:

This is a tourist that really likes to purchase a lot. Although I don't like to generalize, the majority of the African American tourists do buy a lot while they're here. They are completely different from the white European tourists. I spend the whole year bringing European tourists to the same stores and they barely buy anything, while this group that I am guiding now, they always manage to find something to buy everywhere they go. Although we shouldn't generalize, this group in particular is a caricature of this [of the consumerism.] And it's not that they have more money than the other tourists. I would even say that they probably have a bit less money, but they definitely buy more![56]

Another tour guide I interviewed in 2011 made a very similar remark: "The African American tourist is a client that likes to spend money!" When I asked her what kinds of things they buy, she replied, among laughs, "They buy everything! They'll buy whatever you put in front of them: precious stones, dolls, arts and crafts, and jewelry. They like to beautify themselves."[57]

Consumption is a major component of these heritage tours, and all the itineraries that I examined listed time-slots that were set aside specifically for shopping. African-themed paintings, crafts, jewelry, and clothes are among the items most coveted by the African American tourists. A visit to one of Salvador's well-guarded, expensive jewelers is also included in most of the itineraries. Due to security concerns, some of these stores are not open to the general public, and they receive clients by appointment only, to whom they sell jewels and precious stones. Revealingly, the only ad included in the printout of the program of the 1978 First New World Festival of the African Diaspora was by H. Stern, one of Brazil's largest jewelers, and it featured a black female model sporting a matching set of earrings, necklace, bracelet, and ring made of what looks like topaz and silver.

Paulla Ebron also observed the practice of conspicuous consumption among the members of the African American tour group that she accompanied to the Senegambia in 1994. In this case too most of the purchasing revolved around heritage objects and services, ranging from arts, crafts, and fabrics to naming ceremonies, which also involved some kind of money transaction. Critical of the consumerism that permeated the roots trip as well as of the fact that it was sponsored by the McDonald's fast food chain, Ebron argues that a significant and regrettable shift has occurred in the way U.S. blacks engage with other oppressed groups around the world. In her view, the left-oriented internationalism and solidarity thrust of Pan-Africanism has been replaced with consumerism and unsustainable tourism in a context where U.S. minority groups are sponsored by the very corporations that benefit from the neoliberal logic of the late twentieth and early twenty-first century.[58]

Tillet is also critical of the commercial character of African American heritage tourism in West Africa, which she contrasts to the larger international movement for racial freedom that had marked previous movements of black internationalism and Pan-Africanism. Similarly, Hernandez-Reguant argues that symbols that emerged in the revolutionary context of the 1960s as the result of the black power movement were later mainstreamed and commodified, and have ultimately become symbols of middle-class multiculturalism. The African-inspired aesthetics in clothes and hairstyles as well as the African American holiday Kwanzaa are examples of references that have moved from a radical position to become ordinary celebrations of ethnic heritage: "After the civil rights movement and the following decade of Republicanism, black nationalist discourses downplayed Marxist politics and class confrontation in order to appeal to a black professional and entrepreneurial middle class."[59] An example of the commodification of heritage for African American consumption in the specific context of roots tourism in Bahia is that the African American coorganizer of the 1978 festival has been described as the person to have introduced to Afro-Bahians black-themed commodities such as Christmas cards portraying a black Santa Claus and hair products designed to fit the specific needs of black people's hair.[60]

Undeniably, the institutionalization of cultural heritage has been accompanied by, and is to a great extent carried out through, an intense process of commodification, and it must therefore be analyzed in light of the power of contemporary capitalism. At the same time, although these critiques of consumerism are of crucial importance, I agree with Garcia Canclini's observation that "consumption is good for thinking" if we are to understand the interconnectedness between capitalism and identity construction.[61] Although African American roots tourists are undeniably avid consumers, and although roots tourism must be understood as inserted in a market economy, this does not diminish the legitimacy of what these tourists are searching for in order to construct their identities. Furthermore, as the next chapters will show, commodification has coexisted with, instead of having replaced, transnational black solidarity, which figures as a central component of African American roots tourism in Bahia.

Also, if the purchasing power and consumption habits of the majority of the African American tourists are, and in fact should be, critically analyzed by progressive academics, it is at the same time appreciated by the local Afro-Brazilian artists and artisans who benefit from their prioritizing black producers and businesses. The impact of the African American presence in Cachoeira, for example, has certainly contributed to challenge some of the dominant antiblack racist views both because of the attention and valorization it has brought to the Sisterhood of the Good Death and because it has created competition among sectors of the elite business owners in catering to the black tourists. The Bahiatursa employee that coorganized the 1978 festival explained that the African American tourists are perceived locally as a "select clientele" (*público seletivo*), and their presence in Cachoeira as well as their consumption of heritage contribute significantly to the town's overall tourism sector. "Cachoeira gets to be promoted with the visit of the African Americans. The municipal government would never be able to pay for the publicity that is generated with the media, newspapers, TV, etc., that comes here during the Boa Morte Festival."[62]

In interviews with two former tourism secretaries of Cachoeira, I heard the same depiction of African Americans as "first rate" tourists to whom the Festival of the Good Death should cater. In contrast to "local tourists" who supposedly attend the festival with the sole intent of partying and getting drunk, African American tourists are depicted as the true appreciators of Bahian heritage, who spend money on food, lodging, and arts and crafts. One of the consequences of this binary typology of the local vs. foreign tourist is that the date of the festival went from being "movable"—that it, scheduled for the closest weekend to August 15—to becoming "permanent"—that is, scheduled for August 13–15, independently of the days of the week. Circumventing the weekend results in a smaller concentration of "locals" who not only are viewed as potential troublemakers, but who do not have the purchasing power to sustain the heritage businesses that have blossomed as a consequence of the valorization of the festival.

In addition to analyzing the local meanings attributed to the roots tourists, in order to more fully identify them, it is necessary to recognize that Brazil is one among the many countries to where they travel in search of African roots. Because they are constantly seeking out their historical and cultural heritage, roots tourists (African American or otherwise) have also been defined as "existential tourists."[63] For Cohen, who coined the term, existential tourists are not totally centered in their place of residence and feel that there are homes away from home. These are tourists "who adhere simultaneously to two or more heterogeneous 'spiritual' centers, each giving rise to equally authentic, though different, forms of life. Such persons may feel equally at home in two or more 'worlds,' and even enjoy 'existential' experiences from their sojourn at another center or centers, without being alienated from their own."[64] Cohen cites, among the quintessential examples of existential tourists, diaspora Jews visiting Israel, descendants of Europeans in the Americas who visit the "old countries" of their forebears, and black Americans visiting Africa.

For black American existential tourists, there are, however, "centers" that are located beyond the borders of the African continent. Because diasporas are multicentered configurations, diaspora tourism has entailed travel not just to those places that have been historically constructed as homelands. Other locations within diasporas have acquired the status of "centers" for people who are seeking out their historical and cultural roots. Thus, if these "centers" are places that the existential tourists consider as being important for their identities, it is then necessary to also examine the ordinary lives of tourists instead of just the moment in which they are vacationing. Rather than just looking at "people while tourists," it is important to follow MacCannell's suggestion of examining the relationship between the tourists' everyday life and beliefs and their motivations to travel.[65]

African American roots tourists travel in search of elements that can enhance their cultural identities, and which are not always considered to be readily available at home. I argue that the construction of Brazil as a "center" for African American tourists has been motivated by three intersecting desires. The first is a yearning to partake in the African traditions that are often described as having been lost among U.S. blacks, yet preserved by Afro-Brazilians. The second is a longing to be among a black majority without the discomfort, frequently felt when visiting West African countries, caused by the history of local peoples' involvement with the slave trade. Last but not least is the desire to "blend in" with such a black majority, which is usually perceived as more readily attainable in Brazil than in Africa due to the commonalities shared by diasporic blacks. These desires, and the representations that they generate, point to the importance of analyzing the specific meanings of Brazil for African American tourists alongside the meanings attributed to the other countries that they visit, or within the wider system of meanings that I call the map of Africanness.

The Map of Africanness

The search for African roots has stimulated African American tourism to some countries more than to others. Although African Americans travel all over the world, the map of Africanness contains only those countries that the tourists interpret as places that heighten their black, Afro-referenced, identity. One could correctly argue that visiting specific European countries could also be valuable for that effect. The historical importance of Paris in the first half of the twentieth century, for instance, as a point of convergence for African American intellectuals and artists and their Caribbean and African counterparts is widely recognized.[66] The transatlantic histories of cities in Portugal and England could also make them into important tourism destinations for those seeking out their diasporic heritage. However, in the roots tourism discourse, the map of Africanness includes only countries located in the African continent and within a narrowly defined African diaspora.

The map of Africanness is a metaphor; it is not a material representation printed out on paper or readily available on websites. It is a map that has not really been physically drawn. Yet, as an imaginary description, it is widely recognizable among the African American tourists that I have interviewed. Before visiting Brazil, most of these tourists have traveled to several African countries. Sylvia Marie, for example, when I first interviewed her in 2004, had already visited Angola, Benin, Botswana, Cameroon, Cote d'Ivoire, Egypt, Ethiopia, The Gambia, Ghana, Guinea-Conakry, Kenya, Mali, Morocco, Mozambique, Namibia, Nigeria, Senegal, South Africa, Tanzania, Togo, Zambia, Zanzibar, and Uganda, in addition to several European and Caribbean countries. Brazil was the only country she had visited in South America.

Over time, these countries have acquired specific meanings in roots tourism discourses. For example, Egypt is frequently represented as the "place of black pride" since it is understood as proof of the existence of a magnificent black civilization prior to Rome or Greece. West African countries—especially Ghana, Senegal, Benin, and Nigeria—are depicted as the "place of origin," from where the ancestors left to face the horrors of the Middle Passage, and where, with the exception of Nigeria, the dungeons and "doors of no return" feature as the main tourist attractions. South Africa is mostly depicted as the "place of black resistance," where tourists visit the sites that have become symbols of the fight against Apartheid. Brazil has become, in the discourse of these visitors, a "place to find traditions," thus reflecting the desire to "recover" the cultural roots that are believed to have been lost among blacks in the United States. Borrowing from Gilroy's homophony, the map of Africanness is a diagram that traces the *routes* that are followed in search of *roots*.[67]

A statement by William, one of the tour leaders mentioned earlier in the chapter, sums up so well the map of Africanness that it is worth quoting at length:

> As we reached the end of our ability to travel because of the age and health of our members, we decided that we should make one more attempt to find a deeper meaning for ourselves. So I asked the travel agency that we do business with to help me plan a tour of the Motherland and the lands of the diaspora. So when we went to Africa last year we were consciously looking for signs of our heritage, and we went to six or seven countries in West Africa. We presumed that we were all from West Africa since that's where most of the slaves came from. And we visited Benin, which was Dahome and a great slaving area, Togo, Ghana, Cote D'Ivoire, Senegal, and The Gambia. In earlier trips we had been to the Republic of South Africa, Tanzania, Egypt and Ethiopia and even Morocco. So this was sort of a summing up last year. The second part of the effort was to come to Brazil because we understood that there were more black people

in Brazil than in any country other than Nigeria. We understood that most of the blacks who had been forcibly exported from Africa to the New World came to Brazil. So if one wanted to really see what this transplanting had done to those who were transplanted as well as to those who did the transplanting, one had to come to Brazil. And Salvador naturally figured very prominently in this visit to Brazil.[68]

John, the aforementioned professor of social work, also emphasized West Africa, in general, as a place of origin. When I asked him what was the most significant country he had traveled to, he responded that it was not possible to highlight one country over another because it was the broader West African region that had left a mark on him: "West Africa is the most important because most of the African Americans came from West Africa. It is very significant for us to visit a slave fort. So a lot of African Americans visit Senegal—they go to Gorée Island—and they go to Ghana—Elmina and Cape Coast. And just to feel that sense of connection is almost like a mourning process. I cried like a baby. It was very meaningful. And just the return! And our problem in North America is that we can't point to a specific place to say that this is where my people is from, so we embrace all of West Africa. We can't say if we are Yoruba, Asante, etc."[69]

Although West African countries have become marked generically as the "place of origin" of African Americans, there are also, undeniably, important differences in the meanings conferred upon each specific country. Furthermore, the meanings of the different places in the map of Africanness have not always been the same; they have shifted over time as these destinations have competed to attract African American tourists and, more important, as they have struggled over how to represent themselves both nationally and internationally. Although a few pragmatic reasons, such as whether English is one of the official languages spoken in the country, have served to attract African American tourists, the two major, intersecting factors that have contributed to promote nations in West Africa as roots tourism destinations are the level of state engagement in tourism promotion, including support for international events that appeal to diasporic constituents, and the narratives through which these nations have represented their histories vis-à-vis slavery and the slave trade.

Within West Africa, Ghana is undeniably the most important roots tourism destination for African Americans. To a great extent, tourism builds on previous African American representations of the country. W. E. B Du Bois, Richard Wright, Malcolm X, and Maya Angelou produced some of the most well-known portrayals of Ghana as a black homeland for African Americans. Ghana is also the African country that has received the greatest attention from diaspora tourism scholars. Bruner's pioneering article on the divergent meanings of Elmina Castle for African American tourists vis-à-vis Ghanaian social actors has become an important reference in the field of tourism studies. He argues that, while Ghanaians, seeing tourism as a route for development, perceive the castle as embodying several and distinct historical moments, all of which should be represented, African American tourists are interested in how the castle symbolizes their origins, thus their focus is exclusively or mostly on slavery. For these tourists, the castle is above all a slave cemetery and it should therefore represent the history of slavery.[70]

Analyzing Bruner's article on African American roots tourism in Elmina Castle, Naomi Leite makes an important point about the tourists' narrow focus on only one moment of the Castle's history: "For if Elmina is indeed a pilgrimage destination for some African American tourists (and Bruner's description of the emotional and spiritual experiences of these visitors strongly suggests that it is), we must ask not simply *where* the destination lies, but *when*. For these visitors, Elmina Castle is not of interest for its long colonial history, nor is it merely a physical place to be toured. It represents enslavement."[71] Leite's critique confirms the temporal character of the map of Africanness, especially as the narrow temporality of the representation of Elmina Castle ultimately extends itself onto the country of Ghana, more generally, as a roots tourism destination. It also raises the important question of which distinct moments of the past are to be found in each area of the map of Africanness. I argue that the entire map of Africanness is made up of projected pasts, which can be understood as reflections of a U.S.-centered African American identity. Reflection is a useful term to employ in this context because, as Seigel argued elsewhere, it avoids the notions of "accuracy" or "authenticity," since "imperfect understanding is often necessary to the lessons people hope to draw from their contemplations of each other."[72]

In her important book on the contemporary discourses on slavery in Ghana, Bayo Holsey, although departing from what she defines as Bruner's radical dichotomy, makes a similar critique of the narrow focus of the diaspora tourists on Ghana's colonial past. Analyzing the conflation of time and space whereby historical periods are mapped onto places, she sees the projection of the indelible stain of the slave trade onto the African continent as part of a narrative of Western modernity. By arguing that the high visibility of the slave trade in the tourism sphere stands in contrast to its overall invisibility in other arenas of Ghanaian society, Holsey condemns the African American narrative that establishes the slave trade "as the prelude to 'modern' freedom in the West."[73] She contends that the romantic idealization of Ghana by African American tourists reduces the dynamism of a continent filled with ongoing struggles to a mere "prehistory" of blacks in the diaspora. Conversely, the Ghanaian refashioning of this historical discourse demonstrates that Ghana is not merely the homeland of the African diaspora, but it is instead "a site of struggle against contemporary forms of racism in which it too can make use of the figures of both the slave trade and the diaspora."[74]

Favored by the fact that it has the greatest number of forts and castles that held enslaved Africans in anticipation to the Middle Passage, the Ghanaian state has actively employed the images of the slave trade to further its own agenda. Among West African nations, Ghana has been unparalleled in terms of state promotion of tourism generally and diaspora tourism specifically. But the images of Ghana in heritage tourism are not restricted to the horrors of slavery. Ghana promotes itself also through the trope of "redemption" and as the "Gateway to Africa," example of this is that the infamous "Door of No Return" at Cape Coast Castle was renamed "Door of Return" in 1998.[75] Analyzing the complex roles of the Ghanaian state in promoting heritage tourism, Pierre argues that, in its festivals and reenactments, the state predominantly portrays diaspora blacks as the triumphant survivors of the history of slavery.[76]

PANAFEST, a Pan-African arts and culture festival held annually in Cape Coast and Elmina since 1992, has contributed significantly to consolidate the castles into tourism destinations. While important international events geared toward the diaspora have been held in several West African countries since the 1960s, all of which have contributed to attach specific meanings to these countries and to promote them as important destinations for roots tourists, Ghana has taken these events to a whole other level. In July and August 1998, Ghana invited the "dispersed children of Africa" to participate in the first edition of Emancipation Day, where they would "embark on a pilgrimage" of rediscovery of their roots, according to the words contained in the official program of the event. Until then, the date had been celebrated by some Caribbean nations to mark the abolition of slavery in the British colonies.[77]

Yet these international events are not only promoted to market an image of the nation for outsiders, and especially so for African American tourists. These events are also the stage for the refashioning of national and regional identities, and are therefore of great local significance. Emancipation Day was the first time an African nation expressed public concern for the slave trade. One of the high points of the event was the reinternment of the remains of two slaves, one from the United States and one from Jamaica, in Ghanaian soil.[78] The reinternment ceremony was accompanied by a ritual of atonement carried out by chiefs of Oguaa, which complemented Ghana's official apology for the involvement of some chiefs in the slave trade. When asked about the motivation for the atonement ritual, the president of the National House of Chiefs responded that this was done to correspond to the expectation of African Americans.[79] In a similar fashion, Holsey argues that Emancipation Day has marginalized Ghanaian experiences to the detriment of the celebration of the triumph of emancipation and achievements of diaspora blacks. As a consequence, the African diaspora tends to view the African continent less as a site of contemporary struggles and more as "its pre-history, as a remnant of a time that is now dead."[80]

Analyzing the work of two prominent African American photographers, Chester Higgins and Carrie Mae Weems, and the images that they produced of Senegal, Tillet also criticizes the African American projection of a specific U.S. history onto the histories of non-U.S. subjects and places.

> Instead of interacting with present-day Senegal, Higgins and Weems, through their photographs, recreate the sense of displacement and rupture felt by the enslaved Africans and reestablish the feelings of loss and mourning experienced by the heritage tourists. Because of their deliberate emphasis of absence, they represent the House of Slaves as a silent witness to the trauma and the forgotten histories of the millions of Africans forced to travel to the New World. However, the emptiness of the slave fort here also relegates all Gorée Island to the mnemonic domain of the African American heritage tourists who feel compelled to travel to Africa in order to supplant the national amnesia of slavery in the United States and locate alternative ancestral origins.[81]

Also analyzing the discrepancy between African American and African interpretations of festivals and events held in West Africa, Peter Sutherland examined the Vodun Festival that has been carried out in Benin since 1992, when a triumphal arch called "The Door of No Return," built by UNESCO to mark Whydah Beach as a World Heritage Site, was inaugurated. Although interpreted by African American tourists as a ritual of atonement where Africans supposedly ask diaspora blacks for forgiveness for their participation in the slave trade, the festival is, according to Sutherland, an occasion where Vodun priests seek the revalorization of the Vodun religion and the maintenance of their own power in a modern, secular nation where they have been disenfranchised. Sutherland focuses on the agency of the Vodun priests as they deploy diaspora tourism as a resource in their attempt to establish

Whydah (Ouidah) as the center of dissemination of African culture to the Americas.[82]

Forte also sees the Vodun Festival from the point of view of African agency, although her focus is more on the role of the state than on the position of the priests. She argues that the festival marked the beginning of the state of Benin's promotion of heritage tourism. By attracting the descendants of slaves that had been taken from Africa, the festival attempted to establish Benin as a homeland and place of return for diaspora blacks. This then novel support for the tourism industry was part of the country's new developmentalist agenda. Ironically, modernity was to be achieved via the revalorization of the precolonial religion of Vodun. Forte sees the state's employment of Vodun as both a developmentalist strategy and as producing an alternative narrative of slavery. Instead of emphasizing the horrors of the transatlantic slave trade, the festival represented it as a "foundational moment for diasporic cultures."[83] Furthermore, Benin distinguishes itself from other West African destinations because it offers spiritual Vodun journeys. "A trip to Benin means not only learning about the history of slavery but also making it come to life by experiencing the commonality of Vodun. Experiencing the performance of rituals and ceremonies provides tourists with a profound sense of renewal that materializes the bond with the homeland and establishes a spiritual ancestry."[84]

African American tourism to Nigeria has also significantly revolved around religion and spirituality. Many U.S.-based Yoruba revivalists, for example, visit the country in search of what they consider to be the source of the original Yoruba religion.[85] The visits of African Americans who are not members of Yoruba religious congregations, however, are similarly informed by the allure that Yoruba religion and culture have obtained among black communities in the diaspora. Nonetheless, African American tourism to Nigeria today is not as prominent as it used to be in the late 1970s and 1980s, when the nation established itself as the exporter of black and African culture. Predating the use of international festivals as magnets for members of the African diaspora as is evident in the case of Ghana, the Nigerian government carried out FESTAC 77. The First World Festival of Negro Arts had been hosted in Senegal in 1966, under the auspices of Leopold Senghor. Although drawing on the same goals of promoting African unity and attracting members of the diaspora, Nigeria's FESTAC 77 broke from previous discourses of Negritude and Pan-Africanism and promoted above all narratives of black progress and modernity even while grounding this on traditional and precolonial African cultures. According to Apter, Nigerian cultural expressions were used by the petro-state as a mechanism of national development, for whom the festival contributed to homogenize and commercialize national culture. Although the oil boom contributed to position Nigeria as a cultural center in the black Atlantic world during those decades, the country's political instability deterred the development of diaspora tourism.[86]

The Gambia is another West African country that has not been able to establish itself as a roots tourism destination, despite having been made famous by Alex Haley's book *Roots: The Saga of an American Family*. Very few of the tourists I interviewed mentioned The Gambia among the several West African countries they have visited. In his classic work on Niumi, Donald Wright described the process through which the small village of Juffure became famous almost overnight in 1976, following the publication of *Roots*.[87] This is the place where Haley claims to have encountered his kin, the relatives of his ancestor, Kunta Kinte, who had supposedly been captured and taken to the United States as a slave. In addition to demonstrating the flaws of Haley's oral history methods, Wright argues that Gambian government officials capitalized on the opportunity to transform Juffure, and by extent, The Gambia, into a slave site that would become attractive to heritage tourists. After all, he argues, Haley had made known very explicitly what he was looking for. It was not difficult, therefore, to find people who were willing to correspond to his needs and corroborate his story.[88]

However, despite Juffure's fame, it has not consolidated The Gambia into a highly visited roots tourism destination, and this is mostly due to the pragmatic reason of its remote location and difficult access for international tourists. Paulla Ebron described the 8-hour bus trip from Senegal to The Gambia as a grueling experience for the group of African American tourists that she accompanied. The tourists were disappointed also by the poor infrastructure as well as the village's excessive reliance on the images of Haley's *Roots*. The major attractions revolved around the people who claim to be Alex Haley's relatives but whose interactions with the tourists were limited by the language barrier. Jean Rahier's more recent research shows that the difficult access to the potential tourism sites and the overreliance on the iconography of *Roots* continue to function as obstacles for heritage tourism in The Gambia. Rahier argues that the renaming of St. James Island to Kunta Kinte Island and the pictures of the actors of the TV series plastered on the walls are important indicators of the power of mediatized representations and of the centrality of the United States in shaping the meanings of places.[89]

The inclusion of some African countries and the exclusion of others in the itineraries of African American roots tourists do not objectively reflect the history of the enslavement of Africans and their exportation to the Americas. Gorée Island, in Senegal, for instance, played a minor role in the overall transatlantic slave trade, but the governmental promotion of the site, the narrative developed by the curator of the House of Slaves, and the island's addition to the UNESCO's World Heritage List have all contributed to establish its notoriety among international tourists, especially African Americans.[90] Holsey makes a similar point about the discrepancy between Ghana's magnitude as a roots tourism destination and its more limited importance in the broader context of the slave trade. "The grand scale of Ghana's castles coupled with the nation's status as an English-speaking, politically stable West African nation has led to its emergence as a primary imagined homeland among African-Americans, despite the fact that it accounted for only 13 percent of the British slave trade."[91]

On the opposite side of the spectrum is present time Angola, from where the highest numbers of enslaved Africans were exported to the Americas, but which has not been included in the itineraries of roots tourists. The lack of active promotion of Angola's potential slave heritage tourism sites is due, in great part, to the fact that governmental and civil society efforts have focused on the more urgent post-civil war recovery needs.[92] The second most important port of embarkation after Luanda, Angola, was Ouidah in Benin that is estimated to have supplied more than one million enslaved Africans to the Americas between the 1670s and the 1860s. However, as Forte explains, traces of the slave past in Benin were rare and had to be either explicitly marked or built from scratch. Among the locations chosen to be highlighted as diaspora tourism sites are the mass grave areas that were marked by commemorative monuments, the Sacred Forest—a community spiritual site—a sandy route to the Ocean that was then renamed as the Slave Route, and "The Door of No Return," a memorial that was built at the beach to mark the slaves' point of departure.[93]

There is a dearth of scholarship on African American tourism to South Africa, thus not allowing me to discuss in-depth the ways in which the country fits into the map of Africanness. There is no question that South Africa is an important part of the map of Africanness as it is a frequently visited destination by African Americans, including those who seek out their roots in Brazil and West Africa. Several of the tourists that I interviewed in Brazil mentioned how important it was for them to visit South Africa. Based on their comments, it is safe to say that the meanings attributed to South Africa merge the feelings of pride for the anti-Apartheid resistance movement that ultimately toppled the regime with feelings of anger and sorrow for the many people who were killed and tortured by the racial state. One of the most important destinations for African American as well as other tourists in South Africa is Robben Island where Nelson Mandela was imprisoned for twenty-seven years. A visit to the island certainly generates a feeling of "triumph of the human spirit over adversity, suffering and injustice" as advertised by the public organization responsible for managing Robben Island as a World Heritage Site, but it also brings about an intense pain for those who suffered and died at the hands of Apartheid.[94]

The absence of important slave heritage sites as well as the overstatement of less historically significant locations in the itineraries of roots tourists equally reveal that places are culturally constructed and that their representations are not automatic reflections of their histories. The representations of tourism destinations result from several factors, including the actions and projections of different social actors whose narratives do not always converge. The unevenness of the African diaspora, which reflects wider geopolitical asymmetries, contributes to explain why some places, despite being steeped in the entangled histories of the enslavement and dispersal of Africans, such as most Caribbean countries and a number of European cities, have not become roots tourism destinations for African Americans.

The concept of the map of Africanness sheds light on the processes through which places have acquired meanings for African American tourists. Like other signifying systems, the map shows that places are conceived—whether by national governments, foreign funding agencies, local actors, or international tourists—always in connection to one another. The meanings attributed to one spot on the map are produced in relation to the meanings attributed to other places. It is, therefore, a map built by complementariness and opposition. After all, instead of naturally disconnected, spaces have always been hierarchically interconnected.[95] Furthermore, maps indicate a sense of shared connotations, a collective system of representations in the vein of what Hall defined as "maps of meanings"—"the systems of shared meanings which people who belong to the same community, group, or nation use to help them interpret and make sense of the world."[96] Having a position within a set of shared meanings gives us a sense of our own identity. Thus, the uniqueness of each place on the map of Africanness is established in relation to what is supposedly absent in the other places but most of all to what African American tourists believe is lacking in their own lives and in the places where they live.

From the Pain of Dark Tourism to the
Joy of Finding One's People

Understanding the different places visited by the tourists as complementary pieces of the same map of Africanness also highlights a fundamental distinction between the roots tourism developed in West African countries and the one that is carried out on the "diasporic side" of the Atlantic, and that distinction is one that involves, respectively, pain and pleasure. Whereas Brazil, and more specifically, Bahia has been predominantly associated with *alegria* (joy), West African countries have been mostly connected to sorrow. The experience of visiting the daunting African slave dungeons and "Doors of No Return" evokes the horrors suffered by the ancestors, and many tourists are reported to have wept and wailed, expressing shock, anger, pain, and grief while visiting these places. For example, in describing the visit to the Maison des Esclaves in Gorée Island, Senegal, Ebron highlights the pain that she and the tourists that she was accompanying experienced: "The mood, now dreadfully solemn, remained subdued for several hours after our visit. After exiting the fort we approached a church, and a few pilgrims prayed."[97]

Timothy and Teye, having had access to Elmina Castle's guestbook, where visitors are invited to record their experiences as well as identify themselves according to such markers as nationality and ethnicity, sorted through more than 14,000 entries that were recorded throughout the 1990s.[98] Reiterating the often described painful experience of African American tourism in West Africa, the authors identified seven themes in the entries written by African Americans: grief and pain, good versus evil, revenge, forgiveness and healing, coming home, in memory of our ancestors, and God and holy places: "Aside from many mentions of sadness, the element of grief was commonly reflected in the shedding of tears. One woman simply wrote: 'Tears, tears, tears.' One African-American man was so moved that he wrote Elmina Castle was 'A place which can bring an unemotional man to tears of a child. I was deeply moved.' Many black Americans expressed pain: 'This is painful,' 'I'm hurting.'"[99] These findings corroborate my argument that very distinct emotions are invoked in the different places visited in the map of Africanness. Although, obviously, there is not just one exclusive feeling triggered in each place, but several and at times, conflicting sentiments, it is, nonetheless, possible to claim that certain feelings are more elicited by, and therefore become dominantly associated with, certain places.

In an interview in August 2004, Maryanne, a retired educator in her late sixties, and who was visiting Brazil for the first time after having traveled to over a dozen African countries, enthusiastically described her thrill and amazement upon discovering how much African culture has been preserved in Bahia. When I asked her what it felt like to visit the dungeons and the "doors of no return" in Ghana and Gorée Island, she paused, took a deep breath, and solemnly responded: "I felt for my great-great-great-great-grandfather and the sacrifice that my great-great-great-great-grandfather and my great-great-great-great-grandmother made to give me the opportunity to live in America, which is really a great country to live on. Before the grace of dawn, I would still have been in Africa. But it was very, very, very, very, painful to know that this happened to somebody in my family. It was very moving and very painful." She explained that the pain she felt in Ghana's Cape Coast Castle was so deep that when she visited Senegal two years later she did not want to spend much time in Gorée because she did not want to go through that feeling again. Several other tourists echoed Maryanne's description of slavery as having a redemptive character, a topic that I analyze in the following chapter.

The profound engagement with pain and grief experienced in West African slave sites merges roots tourism with what has been called dark tourism, a practice that has been defined as travel to places marked by histories of death, terror, and trauma. Cemeteries, battlefields, prisons, and war and genocide sites are among the major locations visited in the practices of dark tourism. Although experiencing pain and profound sorrow within the predominantly superficial and hedonistic realm of international tourism may seem surprising, and even contradictory, dark tourism has become an increasingly important phenomenon around the world, alongside other postmodern forms of tourism, such as travels to sites marked by extreme poverty and by histories of revolutions.[100] The concept of dark tourism is broad and encompasses quite distinct practices and motivations to travel, including the desire to visit the places of the death of famous politicians and celebrities—for example, the building in Dallas from where president JFK was shot, or the road tunnel in Paris where Princess Diana died. It also includes the touring of places that are considered central for the construction of a group's collective memory and cultural identity. African diaspora tourism to slave sites in West Africa and Jewish diaspora tourism to Holocaust sites constitute the quintessential examples of the convergence between roots tourism and a form of dark tourism where it is possible to experience shared grief and honor the memory of the ancestors who were victimized by atrocities.

In *Wonders of the African World*, a PBS documentary that aired in 1999, Henry Louis Gates Jr. establishes a direct association between these two diaspora identities. Explaining that "his obsession with finding his roots" was one of the reasons why he made the documentary, Gates traveled throughout the African continent, stopping in some of the countries that constitute the map of Africanness. It is during his visit to Elmina Castle that he compares West African slave sites to Holocaust sites: "We feel at home here because we are surrounded by black people. That's why we come. But the memory of slavery and of what our ancestors must have gone through is always lurking. Even a pretty little harbor town like Elmina is dominated by a slave castle. And for us a slave castle is like Auschwitz."[101] This is a strong statement and it is certainly not the first to compare the horrors of the enslavement of Africans to the Jewish Holocaust. Indeed, there are more commonalities shared by African American tourism to the slave dungeons in Africa and Jewish tourism to Holocaust sites than the fact that both forms of travel engage with the practices of dark tourism.

Similar to my map of Africanness, a map of Jewishness could also be drawn, based on the specific and complementary meanings of the different heritage destinations toured by Jews. As Ioannides and Cohen Ioannides explain, for Jewish existential tourists, journeying to a few specific places brings them closer to the center of their world, not necessarily in religious terms but in ways that "embodies in a cultural sense what it means to be Jewish."[102] They argue that for diasporic Jews, the need to encounter the past requires travel not just to the "homeland" but also to other sites of the diaspora, from a Jewish hamlet in Eastern Europe to a cemetery in North Africa, from the homes of famous Jewish personalities to the death camps of the Holocaust or a neighborhood in Brooklyn.[103]

Also comparing the Jewish diaspora after the Holocaust with the African diaspora, Schramm argues that West Africa, and more specifically Ghana, would correspond symbolically to *both* Poland—place associated with death and suffering—*and* Israel—that represents the homeland and the place of redemption.[104] While this is a productive analogy in that it points to the complementariness of the meanings of the different places visited, Schramm's mapping leaves out a number of other places, or "centers," that are toured by members of each of these diasporas. Besides, a fundamental commonality that Schramm overlooked in her comparison is the desire shared by many diaspora tourists to be among one's "own people," and where they constitute the majority of the local population. As we hear in Gates' statement, African Americans visit Elmina and other slave sites in West Africa not only to mourn the memory of their ancestors but also "to be surrounded by black people."

The desire to be in a place where blacks are the majority of the population was frequently expressed by the African American tourists that I interviewed.

Commenting on her preference for visiting countries that are populated by people of African descent, an African American visitor explained how roots tourism allowed for her reconnection with other members of the African diasporic family: "I prefer to go to countries of African descent, and I enjoy it because I have a connection with them. It's like a searching. Maybe it is [that] . . . I don't know where I belong. So I guess I am in search of my beginning. . . . I feel a kinship; I feel a relationship. The first time I went to Africa was just overwhelming. It was so emotional. . . . The string has been cut, and it can't be mended right there, but I can connect somewhere else with other people of African descent."[105]

In my view, in addition to the desire to reconnect with other members of the diaspora, the history of antiblack racism also accounts for the preference of African Americans to travel to places where blacks constitute the majority of the population. Analyzing the effects of prejudice and discrimination on tourism in the United States, Philipp explains that, in comparison with whites, black tourists are much less likely to make unplanned stops, walk on unknown streets, or eat at restaurants not previously recommended by friends. Also noteworthy is information that may help explain the importance of preestablished itineraries in African American travel: "Blacks are significantly more likely to agree with the statement 'When I travel I like to be part of a large group' than are whites. Likewise, . . . blacks are also significantly more likely to agree with the statement 'When I travel I like to have every minute occupied with activities' than are whites."[106]

Racism plays an important role in the tourism practices of other black groups as well. Analyzing tourism among members of the UK Afro-Caribbean diaspora, Stephenson explains that racism shapes their itineraries and patterns, and it informs the choice of the places to be visited as well as those to be avoided. Likewise, the preferred destinations of these tourists are also those where blacks are the majority of the population, since the tourists believe that in these places they will feel more secure and at ease. "Consequently, individuals may prefer to travel to destinations that limit their exposure to racialism. Although the ancestral homeland is one obvious destination where Afro-Caribbean visitors are likely to feel comfortable, especially as racialized encounters are limited and opportunities for ethnic and cultural familiarization prevail (Stephenson 2002), travel may be less threatening in destinations where there is a significant presence of 'black others.'"[107]

Neither Philipp nor Stephenson explain whether blacks were also the majority within the tour groups that they examined; however, in my research

I found that African American roots tourists travel to Brazil in groups composed mainly or exclusively of black members. Besides functioning to foster the collective nature of ethnic identities, travel in groups also promotes what Urry defines as the "romantic tourist gaze," an experience that is enjoyed either in solitude or in the presence of people to whom one feels closely connected. The presence of "strangers" spoils it.[108] Several authors have analyzed the desire—at times transformed into a concrete demand—of African American tourists to visit the slave dungeons in Elmina Castle only with other blacks, since they view the presence of whites as disrupting this unique moment.[109]

Being among a black majority is undoubtedly one of the main reasons for African American tourism to Brazil as well. A major difference, nonetheless, is that in their visits to Brazil the tourists do not have to deal with the suffering generated by the question of whether the local black people are descendants of slave owners and slave traders, which is always a daunting issue during their trips to West Africa. There certainly were Afro-Brazilians who were actively involved in the slave trade, but this information is predominantly erased by the Brazilian tourism industry. References to the Afro-Brazilian involvement with the slave trade would certainly affect the roots tourists' attempts at reconnecting with their Afro-Brazilian "brothers and sisters," who are perceived as "siblings in destiny." African American tourists constantly comment that they could have been born in Brazil instead of in the United States. The unpredictability of the destiny of their ancestors is conceived of together with the certainty of their own common fate, marked by slavery, oppression, struggle, and resistance. Roots tourism thus allows for a scattered people to reunite, as we can hear in the words of this visitor: "I have been amazed at the large number of black people [in Brazil], even though I did know that Brazil was the largest black country outside of Africa. But just to see them living and thriving, and to know that they have been here since the same amount of time that my ancestors were in the United States. . . . That's just amazing! . . . We were separated. We've been scattered but now we're being brought back together. . . . And I found that here."[110]

Roots tourism also allows the tourists to connect with a culture that was able to "survive" because their Brazilian counterparts have supposedly managed to preserve the cultural connections with Africa. In the following statement, the conflation between the notions of "cultural roots" and "family roots" is revealed in the African American tourist's use of the term "we" to refer to Afro-descendants at large. In fact, in many interviews, the tourists frequently alternated between the pronouns *we/our* and *they/their* to refer to Afro-Brazilian people and Afro-Brazilian culture:

> I'm very proud of the Africans who came from the Bantus and the Yorubas that *they* were able to maintain their particular beliefs, spiritual beliefs, even though *they* were forced into Catholicism by the whites. Even though *they* pretended *they* believed in Catholicism, deep down in their hearts *they* stuck to Candomblé to keep their spirits alive. And because of that *we* have Bahia as it is now. Because if it wasn't, *we* wouldn't have Candomblé, and *we* wouldn't have a lot of the spiritual things that came with the Africans to South America. My feeling is that I am very proud that *we* were strong enough, at least in that particular part, to maintain some dignity, and to hold *our* religion together by using Candomblé.[111]

The jubilation of the reconnection that the tourists feel in Bahia contrasts sharply with the feelings of pain, anger, and sorrow experienced in West African countries. The historical roots sought after in West Africa which, although not limited to, necessarily engage with, the painful memory of slavery, contrast sharply with the cultural roots found in Bahia, where the abundant African heritage contribute to confirm the slogan, promoted by the state tourism board, that Bahia is the "terra da alegria," the "land of joy." The joy is then intensified by the sensation that one is arriving in a closer, and cozier, version of Africa in the Americas where it is possible to reconnect with the "past" without having to deal with the painful memory of slavery. Feelings of pain, anger, and the joyfulness of reconnection are triggered by the different sites visited on the map of Africanness, serving therefore to confer an identity on each place.

Because most of these tourists have also traveled to Caribbean countries, it is important to examine the meanings attributed to Caribbean destinations in light of the interconnectedness of the map of Africanness. One of the surprising aspects of the tourists' portrayal of Caribbean nations is that very few of them commented on the African heritage of the islands. Although most of the tourists described the comfort they feel in being among majority black populations during their visits to the Caribbean, they did not highlight the Africanness of these islands. With the exception of Cuba, which the roots tourists did acknowledge as having a strong African culture, there was very little mention of the African roots of the other Caribbean nations. Once again, this reveals that the meanings attributed to the different tourism destinations are not objective reflections of their histories and cultures, but are instead the result of complex processes of cultural construction.

The lack of emphasis on the African heritage of Caribbean destinations in the roots tourism discourse represents a shift from previous African American portrayals of Caribbean countries, which had highlighted the cultural roots of several of these islands. In the 1930s, for example, Zora Neale Hurston researched and published on the Africanisms she encountered in Haiti and Jamaica, while Langston Hughes wrote about his enthusiasm for "the heartbeat and songbeat of Africa" that he encountered among Afro-Cubans.[112] Throughout the twentieth century, several African American writers also represented the Caribbean as a home-place, among them Katherine Dunham in the 1940s, and Paule Marshall and Audre Lorde in the 1980s, just to name a few. The present time representations of Caribbean destinations for African American tourists not only do not emphasize the African heritage of these nations but are, in fact, virtually undistinguishable from the dominant mainstream tourism depictions of these places in the United States. It therefore makes sense to state that Caribbean countries are not part of the roots tourists' map of Africanness, despite the undeniably strong African heritage of these countries.

The statements of the tourists regarding the meanings of Caribbean destinations resonate with the information that I found in tourism promotional material, including, for example, the reports and advertisements contained in African American magazines. Even when Caribbean black cultural expressions or events are mentioned in these magazines, such as the Calypso based-Carnival in Trinidad, the Maroon Festival in Jamaica, or the Crop Over Festival in Barbados, they are depicted as just common tourist attractions, and not as examples of the cultural heritage of black communities in the diaspora. The African origin of Caribbean black cultural expressions is sometimes incidentally mentioned, but it is certainly not emphasized. Most important, these expressions are not promoted as *cultural roots*.

It is also very common for several Caribbean islands to be portrayed as almost interchangeable destinations, and composing a kind of menu of beaches and shopping experiences to be chosen by the tourist. There is, in fact, very little difference between the content of the articles and ads geared specifically to African Americans and those geared toward mainstream tourism promotion. The most common themes are in tandem with the usual portrayals of the Caribbean as they invite tourists to "escape the winter," enjoy "tropical paradise," or bask in the sun at day and hit the shopping, dining, and casino scenes at night.

An article on the importance of visiting Senegal for African American tourists, published in *Savoy* in 2005, is a good example of how the map of Africanness excludes the Caribbean. While making the case that it is possible to have fun in Senegal, *despite* its history of slavery and colonialism, and even arguing that "there's more to Senegal than Gorée," the article reiterates the notion that the Caribbean is where one travels for relaxation: "The idea of a 'trip to the Motherland' sounds too serious, even daunting, and surely requiring a lot of time—unlike a 'real vacation' that you take 'for fun,' like going to the Caribbean. But one can certainly do both."[113]

Evidently, not all Caribbean nations are represented as tourism destinations in African American magazines and other contemporary sources of tourism promotional discourse. The Dominican Republic and Haiti, for instance, are hardly ever mentioned. The most promoted are the English-speaking islands, especially the Bahamas, Jamaica, Barbados, Trinidad and Tobago and, above all else, the U.S. Virgin Islands. The fact that the latter constitutes a U.S. territory is frequently alluded to in the reports and ads as a convenient tourist destination for African Americans.

This is strikingly different from the way in which Brazil is represented in the pages of these magazines as well as in tourism promotional material more broadly. While Brazil, and especially so Bahia are portrayed as a place to find cultural roots, Caribbean nations are more often than not depicted as sites where one can find fun, sun, sand, and sex, when of course all of these attractions are available in all of these locations. Despite Brazil's global reputation as a sex tourism destination, neither of these magazines portrays the country in such light, with the exception of a widely mentioned article published in *Essence* in 2006, which describes the "secret," growing trend of African American men who travel to Rio de Janeiro in search of sex. But even this article describes Brazil as a place that is mostly associated with cultural roots as it states that the country's name conjures up "the strong African cultural traditions that have survived and flourished here for centuries."[114]

When I asked Lidia Matos, a Brazilian tour guide who has worked with African American roots tourism since the early 1980s, whether the African American tourists also visit Caribbean countries, she replied that they do, but not with the purpose of seeking out cultural roots. Her thoughtful and nuanced answer is worth quoting at length:

> Many places in the Caribbean today are too Americanized because white Americans bought a lot of the hotels there in all those islands, and the people there have become contaminated by that. *So they don't see black Americans as different from the other Americans that they are catering to on a daily basis.* There is also the fact that Bahia, regardless of anything else, is one of the places in the continent that has the strongest retention of [African] culture. . . . They mention that in the Caribbean everything is

too commercial. . . . Although these places are proportionally blacker than Brazil, they have a much less African culture than we have here. *So they might be blacker in the color maybe, but they are less black in their culture.* Haiti is also extremely poorer than here, and those who travel want a bit of comfort. *So Bahia is a halfway: Bahia is what they don't have*—of course you see the traces of black culture in the U.S., whoever wants to, sees it, in the music, the dance, you see traces, [but] you have to seek it out, it's not something so clear. Bahia is a place that really has a retention of Africa that is much stronger.[115]

The viewpoints outlined in Lidia's response were echoed in the interviews that I carried out with many tourists over the course of the research. Most of them explained that what made Brazil, and especially Bahia, so attractive was the Africanness that they found there, and which they deemed lacking in their own culture back home. Many of the tourists also drew frequent comparisons between Bahia and locations in West Africa, especially in terms of the similarity among the cultures, religions, and even between peoples' phenotypes. Comparable associations were not made, however, between Caribbean and West African countries, again with the exception of Cuba, which only a handful of the tourists I interviewed had ever visited. Perhaps most important is Lidia's point about how African American tourists in most Caribbean destinations are regarded as regular American tourists, which means that the "American" component of their identities supersedes the "African" part, thus leaving little space for the recognition of the commonalities shared by diasporic blacks.

Brazil, on the other hand, becomes a much more comfortable destination not just because poverty is kept more out of sight than in Haiti or African countries, as Lidia explained, but above all else because the roots tourists experience a sense of shared sameness when they connect with Afro-Brazilian culture and people. When I asked the organizer of the 1978 festival what African Americans and Afro-Brazilians could learn from another in their encounters and interactions, he said that "the lesson is still under construction," but the goal is "to reach a point where the cultures in the Americas can see themselves almost in a seamless sense," similarly to the different peoples in the African continent that, despite belonging to different nations and speaking different languages, "all see themselves as African in a collective sense."[116]

Sylvia Marie, the owner of an African American travel agency whose groups I accompanied several times in Brazil, made a very similar remark in response to the same question. She explained that the shared commonalities and interconnectedness among African Americans and Afro-Brazilians make up the most important lesson to be learned in these visits: "One of the major things that I experience myself and I actually hope that participants in my group will experience is that we, as people of African descent, are inextricably connected, no matter where we are. And we are indeed everywhere. Hopefully it will enhance our own pride in our culture and strengthen our self-esteem as a people. That's why I've visited so many African countries and that's why I want to continue visiting destinations that I think have a like past. It's my people, it's my place, it's my history!"[117]

Conclusion

The search for sameness is therefore a crucial component of African American roots tourism in Brazil, and it is one of the major reasons why Bahia has become a cultural and heritage center for these tourists. This yearning was already evident in the 1978 festival, which was described in the aforementioned article written by one of its attendants as an opportunity provided for the celebration of the identity shared by diasporic blacks. Although the article is critical of both the touristic nature of the festival and the extreme poverty affecting blacks in Brazil, it ends on a positive note: "For many the end [of the festival] was the beginning of an exchange that will continue and blossom between the Afro-American and Afro-Brazilian communities, an exchange that may eventually have international ramifications, culturally and politically."[118]

It is not a coincidence that Thomas Allen Harris's documentary on Bahia, with which I began this chapter, is called *That's My Face* (*É Minha Cara*). This is a popular slang that Brazilians use to describe something that *looks like them* and with which they *identify*. Harris picked this up while visiting Brazil and hanging out with newly found Brazilian friends. Harris found "his face" in Bahia, reflected in the smiles of the little black children he encountered and who supposedly refused to see him as a gringo because he looked too much like themselves. This is in stark contrast to what happens in West African countries, where African American tourists are frequently referred to by terms that somewhat conflate, although in complex ways, the meanings of "foreigner" and "white" such as *Oburoni* in Ghana, *Oyinbo* in Nigeria, *Yovo* in Benin, and *Toubob* in Senegal.[119] Ultimately, it also confirms Lidia Matos's point about African American tourists seeking to be regarded as *different* from generic Americans and *similar* to the local black populations.

To a great extent, the map of Africanness functions like a mirror where African American tourists see themselves while gazing at Others, but also where they reflect on these Others while assessing their own trajectory in the United

States. As Adrienne Rich famously observed several decades ago, "a place on a map is also a place in history."[120] The map of Africanness thus highlights those elements that are considered to be both lacking and abounding in the different places and peoples. African American representations of Brazil and other areas of the world have always been, to a great extent, a reflection of the events happening at home.[121] Over the course of the twentieth century, Brazil went from being the "land of the future"—as stated among others by journalist Cyril Briggs in 1920—to becoming a "land of the past" as it has been portrayed by African American roots tourists since the late 1970s.

Harris's documentary, informed by a postmodern reflexive approach, attempts to show both sides of this mirror as it also incorporates the contemplations of Harris's Afro-Brazilian guide/boyfriend, Jorge, about the African Americans who visit Bahia: "So, you've come to Salvador to find your Orixás? Here, things are not what they seem. . . . You, people from the USA, are always coming here searching for something. . . . You say you want to find the Orixás. But, in reality, is that what you're looking for? Aren't you really searching for a connection to a world that no longer exists, like all the other black Americans who come to Bahia in search of their roots?" Harris responds to this disconcerting scrutiny with a courageous critique of the African American privileged position within the black diaspora: "Am I so different from the Christian missionaries who impose their own view of the world on the heathens they find on faraway lands?"

Harris's awareness of the temporal character of the map of Africanness is noteworthy and quite uncommon when compared to the dominant African American reflections on Brazil. Yet, because Jorge's contemplations do not come out of his own mouth, and are instead conveyed through voiceovers in a Brazilian-accented English scattered throughout the documentary, this leaves the viewer wondering whether Jorge's remarks are in fact his, or if they ultimately express Harris's own reflections. The same ambiguity applies to the perspective of the children who readily welcomed Harris as one of their own. Overall, and in tandem with the dominant African American reflections on Brazil, Harris's Bahia is represented as a soothing, spiritual, and magical place that exhales a long lost Africanness. This is another indication that the map of Africanness is temporal as much as it is spatial. As the African American roots tourists travel to other countries, they are, simultaneously, traveling to past time periods. What stages of the past are then to be found in Brazil? In order to engage with this question, the following chapter leaves the aerial view of the map of Africanness to zoom in on Bahia and examine more in-depth the meanings of Brazil in the African American roots tourist gaze.

CHAPTER TWO

The Way We Were

Brazil in the African American Roots Tourist Gaze

We're here because we're looking for something. I know this sounds kind of corny, but we are looking for our past. I remember growing up in New York City, and once I got into high school I, then, for the first time, started to go to school with white [and other nonblack] kids, and they would go to Israel, to China, to Japan, they would go to these countries, they spoke the languages. . . . And I always felt a gap. Where do *my* ancestors come from?

—Louise, African American tourist, Salvador, August 2012

Louise, an African American lawyer in her mid-sixties, and visiting Brazil for the fourth time when I met her in 2012, explained with the words quoted above why so many African American tourists are drawn to the country. Intrigued by that idea, which I had heard several times before, that Americans could find their past in Brazil, I jokingly asked her if Africa would not be the best place to look. Her unwavering response made clear that it is Bahia's abundant African heritage that allows for a reconnection with the past: "I *am* finding my past here. I am finding people who are still practicing African culture. We are going to see some of that today," she said, referring to the Festival of the Good Death, in Cachoeira, to where we were just about to head off.[1]

Louise's enthusiasm for Afro-Bahian culture represents one of the most important motivations for African American travel to Brazil. In one way or another, all the African American tourists that I interviewed expressed how delighted they were to be able to engage with African cultural expressions in Bahia. They described savoring the palm oil-based cuisine, listening and dancing to the drumbeat of Afro-Bahian music, and witnessing so much "Africanness" in the culture as extraordinary experiences made possible by their encounter with Afro-Brazilians, who they conceive of, simultaneously, as "diasporic counterparts" and as inhabitants of an imaginary past.[2]

But how and why has Brazil, and especially Bahia, become associated with a place to find the past within the African American imagination? In order to understand how tourist destinations acquire distinctive connotations it is necessary to examine the processes through which meanings are mapped onto places. In the context of transnational black relations, African Americans—especially scholars and cultural producers who, nonetheless, have also been travelers—have enjoyed greater access to global currents of power than their diasporic counterparts. This is expressed in the abundance of books, feature films, documentaries, magazines, and other media through which African Americans have yearned for, imagined, and ultimately represented places in the African diaspora. Evidence of the overall economic power of African Americans when compared to other Afro-descendant groups that inhabit other countries is, for example, the sheer number of travel guides geared specifically to African American tourists.[3] These media-produced representations have been influential for the construction of an African American roots tourist gaze.

Although there is no single African American tourist gaze on Brazil, it is possible to identify the dominant discourses and representations among the tour groups that seek out their heritage in Bahia. Upon contrasting the discourse of the tourists with the narratives found in various sources, I identified three major intersecting tropes. The first trope is that of Bahia as a "closer Africa" and therefore as a place where African Americans can engage with their cultural roots and reconnect with their past. Second, but equally important, is the trope of the "happy native," or the perception that because Afro-Brazilians—represented specifically by Afro-Bahians—supposedly inhabit the African American past, they are imagined to be essentially more culturally fulfilled than African Americans. The third and interconnected trope is that of "black evolution," which is based on the notion that, despite abounding African tradition, Afro-Brazilians supposedly lack black modernity, and should therefore look up to African Americans for guidance. This chapter examines these tropes in light of the temporal character of the map of Africanness and the specific location of Bahia within these diasporic representations of the past.

The Tourist Gaze

The concept of the tourist gaze was developed by John Urry to explain that much of what tourists see in their trips is shaped before the tourists even leave home, a process through which different types of media systematize the tourist gaze and organize the overall tourist experience. Inspired by Foucault's theory of the medical gaze as a learned ability that participates in the reorganization of knowledge and power, Urry argues that the tourist gaze is also "an epistemic field, constructed linguistically as much as visually."[4] Tourism professionals produce objects to be gazed upon, and they employ media to influence where, when, and how tourists should gaze. If the tourist gaze is socially organized and systematized, an "archeology" of the gaze can be undertaken. The theory of the tourist gaze does not contend that there is an automatic effect of the images that tourists see prior to their trips on how they will experience tourism destinations. This is a much more subtle and unconscious process whereby exposure to specific ideas and representations gradually shape tourists' perceptions of the destinations and their inhabitants. It is certainly possible to challenge dominant representations and to produce new ones in the processes of touring and gazing. Because meanings are produced culturally, they can never be finally fixed, which means that regimes of representation can always be contested and transformed.[5]

Different gazes develop within different societies and social groups and in different historical periods. One's class, gender, age, nationality, and education shape one's gaze. Moreover, if tourists usually seek to gaze at what seems to be *extraordinary*, then the tourist gaze is necessarily related to the tourist's *ordinary* life. "What makes a particular tourist gaze depends upon what it is contrasted with; what the forms of non-tourist experience happen to be. The gaze therefore presupposes a system of social activities and signs which locate the particular tourist practices, not in terms on some intrinsic characteristics, but through the contrasts implied with non-tourist social practices, particularly those based within home and paid work."[6]

Urry's theory has been criticized for overvaluing the gaze to the detriment of the other human senses. Crouch, for example, argues that when vision is understood as detached and disembodied, space is then conceived of as an inert medium prescribed by inscriptions on it. It would be therefore necessary to pay greater attention to the embodied experience of tourism and move beyond a "dematerialized geography of representations."[7] Cartier makes a similar point: that it is necessary to challenge the visual in order to examine landscapes as always read by multisensory and located subjectivities.[8] Undeniably, the ways in which tourists experience places go way beyond what is prefigured in text as tourists practice their own subjective and embodied semiotics. Tourism brochures, sites, and maps do not determine how tourists will engage with landscapes or define their embodied experiences with places.[9]

Although I agree that tourism is much more than a "two-dimensional detachment of the gaze onto inscripted surfaces by a non-involved bystander," I do not see embodiment as opposite to representation.[10] There is no actual division between geographies of representation and geographies of embodied experience. To highlight the power of the gaze does not require downplaying the agency of individual tourists, nor does it "over-emphasize external constructions of what makes tourism."[11] As Hall explains, representations are not symbols of a material reality that exists "out there," waiting for human systems of classification.[12] Nothing has meaning outside of representation, including our very embodied existence. Instead of a semiotic approach, concerned only with how representations are produced, the tourist gaze is a discursive approach, which also seeks to understand the political effects of representations. It is therefore concerned with how discourses provide a way of talking about a particular topic in a particular period. Although dominant discourses do not *determine* or account for the full range of utterances and actions, they do play a role in *regulating* conducts and practices.[13]

Furthermore, if in his initial theorization of the tourist gaze Urry had already explained that the gaze is more than merely circumscribed to the visual, in the third edition of the book,[14] Urry and his coauthor Larsen further develop the understanding that despite the fundamentally visual nature of tourism experiences, sight is not the only sense involved in tourism.[15] Travel is, necessarily, corporeal travel, thus tourism and the tourist gaze itself are also intrinsically embodied and performative. In addition to seeing, tourists also eat, smell, walk, dance, and feel textures. Contrary to some of Urry's critics, I understand that the focus on the gaze is not meant to further empower eyesight as the major sensory mode.[16] It is meant, instead, to account for the power of discourses in organizing the world and regulating the embodied human experience of our journeys within it.

Sources That Inform the Roots Tourist Gaze

When I asked Sylvia Marie, the owner of a New York-based African American travel agency whose tour group I accompanied in Brazil in 2004 and 2012, if she remembered the first time she had heard about Bahia, her answer was anything but precise: "I can't remember the first time ... Bahia is just somewhere in your body of knowledge."[17] Sylvia's apparently vague response is in fact quite informative. It reveals that Bahia is imagined as an important part of a wider African American heritage. Seeking to understand why this is so, I pressed Sylvia for more detailed information. What had she read, heard, and been exposed to that triggered her interest in visiting Bahia in the first place? And how did she allure so many others to follow in her footsteps? After all, this was her tenth visit to Brazil, and it was the ninth time that she was leading a tour group there.

Seeking to identify the major sources of information on Brazil in general, and on Bahia specifically, I posed similar versions of this question to all the African American tourists that I interviewed. I asked them: "How (or where) did you first hear about Bahia/Brazil?" "What references might have shaped your perception of Bahia/Brazil before your first visit?" Most of the initial responses were similar to Sylvia's in that interviewees could not pin down their first or most important source of information. Upon further reflection, however, many of the tourists were able to cite specific books, movies, and documentaries, a few magazine and newspaper articles, as well as particular websites and brochures as having provided them with knowledge on Brazil.

The websites and brochures put together by the U.S.-based tourism agencies that organize roots trips are undeniably the most systematized sources that inform the roots tourist gaze. Yet no other reference has been as influential as word of mouth.[18] Most of the tourists interviewed mentioned friends' and relatives' enthusiastic accounts of their first-hand experience visiting Brazil as having played a major role in triggering their desire to visit the country. A female tourist that was in her early sixties when I interviewed her in 2004 explained that she became interested in visiting Brazil because of a close friend's account: "A dear friend of mine, who was my roommate when we traveled to Africa, she came to Brazil a year before she passed away, and she talked about it so fervently. So I felt like I had to come to Brazil. She told me so much about the Boa Morte Festival. And so today, when I was there [at the Festival], it was really emotional for me because she talked about it so much. I also have another good friend who has come to Brazil five or six times."[19] Another tourist mentioned that she first heard about Bahia's Africanness through a friend's neighbor, who had traveled to Brazil: "That was the first time I ever heard someone mention Bahia. And this woman was telling me about Bahia, and the rich black cultural heritage here, so after that we started paying attention. . . . I didn't have anything too specific in mind, just that there was a lot of African history here and that a lot of the practices were pretty much as they were in Africa centuries ago."[20]

If word of mouth has played an important role in consolidating Bahia's reputation as an important travel destination for African American tourists, travel agencies have certainly relied on this "method" to publicize their tours. Peter Johnson, a retired university professor based in New York City, and who has been taking groups of African American tourists to Brazil since 1984, explained that he has never formally advertised his tours. "It's all based on word of mouth. People call me, 'Are you going to Brazil this year? I want to come!' And that's how my groups are formed." According to Peter, word of mouth has played a major role not only in making Bahia known among African Americans, but also in having transformed it into a desirable travel destination: "When I first started going to Brazil in the 1980s, people would say: 'What? I've heard of Brazil, but where are you going? Bahia?! Is that in the South Sea Islands?'

They didn't know where it was! Now everyone knows where it is, even if they can't pronounce it sometimes. People call me and say I want to go to Bahhhhia [he said, making fun of the incorrect pronunciation frequently made by English speakers who do not realize that the 'h' in Bahia is silent]. They still might not be able to pronounce the name, but now they want to go there! [Smiles.]"[21]

Lidia Matos, a tourist guide that has worked with this tourism niche for almost thirty years, confirmed the importance of word of mouth in disseminating among African Americans the idea that Bahia is a special travel destination. I asked her what sources of information trigger their interest in visiting Brazil, and she replied that she has also asked them that question several times. The answer, she said, is that they are interested specifically in visiting Bahia, and that they are motivated to do so mostly because of the enthusiastic comments that they hear from friends and relatives who have already traveled there. "They do not have much previous information on Brazil. All they know is that Bahia is a halfway between the USA and Africa." I asked her if this expectation is fulfilled once they actually visit Bahia, to which she enthusiastically replied, "Oh, yes! The expectation is more than fulfilled! It is overwhelming! Of course it depends a lot on the guides too, on how they present Bahia to them."[22]

Undeniably, the tourist guides are major providers of knowledge on Brazil, and they can also be understood as essential sources that inform the roots tourist gaze. The guides have played a key role in both disseminating and confirming the trope of Bahia as a closer Africa, as illustrated in Lidia Matos's comment. Another very important tour guide, also based in Bahia, and who is also a long-established Afro-Brazilian political activist and cultural producer, made a similar comment about Bahia's cultural proximity to Africa. When I asked him what African Americans and Afro-Brazilians have in common, he responded by emphasizing what he sees as the major *difference* between both groups: "What both groups share is the need to rescue the links to our ancestors. So, this need, this search, we both share. But for us [Afro-Brazilians], the path is shorter. The path for us is shorter because we continue to have the African references. Look [he said, pointing to a group of people dancing samba on the street as our van was starting to leave Cachoeira], we have *samba de roda*, and they don't." During the conversation, he also reiterated some ideas that are commonly shared among black cultural producers in Brazil, including the notion that African American musical rhythms, such as jazz and blues, are more distant from the original African source.[23] Because Afro-Brazilians are closer to the African source, he said, "We don't have this need to return to Africa. Our Africa is here."[24] One of the Sisters of the Good Death that I interviewed in 2013 made a similar comment about African

Americans being supposedly disconnected from their Africanness, and thus traveling to Bahia in search of what they do not have: "They come here because of the *axé*, because there [in the United States], they don't have *axé*. They come here to see us because we have kept alive the knowledge of our ancestors."

For many African American tourists, the orientation sessions that are offered by the tour leaders in preparation for their trips constitute the most in-depth exposure to information on Brazil. Sylvia Marie explained that she carries out one or two meetings before the trip, depending on how early the group is formed. In addition to discussing the practical aspects of the visit (such as visa requirements, safety tips, currency conversion rates, and how to dress for the weather), these orientation sessions also play a crucial role in shaping the tour-ist gaze.[25] This came across very clearly in Sylvia Marie's explanation of the purpose of these sessions: "The idea [of the orientation] is to enhance the visit, to make it more meaningful than just coming to see a beautiful place with, like, nice beaches, etc. It's really to enhance their knowledge, their excitement, their identification with the destination. And I gather information from various sources to do that."[26]

"Can you tell me a few?" I asked her. Sylvia replied:

> The Internet [chuckles]; various travel guides that I use—the *Lonely Planet* publishes a series of excellent travel guides; I've done some books. In fact I brought an article that run last Sunday in the *New York Times*, a travel section on Brazil.[27] I clip all kinds of articles. The Brazil Tourism Association in Washington, D.C., has supplied me with brochures. [They] ran an advertorial in *Condé Nest Traveler*, which gave a one-page overview of several destinations in Brazil, including Bahia and Rio, etc. so they supplied me with reprints of this, which I distributed with the group. I can't think of the name of any particular book.[28]

The analysis of the different media that were referred to by the tourists as sources of information on Brazil reveal a constant reiteration of ideas that con-tributes to establish some representations as dominant in the tourist gaze. Bahia's "Africanness" is undoubtedly the most important of these notions, and it constitutes the innermost motivation that draws African American roots tourists to Brazil. In Sylvia's orientation sessions, for instance, she constantly highlights Afro-Brazilian culture as the major attraction of her tours: "I talk about our day-to-day itinerary; I talk about some of the African influences that I'm aware of—I don't know everything about it—but I try to get them in tune to the Afrocentric aspects of Brazil talking about Candomblé in the limited way that I can, and how it is based upon the Yoruba religion and how it is also similar to other religions like Voodoo in Haiti, to the religion in Benin where it all began, and Santeria in the Spanish speaking areas."[29]

In addition to analyzing all the different media that were referred to by the tourists as sources of information on Brazil, I also looked at other sources that, despite not having been directly mentioned by the tourists, certainly contribute to inform African American discourses on the country. I examined feature films and documentaries, the websites and brochures of travel agencies that carry out heritage tours to Brazil, and I also studied how popular African American magazines, especially *Ebony* and *Essence*, portray Brazil as a tourist destination for African Americans.[30] According to a recent report, "*Essence* is the most widely read magazine among African American travelers, with two-fifths saying they read it. This magazine is particularly popular among those with an active interest in African American culture and history."[31]

An important indication of the involvement of *Essence* magazine in promoting African American tourism to Brazil, albeit after this niche had already been established, was the creation of Avocet Travel by *Essence* magazine co-founder and president emeritus Clarence Smith. In February 2005, Avocet Travel announced that it would be establishing nonstop charter flights with VARIG (Viação Aérea Rio-Grandense) airlines from New York City to Salvador, Bahia. The slogan was "Awaken in Brazil. The Experience Begins in Bahia." The venture was short-lived, however, and after a few years, Avocet Travel ceased its business in Brazil. Some people in the tourism industry that I interviewed in Bahia said that the reasons were the economic crisis that hit the United States in 2008 and the insufficient investment on the part of the Bahian state government. My point here, however, is not that the tourists necessarily read these magazines, but rather that the same ideas are present in different sources. Because tourism in not a closed-off realm, tourism representations are produced in connection with wider cultural discourses that are not always necessarily linked to tourism.

In that sense, the "hermeneutic circle" identified by Albers and James in their analysis of tourism photography can also be applied to tourism discourse more broadly. These authors argue that photographs already seen before the trips inform the photographs that the tourists take during their trips. Equally important is that the images that circulate in tourism photography also circulate in nontourism realms such as mass media and academic and scientific circles. The repetition that occurs in travel photography, and I would add, in tourism discourse at large, is the result of a "commonly shared process of symbolization" where the messages "constitute a more widely held and conventionalized body of discourse."[32] Thus, by contrasting the ideas conveyed by the interviewees with the representations of Brazil found in disparate sources, I examined how tourists participate in the hermeneutic circle.[33]

I analyzed the representations of Brazil portrayed in the different media sources only after I had interviewed many African American tourists in Bahia. This allowed me to contrast the tourists' representations to the ones constructed in and through these various sources. I found great consistency between these sources' portrayals of tourist destinations and the tourists' representations of the places they visited. I do not suggest, however, that any of these sources "determine" the roots tourist gaze. I do, nonetheless, agree that places are chosen to be gazed upon through a process of anticipation that "is constructed and sustained through a variety of non-tourist practices, such as film, TV, literature, magazines, records and videos, which construct and reinforce that gaze."[34] And while these different sources constitute different genres, therefore presenting and arranging ideas in different ways, they contribute to the construction and circulation of specific representations.

Aiming to carry out an intellectual excavation of discursive formations,[35] my goal was not to produce an exhaustive catalogue of the sources that inform the African American roots tourist gaze on Brazil, but rather, following Edward Said, I sought to identify the tropes that are most present in these media and which also resonate in the discourse of the tourists. The recurrence of the same tropes, or conventional ideas, in disparate sources contributes to produce the "internal consistency" of a discourse.[36] While these generalizations provide a unifying set of values, they also create constraints on and limitations to the representations of places and peoples.[37] It is, therefore, crucial to interrogate these tropes and to reflect upon the political questions that they raise. If, as Stuart Hall argues, representations do not merely *reflect*, but more so *constitute* reality,[38] then these political questions include: Who constructs and authorizes the tourist gaze that becomes dominant in a given context? And how do tourist gazes participate in the (re)production of asymmetries and hierarchies? In line with Raiford and Raphael-Hernandez's inspiring work on the travels of blackness and the black body, another question that informs this chapter is how have visual cultures, alongside textual and aural forms, served as "diasporic resources" for transnational black communities? And how have these sources/resources, in turn, shaped diasporic imaginings and interconnection, but also unevenness, among black diasporic subjects?[39]

Trope 1: Bahia as a "Closer Africa"

Whether more or less explicitly, all of the tourists that I interviewed identified Bahia's Africanness as their major reason for visiting Brazil. African American travel agent Peter Johnson, who has been bringing groups to the country since 1984, explained that Bahia is always the core of his trips to Brazil. He takes his groups to Bahia *and* one other destination, usually Rio de Janeiro, but sometimes other cities like Iguaçu Falls, Manaus, Maceió, Fortaleza, or Belo Horizonte. He made clear, however, that these other cities are just the icing on the cake. The "cake," in this case, is Salvador, Bahia. Explaining why so many people make return trips to Brazil with him, two, three, and even four times, Peter Johnson emphasized that, compared with other Brazilian cities, Bahia's "Afrocentricity" is unbeatable:

> People keep coming back because I use Salvador as the base, and most of them love Salvador because of the Afrocentricity. When they go to other places, when they go to Recife, it [the Afrocentricity] is there, but not as heavy. In Belo Horizonte, it's there, but not as heavy. . . . So I mix in other cities [in addition to Salvador] so that they can get an exposure to other parts of Brazil and see the connections. In Recife they would try, you can see that there's an African influence there, but it's mainly European. It's not as heavy as in Salvador.[40]

Peter Johnson's statement about Bahia's Africanness reveals the desire, that was also expressed by many African American tourists, to experience firsthand the flavors, aromas, sounds, and sites/sights of Afro-Brazilian culture. This craving for Africanness has led them to deviate from the predominant route followed by international tourists in Brazil, one that usually takes them to the so-called postcards of Rio de Janeiro, such as the statue of Christ the Redeemer and the Sugarloaf Mountain. By contrast, African American roots tourists prefer Bahia to Rio de Janeiro because they understand that this is where a "purer" and "more preserved" African culture can be found. In Rio de Janeiro the syncretic presence of Umbanda, together with a Carnival that has been transformed into a spectacle, point to a black culture that is considered "too mixed" and "detached from its origins," while in Bahia the palm oil-based cuisine, Candomblé, and the samba-de-roda seem to provide proof of the "preservation of Africanisms" and therefore of a supposedly more authentic black culture.

One of the female tourists who was in her late sixties when I interviewed her in 2000 explained the depth of the cultural fulfillment that she felt while visiting Bahia, an experience that she already knew would not be replicated in Rio de Janeiro:

I am impressed that they have preserved the culture from Africa more so than we did in America because they took away our names, they separated our relatives from the beginning, so it just doesn't seem as though we've kept that connection, the African connection, and I am impressed to see it here! I love the food, and the similarity that it has to the food in Africa. And the dance! It is impressive and amazing to me to see as much as I have and enjoyed as much as I have in Bahia. And I know that I will not have the same feeling in Rio, but then that's ok, I've got my fill up here.[41]

The almost oppositional manner in which Rio de Janeiro and Bahia are represented is certainly reiterated also by key actors in the Brazilian tourism industry, including the tour guides that are based in both states. Denise, a Bahian guide who has worked with African American tourists since 1992, restated this contrast: "Salvador is what really meets their expectations of Brazil. Rio de Janeiro is a huge and beautiful city, it is the Marvelous City, but many of them become disappointed with what they find in Rio because it is too big and they are not able to interact with the city and with the people there as they do in Bahia. They basically do not find themselves there."[42]

Another Bahia-based tour guide also confirmed the idea that, after visiting Bahia, it can be a frustrating experience to visit Rio de Janeiro, although, he explained, the tourist's gender and age may also play a role in shaping their expectations: "After they visit Bahia, when they arrive in Rio, it is like a tumble. They are hit hard when they realize that Rio does not have the Africanness that Bahia has. Usually it is only the younger African American males who tend to prefer Rio to Bahia, especially the single guys, but that is because of the sexual issue. But the older folks, especially the older women, they definitely prefer Bahia. No doubt."[43]

Several years later, when I accompanied Sylvia Marie's tour group both in Bahia and Rio de Janeiro, I was able to experience how these two states are contrasted, both in terms of what I heard from the tourists and how the Rio-based tour guide portrayed the city. When I asked the tour guide about the group's itinerary in Rio, and whether they were going to visit black organizations or sites of importance to the history of Afro-Brazilians, she replied that the group's schedule in Rio would follow the typical itinerary of the international tourist, that is, they were going to visit the Sugarloaf Mountain, the Sambadrome, and the other "postcards" of the city: "After spending eight to ten days in Salvador, they've seen all the Africanness there is to be seen. They're having none of that in Rio!"[44]

Revealingly, in an interview carried out several years before, Lidia Matos had already commented on the importance of the tour guides in promoting the different representations of Bahia and Rio de Janeiro. She was critical of what she sees as a lack of racial consciousness among most of the tour guides in Rio:

> The stay of the African American tourist in Bahia is much longer than the stay of the white American or European tourist. The European tourist usually spends only two or three nights in Salvador and many more nights in Rio de Janeiro or another city. The black American tourist comes to Brazil above all to visit Bahia. Rio is only an extension. And Rio, unfortunately, is a disappointment. There is a lot of [black] culture there, but the guides are not interested in showing the black tourists this culture because it is easier to make money by showing them the conventional Rio. They could visit Saint Benedict's Church [a black saint], where they have the Museu do Negro [Museum of Blacks], where Anastácia's remains are kept, but none of the tours include that. At the most, they take them to the Mangueira Samba School.[45]

If the map of Africanness demonstrates the different meanings of Brazil vis-à-vis other countries visited by African American roots tourists, it also reveals the specific meanings of Bahia within Brazil, and how it compares to other important destinations for international tourists. The tourists I interviewed frequently contrasted Bahia to other international destinations, but they also commonly compared Bahia with Rio de Janeiro, always preferring the former to the latter. This comparison was more often than not expressed through allusions to binary conceptualizations of tradition versus modernity, and cultural purity versus cultural hybridity.

Sylvia Marie also brought up the comparison between Bahia and Rio a few times during our conversations. Sitting under a sun umbrella in Copacabana beach on a sunny afternoon in August 2012, she pointed to a bikini-clad woman that was lying on the sand next to us, and commented on the fact that Brazil was known worldwide for its beautiful beaches and its gorgeous women, but there was more to Brazil than that. She stated that she saw as one of her missions to raise awareness among African Americans about Bahia's similarity with Africa. She defined Bahia's African heritage as "maintained" in a way that could not be found anywhere else in Brazil, or beyond the African continent: "Having traveled throughout Africa, Bahia is just so similar! So many of the practices are so similar; the people look so similar in so many ways. It's fascinating to see how some of the African culture has been brought here and maintained! Far more than in many other places, and this is very good to see! It's very interesting to see the connections!"[46]

The exaltation of Bahia's Africanness is also disseminated in a short documentary that Sylvia Marie, Peter Johnson, and other tour leaders screen in their orientation sessions: *Brazil, a Celebration of Life*, a twenty-six-minute video produced by the, now defunct, Brazilian airlines VARIG. Hosted by African American actor Tim Reid, the video explicitly caters to African American tourists. The tourists featured in the video are black Americans, and they are shown experiencing Brazil's Africanness through the food they eat, the music they listen to, the paintings they purchase, and the history that they learn about while visiting Bahia and Rio de Janeiro, almost always within the luxury of their upscale hotels and the safety of their guided tours.

Sylvia described the role of this video in producing *anticipation* for the trip among her tour members: "It is not intended to give them a whole history lesson; it is intended to give them some of the information of the destination and get them excited about it, get them to see the visual impact of the destination. That's crucial!"[47] The production of anticipation is indeed a crucial feature of the tourist gaze as it creates interest among tourists, or potential tourists, in visiting a particular place. But the VARIG video does more than just trigger curiosity about Brazil among African Americans; it elicits the notion of a shared diasporic condition, creating a feeling of sameness and strengthening the idea that Afro-Brazilian culture is an important part of the heritage of African Americans, a heritage that can be accessed through tourism.

The supposed "sameness" shared by these two groups is constantly alluded to in the video, which begins with shots of the Atlantic Ocean and references to the shared history of the middle passage: "*Our* forefathers came upon this shore for the first time in bondage to the Americas." Several statements throughout the video, which superimpose an African American "us" onto Afro-Brazilian cultural expressions, further emphasize sameness: "*We* are a spiritual people. The traditions and heritage of *our* ancestors were bought over with *us*. *Our* West African religious celebrations mixed with Catholicism and evolved into the Afro-Brazilian religions of Candomblé, Macumba, and Umbanda."[48] Yet, at the same time that it produces a sense of sameness, the video also promotes the idea that the Afro-Brazilian "siblings in destiny" embody the African American past: "Here in Brazil we see the links between ourselves and Africa in many ways. We hear echoes of *our* past in the chants of the Candomblé houses; we experience the taste of Africa in the foods that are used like okra, pepper, coconut milk; and we feel the quiet dignity of our ancestors as reflected in the faces of the people. We share a common history with our brothers and sisters here in Brazil, one that is marked by slavery for *survival* is profoundly rooted in the celebration of life."[49]

The documentary reiterates the trope of Bahia as a "closer Africa" where African Americans can partake in a rich heritage that will bring them closer to their past. This can be found, essentially, in Bahia's capital city of Salvador and in Cachoeira, home of the Sisterhood the Good Death and where many traditional Candomblé temples are located. Showing glimpses of these living samples of Africanness, the documentary articulates the idea that Bahia is frozen in the past, as it explicitly states: "A short drive from Salvador is Cachoeira, where the time seems to have stopped and the past is always the present."[50]

The trope of Bahia as a closer Africa is present also in several *Essence* articles, where Bahia is described, over and over again, as a smaller and closer version of Africa in the Americas, and even at times as a "surrogate" Africa, accessible to those who wish to reconnect with their lost heritage: "I wept. Standing on a hill overlooking the sacred gardens of Casa Branca, viewing the tranquility of its religious shrines, I experienced a surge of emotion. It was the first time in my 37 years that I had ever seen a traditional African place of worship, known as a terreiro. But I wasn't in Africa, I was in Salvador da Bahia, a balmy state in northeastern Brazil. . . . I've never been to the Motherland, but in Bahia the movement, the color, the flavor, are all home—albeit home to a samba beat. Yet it's a beat identifiable to anyone with even a hint of African roots. For me it was a good opportunity to study a culture and lifestyle that related directly to my own heritage."[51]

African American tourists and tour agents frequently brought up in interviews the greater proximity and comfort that Bahia provides. I most recently heard this in August 2013 when I had the chance to interview again African American travel agent Lionel Washington at the Festival of the Sisterhood of the Good Death. Lionel is one of the pioneers of African American tourism in Brazil, and he has been leading tour groups to the country since the early 1980s. I asked how he would compare African American tourism to West Africa with African American tourism to Brazil. He employed the analogy of children visiting grandparents to explain the discomfort felt by African Americans in Africa:

When we go to Africa, we feel at home, but it's like an old home. You don't feel like you're coming to your house, or to your contemporaries' house. You feel like you're going to your grandmother's or your grandfather's house. When you come to Brazil, you feel like you're coming to your own house, or to your friend's house, who is just like you, as opposed to your grandmama's or granddaddy's house. They have these old forms, and you realize that's your foundation, and you have to pay them your respects. But when we're in Brazil, we can relax and feel more comfortable.[52]

The concept of Bahia as a "closer Africa" for African Americans has been promoted ever since African American roots tourism to Brazil first began in the late 1970s. According to Lidia Matos, a Brazilian tourist guide who has specialized in this niche since the early 1980s, African Americans find it easier to identify with Afro-Brazilians than with Africans in part because they have excessively idealized Africa, thus having set themselves up for disappointment.[53] Bahia's abundant Africanness, on the other hand, can be experienced without such frustration: "I think that for African Americans, the movement of return to Africa was and continues to be important, but it has also been, in some moments, disappointing. It's that thing that you arrive in Africa but you are no longer an African. Africans don't consider you African. And you come from a very different reality. And you have idealized Africa a lot more than you have idealized Bahia.... They [African Americans] then begin to discover that Bahia is a closer Africa."[54]

Several African American scholars have reflected critically on the disappointing experience of not finding in Africa the mythical homeland for which they had longed. Probably nowhere else is this more thoroughly dealt with than in Saidiya Hartman's powerful memoir *Lose Your Mother*. Hartman defines the painful feeling of alienation of African Americans in Ghana as that of a stranger in search of strangers. In an insightful analysis of her own at times rewarding and at times distressful trips to Nigeria, Tory Arthur argues that the journey to Africa can create among African Americans a transatlantic double consciousness, where the tourists are forced to deal with the fact that the still unresolved consequences of the slave trade "render them as outsiders in an Africa they had hoped to reclaim."[55]

While it is true that the African continent has featured a lot more prominently than Brazil in the African American imaginary, the process of idealization equally characterizes African American representations of Brazil, and more specifically of Bahia. This idealization is expressed in portrayals of Bahia that glorify the region's "Africanness" through emphasizing the Africanisms contained in Afro-Brazilian religion, cuisine, dance, music, and other cultural expressions while perhaps unconsciously downplaying the interconnections between these cultural "retentions" and a forceful history of slavery. Thus, a major reason that explains the greater comfort felt by African Americans in Brazil is that, in Bahia, they can experience the region's abundant Africanness without having to deal directly with the pain associated with slavery, which is an unavoidable component of their trips to Africa.

Because it is impossible to completely disregard the legacy of slavery, the dominant African American tourism discourse on Bahia tends to subsume the history of slavery to representations of *redemption* and *survival*. In that sense, the trope of Bahia as a closer Africa rests on three intersecting components: the amplification of Bahia's Africanness; the overlooking of cultural hybridity to sustain an ideal of cultural purity; and the silencing of Brazilian slavery. The interviews with the tourists as well as the tourists' sources of information on Brazil, such as magazines, books, documentaries, etc., mutually confirm these ideas. Yet the representation of Bahia as "Brazil's Africa" precedes the phenomenon of African American roots tourism as it has been promoted locally as part of Bahia's public image since the 1930s. There is, therefore, a paradoxical convergence between, on the one hand, a race-conscious African American roots tourist gaze and, on the other hand, the narrative of racial harmony divulged by Bahia's official tourism board. While the latter systematically ignores the history of slavery, thus contributing to its invisibility, the former represents Brazilian slavery through a narrative of social redemption and cultural survival.

Amplifying Africanness, Silencing Slavery

There is an intimate connection between the underrepresentation of slavery in African American tourism discourse on Brazil and the tourists' search for "preserved African culture." As Mintz and Price argued several decades ago, it is crucial to acknowledge the role played by the social institution of slavery in the transformation of African cultures in the Americas. The great cultural diversity among the enslaved "crowds," coupled with the reassembling of their many and diffuse "Africanisms," disrupted any possibility of preservation of entire "blocks of culture," especially when there was no cultural homogeneity to begin with. As the authors of this still important book explain, no group can transfer its way of life and set of beliefs intact from one place to another. Furthermore, slavery dismantled and at the same time reorganized the wide array of cultural traits and expressions brought over to the New World by the enslaved Africans.[56] However, because African American tourists are searching for "old," "traditional," and "preserved" African cultures, there seems to be little acknowledgment of the role that slavery played in the construction of what is, in fact, a creolized and hybrid Afro-Brazilian culture.

FIGURE 2.1 Cover of *American Legacy: The Magazine of African-American History &*
Culture, Winter 2006 edition, featuring a stylized *baiana* posing in Pelourinho, one of
Salvador's top tourist attractions. The article on Bahia, referred to on the cover as "Brazil's
African Heart," served as a major source of information for African American roots tourists.

Several of the African American tourists that I interviewed referred to a
beautifully written and colorfully illustrated article, published in 2006 in *Amer-*
ican Legacy: The Magazine of African-American History & Culture, as an important source of information on Brazil.[57] The cover of this edition of the magazine
(figure 2.1) features a beautiful, smiling, and typically dressed *baiana,* adorned
with turban and bead necklaces, posing in Pelourinho, one of Salvador's major

tourist attractions. Next to her, a large caption reads: "Brazil's African Heart." Sylvia Marie mentioned this magazine a few times in our conversations, and she told me that she includes copies of the article in the literature that she distributes to members of her group in her orientation sessions. Fittingly titled "Where Africa Also Lives," the text's content reflects well the idea that is highlighted in the caption: "African customs brought to Brazil 500 years ago survived slavery and flourish today in Bahia's port city of Salvador."[58] Slavery is certainly present in the article, both textually and visually, yet the focus is on how African culture *overcame* slavery. Afro-Brazilian cultural expressions are represented as if they had been brought fully formed from the African continent, instead of developing in Brazil as hybrid cultural forms. This is especially the case with Candomblé and capoeira, which are portrayed as predominantly unchanged African cultural transplants.

The article's description of capoeira faithfully illustrates this idea, both in the text as well as in terms of how it is visually represented (figure 2.2). On the bottom left hand corner of the page there is a large contemporary photograph of two shirtless, muscular black men playing capoeira, and right above it is the well-known painting by Augustus Earle, from the early 1820s, titled "Negroes fighting, Brazil."[59] The scene depicts two strong enslaved men playing capoeira and being observed by two other slaves. A policeman (or soldier) appears jumping over a fence and approaching the players as if he is about to arrest them for carrying out what was then an illegal practice. The way in which these two images are arranged on the magazine's page, with the recent photograph literally superimposed onto the nineteenth-century painting, provides the reader with a sense of *continuity*. The fact that the figure of the policeman, which represents repression, is replaced in the recent photograph with a group of awe-struck bystanders, represented by white, apparently middle-class, uniformed school students in their teens, signal a shift in how this Afro-Brazilian cultural expression has gone from being repressed to becoming respected. More important, the overlapping of the picture stresses the perseverance and resilience of African culture in Brazil, and its victory over the institution of slavery.

The article depicts the Brazilian variant of slavery as a particular kind of institution that allowed African culture to be preserved. The reasons presented for this include the specificities of Portuguese colonization and the continuous influx of slaves, where new arrivals guaranteed the "Africanness" of the culture. Instead of portrayed as the oppressive framework in which Afro-Brazilian culture developed, slavery is depicted as a faint scenario for the vibrant and colorful Africanisms that today characterize Bahia. Slavery is represented as

THE CAPOEIRISTS BECOME MIRROR IMAGES OF
EACH OTHER, STOPPING, ROCKING, FEINTING, STRIKING.

was a way for Africans to practice their fighting skills without appearing to do so. Pairs of men perform what look like cartwheels, as graceful as gymnasts. They become mirror images of each other, stooping and rocking side to side, feinting, striking, defending, executing moves that look incredibly like break dancing. At no time do they touch one another; they are smiling, joyous. It is a game.

We are standing on the tip of Salvador the next morning, at the southernmost part of the city. To the east are several miles of *praias*, beaches, along the Atlantic Ocean. Stretching north are the bayside beaches (all told, Salvador's beaches span about 30 miles). Nearby, vendors hawk coconut

juice, sold right in the young green husks.

Our guide for the day, Carlos Scorpião, points to a tall black-and-white-striped lighthouse, the Farol da Barra, that sits on top of Forte de Santo Antônio. It is there, he tells us, that the Portuguese landed briefly in 1501 and planted their flag, christening the bay Baía de Todos os Santos—the Bay of All Saints. They ignored the name that the Tupi Indians, who had lived there first, gave it—*kikimuré*, the Sea Inside the Bay. I have since learned that there are today more than 10,000 indigenous people from 20 different tribes living in the state of Bahia.

In the sixteenth century Salvador was the center of the Portuguese sugar industry. As other New World colonists discovered, the Portuguese found that the

Indians could not be enslaved. So, beginning in 1538, they brought Africans to Brazil. Before the abolition of the slave trade in Brazil in 1888, more than a million slaves—from Benin, Nigeria, Togo, the Congo, Guinea, Cape Verde, Gambia—arrived in Bahia, mostly through Salvador, constituting about one-quarter of the total number of captured Africans brought to Brazil.

On the lawn sloping down from the lighthouse, young men in bright yellow pants perform capoeira. It is different from what I saw at the Balé: slower, less intense. I soon find that the martial art is practiced in a multitude of variations throughout Salvador, sometimes on stage, sometimes out in the street.

All capoeira is executed to the music of a *berimbau*, a bow-shaped instrument that makes, according to my friend and Latin-music scholar Ned Sublette, "a singing percussive tone, approximately in the low register of a cello or guitar," when struck with a thin stick called a *vaqueta*. Before each match the two athletes kneel in front of the berimbau player, shake hands, then step into a circle made up of other capoeirists and spectators and begin.

Left: Two men practice the Brazilian martial art called capoeira in front of Forte de Santo Antônio. Inset: Slaves fight with similar moves around 1822.

An elegant stone railing, plastered white, snakes among Avenida Sete de Setembro on the bay side of the city. Below is Barra Beach. Fishermen walk by with substantial catches. A man cooks cheese over charcoal; had I not tasted roasted cheese drizzled with molasses the night before, I might be skeptical, but it is a truly delicious combination. Fall and winter (our spring and summer, remember) are slow seasons in Salvador, but still there are lots of people here, many of them locals. This is a democratic beach, and there are many more here just like this one, from what I understand. Not for Salvador the gaunt, overpolished glitz of Rio. People

FIGURE 2.2 Page 74 of Audrey Peterson's article "Where Africa Also Lives," featured in *American Legacy: The Magazine of African-American History & Culture*, Winter 2006 edition.

having served the purpose of transposing African cultures to the New World, and then discreetly stepping out of scene once that job was completed: "We walk to the Largo do Pelourinho, the street where the infamous whipping post that lent its name to the neighborhood once stood. It was there that slaves were brought to be sold at auction or sent by their owners to be beaten and tortured as punishment for infractions small and large, real and imagined. *Nothing remains but the name.*"[60]

This article weaves together several dominant ideas about Bahia that African American tourists expressed during the interviews. First, it puts forward the notion that African culture *transcended* bondage, and therefore the legacy of slavery is found in the lively Africanisms of Bahian religion, food, music, dance, and visual arts, and not in the history of pain and suffering. Second, there is an emphasis on the *continuity* between the Africanisms brought over to Brazil centuries ago by enslaved Africans and the contemporary Afro-Brazilian traditions, thus overlooking the significant and ongoing processes of cultural transformation and hybridity. Third, the article suggests that Africanness defines Bahia, which is portrayed as a miniature version of Africa in the Americas and, therefore, a place where African Americans can find their cultural roots.

Various types of U.S.-produced media have endorsed Bahia's reputation as a site of preserved Africanisms. Probably no other source has been as explicit in disseminating this notion as the revealingly titled documentary *Bahia: Africa in the Americas*.[61] In addition to reiterating the same three dominant ideas about Bahia found in the article analyzed above, this documentary adds a fourth explanation for Bahia's preserved Africanness: the fact that a very special "ethnic group," the Yoruba, were brought at a later point in time and were mostly kept together in a context of urban slavery.[62] Cultural transplantation, purity, and preservation lie at the core of this documentary, which focuses greatly on Candomblé in order to sustain the notion that Bahia "although geographically located in Brazil, is emotionally rooted in Africa" as stated by African American anthropologist Sheila Walker, one of the film's narrators: "Bahia can be considered the capital of African culture in the Americas. And it can be considered that because, when one arrives in Bahia, if one can read the symbols, it becomes immediately clear that there is a lot going on that is not American in origin. It is African in origin. And what is most interesting about Bahia is that it is a modern city. But in this modern city there is something else going on that is ancestral."[63]

Not coincidentally, these ideas are also present in the previously discussed VARIG video, which many tourists watch in the orientation sessions. Once again, the portrayal of Bahia as a "closer Africa" is done at the expense of the history of slavery. While aerial shots of Pelourinho and some of its pompous Catholic churches built by slave labor are displayed, the narrator does not explain that the term *pelourinho* means slave whipping post, nor that the neighborhood of Pelourinho received that name because it was one of the city's most important settings for the spectacle of the public punishment of the enslaved. Instead, the documentary portrays the area as a place of cultural encounter: "Today Africa meets America again in the shadow of this square at the House of Benin, a museum and restaurant."[64]

The representation of Pelourinho as a site of cultural encounters, and devoid from the history of slavery, was already part of UNESCO's narrative when it added the location to its World Heritage List in 1985. Historian Ana Lucia Araujo explains that UNESCO ignored the site's relevance for the history of slavery in Brazil, and emphasized only the colonial architecture of the locale.[65] In tune with the representations that abound in the African American tourism discourse about Pelourinho, UNESCO did not even mention that this was a site where slaves were publicly punished, preferring instead to depict the area as a site of cultural merging: "Salvador is one of the major points of convergence of European, African, and Indian cultures of the 16th to the 18th century."[66]

The VARIG video similarly opts to portray Brazil as a place where people celebrate life and preserve a culture that survived captivity. The only other moment in which VARIG's documentary mentions slavery is when the narrator visits the basement of the Mercado Modelo, which is erroneously depicted as a place where enslaved Africans were disembarked and kept for sale.[67] But even then, the focus is, once again, on life over death as the narrator emphasizes the exhilarating culture that outlived the experience of captivity. The celebration of Bahia's Africanness contributes to enhance the idea of Bahia as a closer and more comfortable Africa, but this comfort is only made possible because slavery is depicted as having fulfilled the purpose of transplanting African culture to Brazil. Bahia is thus considered a "closer Africa" not only because it requires less time and physical distance for one's arrival from the United States, but also because it is represented as offering African Americans a more intimate and comfortable atmosphere than what is commonly found in the African continent. Revealingly, Bahia's "comfort" derives from a dominant representation that downplays Brazil's history of slavery.

The silencing of slavery in African American tourism discourse on Bahia contrasts sharply with the centrality of slavery in African American tourism to West Africa, where the history of the transatlantic slave trade is not only overt, but is in fact reclaimed. However, similarly to the representations of Bahia, the centrality of slavery in the discourses on West Africa is also imbued with the notion of an African American redemption. As Holsey explains, in African American tourism in Ghana, there is a "redemptive quality to the story of enslavement" in which the "return" to Africa is represented in the discourse of the tourists as an act of triumph over slavery.[68]

Converging Narratives

It is important to emphasize, however, that the correlation between the downplaying of slavery and the amplification of Bahia's Africanness is not exclusive to African American tourism discourse. Brazilian and foreign intellectuals, state officials, members of the Bahian elite, and Afro-Bahian religious leaders all contributed in different ways and with different motivations to forge this ideal. The process that gradually defined Bahia as "Brazil's Africa" began in the first half of the twentieth century and has entered the twenty-first century predominantly unchallenged.

In *Mama Africa: Reinventing Blackness in Bahia*, I analyzed the process through which local politicians and agents of the tourism industry produced the official discourse of *baianidade* (Bahianness) by grounding it on representations of a "joyful" and "infectious" black culture.[69] Diverging from the idea that the black image of Bahia had originated in the 1950s when it supposedly *replaced* the state's earlier representation of Brazil's melting pot, I argued that Bahia's aura of blackness was *compliant* with its image as a site of harmonious racial relations. I also contended that this process began at least as early as the 1930s under the influence of Gilberto Freyre's work, even though the process of construction of the official discourse of Bahianness did not follow a linear path. Some decades were more important than others in the process of emphasizing the "blackness" on which Bahianness was grounded.

The mixture of races and cultures, which before the 1930s had been equated with the incapacity of the Brazilian people to constitute a nation, began to mean the opposite, and was adopted as Brazil's myth of origin. Brazil was classified not only *mestiço*, but as a natural consequence of its *mestiçagem*, deemed to be devoid of racism. Miscegenation thus became the founding condition of the "Brazilian character." In this narrative of the Brazilian nation, Bahia was projected as the locus of the highest expression of Brazilianness, especially because of its black culture that, reduced to a set of symbols, was largely used as one of the pillars of racial and cultural mixture. Still during the 1930s, specific elements of black culture began to be used to compose Bahia's image and to define the characteristics of "Bahianness." Candomblé religion, for example, though still repressed by the police, started to function as a symbol of the celebrated cultural and racial mixture of both Brazil and Bahia, precisely because it "contained Africanisms," a quality that beforehand had justified its repression. Historian Anadelia Romo also argues that the idea of Bahia as racially harmonious was established in conjunction with the notion of Bahia as "traditional" and as a "city of the past." She explains that Bahia's status as the epicenter of Afro-Brazilian culture, although originally produced by Brazilian intellectuals and religious leaders, was later influenced by the arrival of several U.S. scholars in the late 1930s and early 1940s, including Melville Herskovits, E. Franklin Frazier, Lorenzo Dow Turner, Ruth Landes, and Donald Pierson.

It is well known that Herskovits's work played a crucial role in enhancing and divulging for an international audience Bahia's reputation as one of the sites of greater preservation of "Africanisms" in the Americas.[70] This notion was further strengthened in what has become known as the Herskovits-Frazier debate of the 1940s. While both authors agreed that black people in the United States and throughout the Americas had a "distinctive culture," they diverged on the reasons why that came to be. For Herskovits, the explanation lied on the retention of Africanisms, those "pieces of culture" brought from West Africa and which had survived in the New World despite centuries of slavery and oppression among diasporic blacks. For Frazier, the processes of capture, abuse, and discrimination, and not Africanisms, explained the distinctive social patterns of blacks in the Americas. Herskovits's position gained more currency within the academic and nonacademic realms. Romo argues that there was a politics of endorsement and suppression that pervaded the professional and personal relationships between Bahian and U.S. scholars, and which contributed to make hegemonic the depictions of Bahia as "Africanized" and "traditional."[71]

Historian Scott Ickes also analyzes the grounding of Bahia's regional identity on its African culture. Although this process started in the mid-1930s, it further materialized in the 1940s and 1950s with the advent of the State's efforts to establish and develop a tourist industry.[72] In addition to Bahia's colonial architecture, cobblestone streets, and its location on the beautiful bay that names it, Afro-Bahian cultural practices were then being transformed into tourist attractions. Although more significant changes would only come in the 1970s with the creation of Bahiatursa, government officials, businessmen, and journalists were already alerting for the city's potential as a tourism destination in the 1950s. An example of the promotion of Afro-Bahian culture for tourism was the hiring by the Diretoria Municipal de Turismo (Municipal Tourism Department) of capoeira masters to perform in "folkloric" shows for tourists as early as 1952.[73]

In the 1950s, as Bahia could no longer compete with the modern Southeast-ern states for political or economic power, the state became increasingly de-fined as the authentic guardian of Brazil's past. If this idea had already been put forward by institutions such as the Museu do Estado, events such as Bahia's Afro-Brazilian Congress, the narratives of foreign anthropologists, and the famous UNESCO studies, it was further projected in the budding tourism lit-erature produced by the state government to consolidate Bahia's status as the locus of Brazil's essence.[74] It was then that tourism began to occupy a central role in the production of Bahia's public image. This image has since relied on a celebratory Bahian way of life where black culture stands in for rhythm, plea-sure, and joy. The labeling of Bahia as the "land of happiness" had already circulated widely in 1938 with the release of Ary Barroso's song "Na Baixa do Sapateiro," which became an instant hit in Carmen Miranda's rendition. In 1979, Bahiatursa adopted the slogan "Bahia: Terra da Felicidade" in the branding of the state. The term was then included in all the tourism publicity material pro-duced or sanctioned by Bahiatursa. Similar slogans were created to brand Bahia for tourism purposes in the following decades, but none other became as widespread as "Bahia: Terra da Alegria" (Bahia: Land of Joy), created in 2003.[75]

Trope 2: The Happy Native

Answering my question as to why there are so many African Americans com-ing to visit Brazil, one of the female interviewees explained: "It's because many of us have this great deal of pride in African roots, and we now have a real need to begin to start tracing the *beginnings* and how *we* came to this continent."[76] Explaining what she expected to find in Bahia, another tourist, and member of Sylvia Marie's group, responded: "I expected to find 'me,' a part of my past, my ancestors, my culture, my people. I found a great deal of what I was looking for in all that I have learned during our cultural tours. I am most impressed."[77]

The search for roots, beginnings, origins, and the projection of one's imag-inary past onto the present reality of another community are common features of tourism encounters, especially within what has become known as "cultural" or "heritage tourism." And this is where roots tourism, although triggered by a desire to find the "same" converges with ethnic tourism and its search for the Other. I would argue that, despite having quite opposite motivations, roots tourism shares several of the characteristics of ethnic tourism, a concept that has been employed most commonly to refer to the experience where Western tourists seek out the exoticism of those they deem to be primitive peoples.

According to MacCannell, ethnic tourism is grounded on the binary opposites "us" versus "them" and "modern" versus "primitive," and it engages in the practices of stereotyping and fetishism. Another feature of ethnic tourism is that it establishes, at the same time, rhetoric association and antithesis; in other words, one can admire a specific aspect of the culture of the Other but still consider the Other's overall society as inferior or at a disadvantage when compared to one's own.[78] The latter trait, in my view, comes to life in the trope of the "happy native."

Several African American tourists expressed the idea that, despite being poorer than themselves, Afro-Brazilians are generally "happier." This happiness stems from the supposedly greater authenticity of their lives, which in turn is due to the greater "Africanness" of their culture. This idea came across very often in the interviews, and it was clearly stated, for example, by a female African American tourist in her mid-sixties: "Bahia is so rich with African culture that I felt a closer relationship with a possibility of being nearer to those who may be of my own ancestry. In a way I felt that the blacks here, while at a disadvantage economically, perhaps are better off than American blacks in holding on to some of their ancestral culture. I would hope that, through more education and awareness, both blacks in the U.S. and in Brazil will understand their connection and become one with a true cultural and ancestral bond."[79]

Upon visiting Bahia for the first time in the early 1990s, *Essence* magazine writer Lula Strickland-Abuwi made the same observation about local people's possessing a rich culture despite their material poverty: "Bahia is like that. Warm smiles and embraces make you feel welcome and in the middle of a cozy family reunion. Though the overall population of Bahia is humble in material wealth, I feel that I was given a most invaluable gift—a chance to experience a rich and still flourishing African culture."[80] The responses of the tourists to one of the questions in my questionnaire, "How was the connection with the local people?" confirm this very idea: "I could relate to the people in the villages. It reminded me of my own childhood days. They seem very happy with their lifestyle," wrote a female tourist in her mid-sixties. On the box for "additional remarks," this same tourist wrote: "I did not like the fact that the poor people have to live in undesirable houses."[81]

Another tourist, in response to the same question, "How was the connection with the local people?" responded: "There is a serenity and relaxation shown in the faces of people here vs. the more angry/hostile facial expressions one sees in African Americans in the U.S. Although there is greater poverty here, there is no visible anger, cursing, etc., which is a regular occurrence (unfortunately) in the U.S. among young children, teens and adults." Although she did not draw a connection between her answer to this question and her answer to a previous question, "What impressed you most in Bahia?" it seems plausible that these answers may be connected: "The pride and commitment regarding preserving African history and influence as reflected in the prominence of artists and art, music, and religion especially."[82] Another member of the same tour group, responding to the question, "What impressed you most in Bahia?," wrote: "The people are very generous and happy. They seem to enjoy themselves even though their lives may not be what they desire. I felt very much at home walking among the people."[83]

African American writer Rachel J. Christmas expresses a similar idea in her articles on Bahia's Africanness. Despite the racism, poverty, and inequality that afflict the lives of Afro-Brazilians, their connection to their African roots provides them with such a rich cultural life that it seems to function as compensation. Commenting on census figures that provide evidence of black people's economic and social disempowerment in Brazil, she states, "As an American, I found this scenario hauntingly familiar. Yet there was something wonderfully refreshing and uplifting in the way Bahians were still so firmly connected to our common roots."[84] In a similar article, published a few months later in the *New York Times*, Christmas reiterates this notion, but now blending it with the trope of Bahia as a closer Africa for African Americans: "I was not surprised at how refreshing it felt to be among people who were so firmly tethered to our common past." Later on, toward the end of the article she describes Brazil as a kind of surrogate Africa, as other authors have also done: "Brazil's vibrant culture had sent me on my first trip to Africa."[85]

The idea that Afro-Brazilians are more emotionally fulfilled despite their material deprivation was expressed in several interviews, magazine articles, and documentaries, and it can also be found in the lyrics of a moving song, aptly titled "There's Hope," composed and interpreted by India Arie, who visited Brazil with her band in 2002. In an interview on National Public Radio,[86] the famous singer explained the autobiographical nature of the song as it describes her experience of visiting Bahia and meeting a man who, even in the face of adversity, lived a happy life: "Off in the backcountry of Brazil, I met a young brother that made me feel that I could accomplish anything. You see, just like me, he wanted to sing. He had no windows and no doors, he lived a simple life and was extremely poor. On top of all of that he had no eyesight, but that didn't keep him from seeing the light. He said: What's it like in the USA? And all I did was complain! He said: Living here is paradise. He taught me paradise is in your mind."[87]

The African American search for a lost identity in Bahia is widely recognized on the Brazilian side of these tourism encounters, especially among the people that work directly with the tourists. One of the tour guides that has participated in African American tourism since the mid-1980s, explained that the tourists carry within them a kind of cultural void, differently from Afro-Brazilians who interact with African heritage on a daily basis: "A lot of people here have not yet understood why African Americans come here. They haven't understood that they [the African Americans] have this emptiness that they come here to fill."[88] A younger Afro-Brazilian guide, also based in Bahia, and who has worked in this realm since the early 2000s, similarly expressed that there are different levels of cultural fulfillment between African Americans and Afro-Brazilians: "They come here to find their identity. They come here to find what for a long time in their lives was taken from their knowledge. Christianity was their base while our base was Candomblé, the Orixás. So our roots have allowed for a permanence of our identity. So even if they have a different kind of religious faith, they are proud of what has been preserved here. And the roots in Bahia are natural. And to me it is a much greater pleasure to work with African American tourists than with, say, French tourists for whom everything here is *exotique*."[89]

Because Afro-Brazilians are portrayed as more culturally fulfilled, they seem to be permanently engaged with celebrating life. Several tourists expressed the idea that in Brazil people celebrate life more so than in other countries, or at least more than in the United States, despite the fact that they are considered to be living in a less developed stage. Describing her first visit to Brazil in 1998, African American activist and *Essence* writer Evelyn White tried to come to terms with the contradiction that she witnessed between a deprived material life and an advantaged spirituality that fed the joy for life among Brazilians. Upon arriving in Rio, White ran into a nearly twenty-block long street party where "a sea of people gyrate wildly as they dance the most sensuous sit-down-before-you-hurt-yourself-samba that I have ever seen. . . . Swept along by such exuberance, one could easily forget that Blacks in Brazil are still fighting for rights that most African Americans take for granted. Indeed, many Afro-Brazilians still live in dire poverty, shut out of the jobs, housing and schools that could improve their lives. But even in the face of these hardships, Blacks in Brazil seem imbued with a love of self that touches the entire country."[90]

Likewise, several African American tourists that I interviewed also expressed how pleased they were in encountering African heritage in the midst of a joyful people that seems to be constantly engaged with celebrating life. An African American tourist that was interviewed by a Bahian newspaper while attending the Festival of the Good Death also explained that she originally intended to also tour several other Brazilian cities, but after visiting Bahia she had realized that this was no longer necessary: "After Bahia, I don't need to know anything else. This place is very spiritual, there is a lot of magic here, and the people are very warm. Everywhere life should be like this: to work and to celebrate the mystery of life."[91] In a similar vein, a *New York Times* article on the Sisterhood of the Good Death, which was mentioned by several of the tourists as one of the sources they had read, also describes Bahia as a place where life is profoundly celebrated, even in a festival aimed at honoring death: "I did not expect to be doing a solo samba in the middle of a circle surrounded by hundreds of Brazilians, but the Festival of the Good Death turned out to be more fun than the name would suggest."[92]

The VARIG documentary *Brazil, a Celebration of Life* reiterates this same idea, as the title itself indicates. The video is filled with scenes of black people dressed up in colorful "African" looking clothing dancing in the streets, interspersed with shots of African themed paintings and sculptures, short interviews with Afro-Brazilian artists, and, of course, the omnipresence of Candomblé. The concluding statement, which is followed by a festive Brazilian Lambada song of the 1990s, illustrates the documentary's title and overall message: "Afro-Brazilian culture is alive in Brazil. It lives in the heart and the soul of the people. We see it everywhere, in their homes, in their religion, and, oh, how we feel it in the streets. Come to Brazil and celebrate life with your brothers and sisters from other shores. Celebrate life in Brazil."[93]

The myth of the Brazilian eternal celebration is, of course, previous to and expands way beyond African American tourism discourse. Perhaps the first version of the trope of the Brazilian happy native can be found in the letter of Pero Vaz de Caminha, the scribe who sailed with Pedro Álvares Cabral, the Portuguese navigator who "discovered" Brazil in 1500. Describing the newfound land as a tropical Garden of Eden, Caminha's narrative—in tandem with the then dominant language used by other European conquerors to depict the New World—points to the beauty, innocence, and harmony of the indigenous people. Several other iterations of the idea that Brazilians are an inherently harmonious and joyous people have been produced throughout the country's history, by Brazilians and foreigners alike, and from people occupying disparate positions of power.

During the first half of the twentieth century, the transformation of samba into Brazil's official national symbol and the resignification of carnival as the quintessential realm of the production and performance of Brazilianness consolidated the image of Brazilians as a festive people.[94] It was during that time, and more specifically in the 1940s, that a festive and joyful image of Brazil was disseminated in the United States through the wider circulation of Brazilian music, the colorful and stereotypical roles played by Carmen Miranda, and the Latin American characters of Disney cartoons, among other means.[95] The Brazilian government, in collaboration with the U.S. Good Neighbor Policy, was then actively engaged in disseminating the image of Brazilians as a happy people. These images continued to circulate, both domestically and internationally, during the second half of the twentieth century, when the image of the sexy, dancing mulata also acquired the status of national icon of Brazilianness.

Among African American tourists, especially the older generation that makes up the majority of the roots tourists, the festive characterization of Brazil also derives from the 1959 film *Black Orpheus*, which portrayed Brazil as "a postcard idealization" of the favela, revealing to the world the rhythms of samba and bossa nova and establishing Carnival as the main image of Brazil.[96] Most important, the film called attention to Brazil's blackness and the Africanized phenomenon of its Carnival "at a time when advances in aeronautics were making tourist travel available on a vast scale."[97] Several tourists made reference to this film, emphasizing how exciting it had been to watch a movie where everyone was black and happy.[98] Explaining the influence of this movie, one of the tourists stated, "I was about ten years old when I saw *Black Orpheus*. And that's sort of in the back of your mind. Basically I had never seen a celebratory event with the magnitude of *Black Orpheus* where everybody was black, you know? I was like, 'Where is this place where people look like me? Where is this place?' In the back of your mind there's this mystical fantasy. It was like seeing a Walt Disney cartoon."[99]

The trope of the happy native is very common in tourism discourse about the Other, and it can be found in a wide variety of tourism genres. In favela tourism, for example, tourists often comment on the "appreciation for life" that they seem to encounter among impoverished slum dwellers, despite their material deprivations. Describing his visit to the Rocinha favela in Rio de Janeiro as a transformative life experience, a white American tourist stated that one of the most important lessons that he learned from the visit was that "the people with less material goods are the ones that demonstrate greater appreciation for life, and they are the happiest ones, happier than those who have money."[100] In addition to being "happier," "natives" are often imagined as "purer" and more "authentic" than the tourists. In gay sex tourism, for instance, the stereotype of the "real macho" abounds in the tourism portrayals

of native men. Cantú's observation about the "Mexican macho" certainly applies to representations of Latin American and Caribbean men more broadly:
"In the Western queer imaginary Mexico and its men are somehow locked in
a spatiotemporal warp of macho desire. Mexico seems to represent a place
fixed in time where 'real' men can be found."[101]

Maybe nowhere else is the trope of the happy native more common than
in ethnic tourism, where Western tourists seek to observe the so-called fourth
world peoples, who are frequently marketed as the remaining specimens of
humankind. In this case, the lifestyle of the "natives" is often described as "purer"
due to their allegedly harmonious connection to nature. Dennis O'Rourke's
remarkable documentary *Cannibal Tours*, which follows a group of ethnic
tourists visiting a community of "primitive" and "exotic" Papua New Guineans,
highlights the unevenness of these encounters and the processes through
which both groups gaze at one another. One of the most striking scenes takes
place aboard a boat where two male Italian tourists are debating the life style
of the "natives." They conclude that the natives' way of life is, ultimately, better than their own, as they are truly living in nature: "They are happy and well
fed. Nature provides them with the necessities of life. And they don't have to
worry about thinking of tomorrow."[102]

Although the trope of the happy native is not surprising in the representations of ethnic tourism and favela tours, it is at least disconcerting in the context of gay tourism and diaspora tourism, where one of the purposes is to
engage with those with whom the tourist supposedly shares sameness. A common idea exists in ethnic tourism that "primitive" peoples are happy, despite
being underdeveloped, because they are "closer to nature." In the case of roots
tourism, blacks in Brazil are "happy" (or, comparatively, "happier" than in the
United States) because, although poor and not sufficiently organized politically, they have preserved their "original culture" and are, therefore, "closer to
Africa." If the primitive others of ethnic tourism are conceived of as the children
of humankind, the joyous Afro-Brazilian "siblings" are implicitly understood
as inhabiting an imagined African American past, when life was still authentic
and unaffected by the maladies of modernity. My research reveals that roots
tourism has a lot more in common with ethnic tourism than meets the eye. The
major features shared by these apparently opposite forms of tourism is that they
are grounded on the asymmetry of transnational encounters and they are both
sustained by a Western gaze that represents the inhabitants of tourist destinations as living in the past.

Trope 3: Black Evolution

Because they supposedly inhabit a premodern past, Afro-Brazilians are conceived of as not having yet developed the sophisticated tools needed to appropriately and effectively fight racism and advance within their society. Despite Brazil's abundance of roots, or supposedly preserved African culture, there is allegedly a shortage of political mobilization among Afro-Brazilians, which has impeded their social progress, especially when compared to the significant gains obtained by blacks in the United States. As a consequence, a major idea that characterizes the discourse of African American tourists is the notion that there should be an exchange between both groups, where African Americans, while partaking in the much-desired Africanness of Afro-Brazilians, should at the same time share with them their strategies of social and economic success, thus "leading" Afro-Brazilians toward advancement.

Most of the sources I examined confirmed the binary opposites tradition-versus-modernity and Africanness-versus-blackness that many tourists articulated in the interviews. In tandem with these binaries, the sources and interviews reflected a rather evolutionist understanding of blackness, grounded on the notion that Afro-Brazilians are yet to experience the developed forms of mobilization that have already been practiced by African Americans for many years. This idea was put forward, for example, in an *Ebony* article, titled "Blacks in Brazil: The Myth and the Reality," published in 1991, and which resorts to the notion that Afro-Brazilians will evolve as long as they seek the leadership of African Americans: "The realization that people of color remain disproportionately poor and disenfranchised despite government claims that racism was outlawed has helped the Black-nationalist movement grow. It has led Afro-Brazilians *to reach out to other blacks, particularly Black Americans for guidance* as they attempt to gain control of their own destinies."[103]

In fact, several of *Ebony*'s articles published in the 1990s made the case that racial consciousness was yet to be raised among Afro-Brazilians, and in line with the guidance provided by fellow African Americans. Among the cues that Afro-Brazilians should take from African Americans is the adoption of the one-drop rule so as to classify as black all of Brazil's *mestiços*: "Demographers estimate that of the nearly 80 million Brazilians who classify themselves as White, as many as 15 percent have enough of a trace of African ancestry to be considered Black by American standards. Internationally acclaimed actress Sonia Braga (a frequent guest on television's *The Cosby Show* and co-star of the movie *The Kiss of the Spider Woman*) is among the dark, abundantly hipped

'White' beauties about whom Black Brazilians whisper: 'she has more than a touch of the mother country in her.'"[104]

This article is critical to how Brazil's myth of racial democracy supposedly dissolves blackness into many color categories, but it ends on a more "hopeful" note as it explains that Afro-Brazilians, under the guidance of African Americans, are finally gaining racial consciousness: "But in spite of the bleak outlook, or perhaps because of it, *a new day is dawning for Afro-Brazilians*. After decades in which military dictators preached that complete amalgamation was the cure-all for festering racial tensions. Brazilians of African descent . . . *taking their cue from Black Americans*, are in the throes of a consciousness-raising movement designed to help gain political power to the civilian government and to highlight African contributions to the country."[105]

Many of the tourists that I interviewed also suggested that Afro-Brazilians should follow the African American path of letting go of the different color categories in order to unite around an exclusively black identity. Referring to the variety of color categories that set Afro-Brazilians apart from one another as a "divide and conquer strategy," a tourist that was in her early sixties when I interviewed her in 2000, stated that African Americans had also "gone through that" in the past, but that they had overcome it, and so should Afro-Brazilians: "We had to go through that process in the sixties in America, and then the realization came: 'Wait a minute, we are all black, and we are all in this together, we all have a struggle.' It might be a different type of struggle, but it is still a struggle. Within the families there are many deviations of skin color, there is every color within the rainbow, but we are all black, so it is very clear who we are. And I think that hasn't happened here yet. And once that takes place that's when you're going to see a true change in the country."[106]

Also contending that Brazil's widespread racial mixture has not meant the erasure of racism, African American writer Rachel J. Christmas describes how upsetting it was to witness so much racial inequality in Brazil. However, upon attending a rehearsal of a *bloco afro* in Bahia and seeing the youth's adoption of an Africanized aesthetics, she realizes that, finally, Afro-Brazilians have begun to develop racial consciousness. "The welcome profusion of natural hair styles we saw in Bahia was one indication of the healthier consciousness that *has begun to sprout*. This trend made it easier for me to cope with the country's socio-political ills, including its pervasive poverty."[107]

The idea that Afro-Brazilians lag behind African Americans in terms of economic and political achievements is present in circles as seemingly disconnected as commercial media and academic texts. Elsewhere, I analyzed a common trend among African American scholars of unfavorably comparing

Afro-Brazilian forms of struggle, resistance, and achievement to those of African Americans.[108] Anthropologist Sheila Walker, for instance, goes as far as proposing that Afro-Brazilians and African Americans should gaze at one another as if they were looking at a mirror so that they can exchange *Africanity* for *blackness*.[109] A more recent example of this hierarchical depiction can be found in the PBS documentary series *Black in Latin America*, organized and presented by Henry Louis Gates. An ethnocentric perspective that seeks to universalize the specific racial conceptualization of the United States underlies all the episodes, including the one that discusses race in Brazil, and which is revealingly titled "Brazil: A Racial Paradise?"

The evolutionist understanding of blackness is quite visible in a 1997 article published in *Ebony* on the supposedly emerging, not to say overdue, Afro-Brazilian political mobilization process, where Brazil is dubbed "the awakening giant" as it was finally "awakening to color and identity after a centuries-long sleep during which almost everyone avoided the imperatives of color."[110] Confirming the alleged paradox that Brazil abounds traditional Africanness while it lacks a modern form of blackness, the article reads: "The mark of Blackness is everywhere in this undiscovered country—its music is Black, or at least, off-White; its religion is African-oriented and African-influenced; its rhythm and, some say, its soul is Black—but Blacks have little or no power or influence and lag behind United States Blacks' political and social consciousness." Nonetheless, this backward condition of Afro-Brazilians could be solved once they follow in the steps of their American counterparts: "Some commentators have observed that Blacks in Brazil are approaching *a period of social activism similar to the ferment Blacks experienced in the U.S. in the '60s.*"[111]

Another article, published ten years later, also refers to Brazil as a giant, but this time a *sleeping* giant, and it reinforces the evolutionist idea that Afro-Brazilians lag behind African Americans and are therefore in need of assistance: "Brazil is an adventure that all African Americans should experience to glimpse an African presence flourishing in the Americas, as well as to *assist* Afro-Brazilians who are struggling for equality—as we were less than half a century ago—and by all accounts have not achieved. You won't regret the gesture."[112] These articles suggest that Brazil's "awakening process" is due, in large part, to the growing interactions between African American and Afro-Brazilian professionals, activists, and scholars. In my fieldwork, I encountered this same trope in the discourse of African American roots tourists and travel agents. In my first interview with Lionel Washington, the owner of one of the largest African American travel agencies operating in Brazil, I asked him what is it that characterizes the alleged exchange between Afro-Brazilians and

African Americans. His response is worth quoting at length: "I think that for the *African-Brazilians* it's important for them to see *who we are as a people* in the United States. There are certain things that we have attained that have not been attained by the African-Brazilians in Brazil. . . . I mean in terms of certain kinds of levels of education, in the economic advantages [and then he corrects himself and says:] *advances,* not advantages, economic *advances.*"[113]

The notions of "advancement" and "development" figure prominently in the statements of the African American tourists that I interviewed as they do in the pages of the magazines and in the websites that I examined. Another African American male tourist, who was in his early seventies when I interviewed him in Cachoeira, commented on how pleased he was to be in Bahia and to witness such a large concentration of people of African descent. "However," he stated, "I had thought previously that I would find not only a large [black] population, but I thought there would be greater *advancement* on the part of the Africans in this country, in this state, because I assumed that they would have used their political power to create a greater share of the wealth and a greater share of the power." "So, you felt disappointed?" I asked him. "As I learned about it, it was not so much disappointment, but I have to recognize that *that will happen;* but that *the stages of this development are less advanced* than I had thought."[114]

The same notions of development, advancement, and evolution were employed by African American tour leader Peter Johnson to explain the differences between African Americans and Afro-Brazilians. I asked him, "How would you compare, in general, historically, culturally, economically, on the one hand Afro-Brazilians and, on the other hand, African Americans? What are the major differences and what are the major similarities between both groups?"

PETER JOHNSON: To me, when I first started going to Salvador [in the mid-1980s] what I saw was the United States' civil rights struggle fifty years ago. In other words, Salvador was fifty years behind what we were doing here. You see, I talked to So-and-So [an Afro-Brazilian activist] and the things that they were doing there then we had already done here in America in the 1950s. Now, the difference is education. That is the biggest denominator. What I found in Salvador was that the masses were not educated. I think their aspirations were the same, but the advantages that we had here were education, the Negro colleges and things like that. And that's why I support that project they have in Bahia to get black kids into college. I supported them with books, and pens and pencils, from the beginning.

PATRICIA: I believe in an interview in which I don't just ask you questions, but where we really have a dialogue. And this idea that Brazilians kind of lag behind African Americans and are in a state of delay, I have heard this before, and in fact Spike Lee was in Brazil recently to film a documentary and he was there while the Supreme Court voted for the constitutionality of the racial quotas, and when they interviewed him, he said something similar to what you are saying, that Afro-Brazilians are now going through what African Americans went through several decades ago.

PETER JOHNSON: That's correct.

PATRICIA: I, honestly, I question that idea though.

PETER JOHNSON: Ok, come on.

PATRICIA: I think that different groups have different histories. And the moment that we say that Afro-Brazilians are living now what African Americans lived five decades ago, we are assuming that history happens in the same way for everyone, but just in different times. And I don't think that's how history happens. I think that history happens differently. Otherwise we might be establishing, 'these are the steps, and we have gone through steps one through ten, and you've only gone from one through five.' But what if the steps are different for different groups?

PETER JOHNSON: You might be right. That's one viewpoint. As you can tell, I talk to everybody. I want to hear from politicians, I want to hear from bartenders, I want to hear from the women on the streets. I want to get across views. And what I saw was the same thing: that everybody had the same aspirations, that they wanted things to change. They were complaining about Bahia being 90 percent black and they still had discrimination.

PATRICIA: In a way, the fact that you're telling me this, it's kind of good from a research point of view because it confirms this dominant idea, because I've heard this from several people who are serious people, like you. You know, this same statement you made about Afro-Brazilians being behind historically.

PETER JOHNSON: Well, I wouldn't say being *behind*.

PATRICIA: Well, being in a state of delay.

PETER JOHNSON: Going through evolution, that's better.[115]

In 2012, Spike Lee was in Brazil filming a documentary and in an interview to a Brazilian journalist he too reiterated the trope of black evolution. Commenting on the fact that the Brazilian Supreme Court had just voted unanimously in favor of the constitutionality of the racial quotas in higher education, Lee affirmed that affirmative action was absolutely crucial for the social inclusion of black people, and that it had played a major role in allowing African Americans to occupy positions of power in the United States. Although the vote was a big victory in Brazil, Lee cautioned that Afro-Brazilians still have a long way to go in order to obtain recognition, proof of which is the almost complete absence of Afro-Brazilians in the media, a problem that, in his view, African Americans no longer have to deal with. "My ancestors were freed in 1865, and slavery was abolished in Brazil in 1888. It's a small difference, but if we compare the evolution of African Americans and that of Afro-Brazilians, we are 20 years ahead."[116]

In my attempt to understand how these ideas were formed and became conventional, I asked the author of one of the magazine articles cited here which were his sources of information on Brazil. I asked him: "I am really curious to know which books you read, who you talked to at the time, and which sources you looked into in order to provide this information in your article. I am curious about the idea that Afro-Brazilians were looking up to African Americans from whom they were seeking guidance, as you explain in the article." He told me that he didn't really recall which books he read, although he did check out books from a library and he did talk to several people in the United States and in Brazil. "It is quite possible, I realize in retrospect, that my 'sample' was not representative of Afro-Brazilian feelings as a whole, and merely reflected the feelings of the people I stumbled upon in my convenience survey. It is also quite possible that they were merely saying things that they thought I, as an African-American, might want to hear."[117]

The author's response to my query confirms the argument that the reoccurrence of tropes in scattered sources helps to produce the cogency of a discourse. Representations do not emerge out of thin air, but are, instead, the reworking of already existing ideas. To represent is, to a lesser or greater degree, to engage in repetition; to reiterate the "traces"—"vocabulary, imagery, rhetoric, and figures"—left from past portrayals.[118] Furthermore, the journalist's response shares with my interviewees' statements the operations of intertextuality, that is, the presence of elements of other texts, whether written or spoken, in what one says or writes. In written texts, intertextuality tends to be more palpable because it usually, even if not always, takes the form of quotations followed by the attribution of sources. In the case of speech, however, the attribution of sources is less frequently practiced, but ideas and values produced elsewhere are certainly present in one's imagination, opinions, and assumptions, and these are not attributable to specific texts. Besides, the more frequently assumptions circulate, the greater is their power to shape the content of common sense and become hegemonic.[119] This process is no different within the context of tourism discourse production. Intertextuality among the different sources of information is constantly operating in the construction of the dominant tropes about particular places and peoples.

While persistently emphasizing the sameness they supposedly share with Afro-Brazilians, African American tourists are constantly, even if unintentionally, marking out the differences that set these two groups apart. This process occurs through the representation of time as much as it is done through the construction of place, bringing to mind Johannes Fabian's concept of allochronism, or the "denial of coevalness" between Self and Other, whereby the Other is relegated, simultaneously, to a different place and time. As it studied and thus constructed its object, evolutionist anthropology employed a conception of time that was not only secularized and naturalized, but also deeply spatialized. This temporalization of the Other, in turn, necessarily requires the spatialization of time.[120] The ideas disseminated by Western scientific discourses have undoubtedly expanded beyond the boundaries of academic production, seeping into popular imaginaries and representations of Otherness.

An example of the denial of coevalness in African American tourism discourse is the representation of Afro-Brazilians as living in the past, which was very often expressed in the interviews and the sources that I examined. Probably nowhere else is this idea more bluntly put forward than in a 2001 *Essence* revealingly titled "Brazil: The Way We Were." Colorfully illustrated with pictures of "African-looking" *baianas* selling *acarajés*, black men performing *capoeira*, and statues of *Orixás*, the article describes the author's search for whom African Americans "had been": "On my first trip to Africa more than a decade ago, I looked for traces of the ancestors. I'm not talking about gazing on their watery grave from the shores of Goree Island or studying the leg irons that kept them chained to adversity. I wanted to see less of what slavery had reduced us to and more of *who we had been*. Who knew the trail would lead to Brazil? Some people call the Brazilian state of Bahia the Africa of the Americas."[121]

The representation of Afro-Brazilians as "less developed" or "less advanced" than African Americans is coherent with the idea of Brazil as the "place to find roots" since both notions position Brazil in the past. The "past" however is not just any earlier time in history. In fact, the idea that Afro-Brazilians abound Africanness while lacking a modern form of blackness raises the question of which "past" is represented in the African American tourist gaze on Brazil.

Listening carefully to the tourism discourse, it is possible to identify two quite distinct historical periods to which this imagined past alludes. One is more specific and it can be located within African American recent history while the other is more generic and remote, and it is imagined as a past history commonly shared by African Americans and Afro-Brazilians.

The more specific past to which African American tourism discourse refers is the 1960s, a time of political effervescence when U.S.-produced markers of blackness—the black power movement, the "black is beautiful" aesthetics, soul and funk music, etc.—functioned as cultural references for black communities around the world. When Afro-Brazilians are represented in African American tourism discourse as currently inhabiting this specific time period, the comparison places them in an unfavorable position since they are imagined to be in a "previous stage of evolution." Conversely, when the imagined past is the more remote, colonial period when black life seemed to be steeped in the Africanness brought over by the enslaved, then Afro-Brazilians are represented as occupying a more advantageous position since they are supposedly more in tune with the "original" African culture. If the exhilarating encounter with the abundant African traditions of Afro-Brazilians is also a confirmation of the modernity of African Americans, then the travel to the past in Brazil— while not following the straight, centripetal line that marks the tours to West Africa—is still linear because it is imagined as progressing from one stage to another.

It is important to highlight that African American roots tourists are not the only ones who engage with the trope of evolution when imagining their diasporic counterparts. This seems to be, instead, a common feature of diaspora tourism at large. Chinese diaspora tourists, for example, although motivated by a desire to reconnect with their homeland, also tend to produce an othering of the place and the people they encounter by placing them in the past: "The overarching narrative is the genealogical past, which makes the geographic present a scene for negotiating the historic bloodline."[122] Similarly, roots tourists of Scottish descent describe their visits to Scottish Highlands as journeys to the past, where the present time dwellers still engage with a "simpler way of life."[123] Although the search of African American tourists in Brazil is not for biological relatives or to reaffirm identities based on bloodlines, as in the Chinese or Scottish cases, there is still a linear arrangement at play. Lineage in this case is replaced by linearity in a context where modern black subjects encounter their traditional black forebears.

Conclusion

African American tourists arrive in Brazil already bringing with them a set of concepts that were formed previously to, and in anticipation of, their trips and their encounters with Afro-Brazilian heritage. Although in a few occasions some of my interviewees mentioned Brazilian music and literature as having triggered their desire to visit Brazil, the great majority of the sources of information on Brazil cited by the tourists were in fact produced in the United States. This is relevant because it confirms that, despite its recent spurt of economic growth, Brazil still occupies a peripheral position when it comes to the global dissemination of culture and knowledge. The multiple geographies of coloniality that have, to some extent, blurred the dominant-centers-subjected-peripheries configuration of the world-system, have not done away with the unevenness of the transnational influxes of representations. The dominant channels of production and distribution of information remain firmly located in the Global North, and the English language continues to be the major "medium through which conceptions of 'truth,' 'order' and 'reality' become established."[124]

The brochures, posters, as well as the more detailed literature such as the magazines produced by the State of Bahia's tourism board usually reach these tourists only after a specific gaze has been formed. Conversely, although Brazilian-based media has had very little direct influence over the African American roots tourist gaze, it is clear that the mid-twentieth century exchanges between Brazilian and foreign scholars regarding Bahia's Africanness have greatly informed the contemporary representations of Brazilian slavery and Afro-Brazilian heritage. It is not surprising, therefore, that ideas produced as the result of a transnational dialogue are present in different cultural contexts. Thus, notwithstanding their different origins and distinct motivations, African American roots tourism discourse and the Bahian official tourism discourse simultaneously foster the idea of Bahia as a "closer Africa," where a joyful black population was able to preserve the Africanness of their culture, despite the three and a half centuries of slavery.

It is undeniable that the common experiences of enslavement, racism, and racial inequality have affected African Americans and Afro-Brazilians, certainly producing shared structures of feelings among these diasporic counterparts. But transnationally forged identities do not obliterate the unevenness that sets apart different national affiliations. The attempt to ascertain "sameness" has led to the representation of a single chronology for both groups, where Africanness is understood as a previous and thus lower stage in the path toward blackness. If, as Enrique Dussel explains in his critique of European modernity, "chronology reflects geopolitics,"[125] and if, as I have argued here, the chronology of roots tourism sustains an evolutionist understanding of blackness, then it is vital to recognize that any attempt at building transnational black identities must necessarily tackle the asymmetries of the black diaspora.

Louise's ability to find her past in Brazil is thus made possible less because of the African heritage that has been "preserved" in Bahia and more because of the geopolitics of knowledge that has enabled African American tourists to discover, and at the same time, produce places abroad. On the other hand, it is from this same advantageous position that African Americans have sought to establish transnational links of solidarity with Afro-Brazilians. Instead of merely criticizing what they view as the less developed stage of their diasporic counterparts, many African American roots tourists have attempted to deploy their privileged positionality in projects aimed at transforming the lives of Afro-Brazilians. How they have done this and, in turn, how Afro-Brazilian activists and cultural producers have participated in these projects and positioned themselves as coproducers in the processes of diaspora-making, is the subject of the following chapter.

CHAPTER THREE

Black Gringos in Brazil?

Encounters in Sameness, Difference, Solidarity, and Inequality

Look around you. How many black people do you see here?
You should be ashamed of yourselves.

—Carl Hart, opening his keynote address at the International Brazilian
Institute of Criminal Sciences Seminar, August 28, 2015

In late August 2015, the news that the African American neuroscientist Carl Hart was barred at the Tivoli Mofarrej—the five-star hotel that was hosting the seminar where he was a keynote speaker—made headlines in the Brazilian press.[1] The incident generated a frenzy of posts in Brazilian social media under such captions as, "Black American professor is barred at hotel"[2] and "Black and with dreadlocks Columbia Professor is the target of security guards in São Paulo hotel."[3] Hart explained that he was never directly confronted or had his entrance obstructed and was actually only made aware "that something was going on" when the conference organizers poured him with apologies for the fact that a security guard had tried to approach him as he had entered the hotel. Hart was later asked to comment on the incident in several interviews, and while he minimized the impact this had on him as an individual, he took advantage of the occasion to speak on behalf of those whom he views as the real victims of racism in Brazil: the black citizens of the country.

> For me, it was a relatively minor incident because, as I think about what happens in this society every day, this society has effectively shut out its black population. . . . Whereas me, I had people come to my aid and they took care of that incident before it even affected me, so that's minor in my life. But the thing that most concerns me is that there is not the same amount of outrage in this society for the black citizens of this society. For example, in all the spaces that we go in, like that meeting, that conference, there were so few black people there, there are so few black people in the universities, in the middle class, in politics, your politicians. The country has 50 percent African population, but they are shut out. That's more of a concern to me. . . . It's more important to worry about the regular citizens

of this society, so if I can bring some attention to what they go through, that's far more important.[4]

In an article published in the Brazilian newspaper *Folha de S. Paulo*, and aptly titled "O Viral e o Crônico" (The viral and the chronic), Hart once again compared the massive attention that his "non-incident" received with the predominantly overlooked and recurrent forms of discrimination affecting the lives of Afro-Brazilians. He explicitly referenced the police raids of buses in Rio de Janeiro where poor black men from the favelas were being impeded from going to the beaches in the middle-class neighborhoods of Ipanema and Copacabana, and the recent, and as of yet unpunished, slaughter of nineteen impoverished men in São Paulo, where the main suspects are members of the state's military police. None of these horrifying episodes, or the daily racial discrimination suffered by blacks in Brazil, generates a fraction of the solidarity that he has received, declared Hart in his op-ed piece.[5]

Despite the many reactions of embarrassment and surprise that followed this incident, this was not the first time that discrimination of a prominent African American guest made headlines in Brazil. In mid-July 1950, the renowned choreographer and anthropologist Katherine Dunham was barred at the upscale Esplanada Hotel in São Paulo, although she had made an advanced reservation and despite the fact that her white husband, who was accompanying her, was provided accommodation. This event too garnered nation-wide attention, and it is frequently cited as having resulted in the establishment of the Afonso Arinos Law, the first Brazilian law against racial discrimination.[6] Dunham vigorously denounced the incident and attempted to file a suit against the hotel, eventually prompting the president of Brazil to apologize to her. Afro-Brazilian activists joined in the condemnation of this racist act, and publicized it as proof of Brazilian antiblack racism.

The sixty-five-year gap that separates Hart's and Dunham's incidents does not diminish their similarities. Both cases involve high profile African American visitors who were, purportedly or effectively, racially discriminated. Both episodes received a lot of public attention and were broadly reported and discussed in the mainstream media. The foreign and, more specifically, the *American* identity of these visitors contributed significantly to make these incidents widely known. Another major commonality shared by both episodes is that they occurred in the secluded space of upscale hotels, thus pointing to the importance of place for the mapping of race. Whether directly or indirectly, both cases had implications for policymaking in Brazil: the establishment of the Afonso Arinos Law in the case of Dunham, and Hart's advocacy for the creation of nonracially driven drug policies. Most important, however, is that both visitors strategically deployed the attention they received to shed light on the racism affecting black people in Brazil. Instead of emphasizing their individual victimization, both Durham and Hart opted instead to express solidarity with Afro-Brazilians.

These two incidents and their repercussion in Brazil capture some of the central issues analyzed in this chapter: the power of the *Americanness* of African Americans while abroad, their awareness and active use of this privileged positionality to establish links of solidarity with their diasporic counterparts, and the ways in which Afro-Brazilians have responded to and participated in processes of transnational black solidarity, sometimes also expediently deploying the Americanness of U.S. blacks so as to enhance their fight against racism and racial inequality. Although the Americanness of African Americans is not in itself a novel research topic, the phenomenon of roots tourism offers a specific and enriching context to examine the national components of diasporic identities. International tourism constitutes an encounter between groups that, although occupying unequal positions of power, are undoubtedly *agents* in the process,[7] and are therefore, *coproducers* of the meanings and practices that result from this encounter.[8] In this case, African Americans and Afro-Brazilians are both counterparts in the production of Afro-Atlantic dialogues and in the processes of diaspora-making.[9] To understand how these factors unfold in the specific context of African American roots tourism in Brazil requires investigating how national affiliation affects the construction of transnational racial solidarity, and the intricate ways in which difference and inequality challenge the attempts at constructing sameness.

African American Leadership of the Black Diaspora

As a historically oppressed minority in the United States, African Americans have been at the forefront in establishing links of solidarity with subjugated communities around the world, and especially so with their counterparts in Africa and the diaspora. Examples abound. In the 1920s, for instance, African American activists and intellectuals campaigned for the end of the U.S. occupation of Haiti. Protesting against U.S. imperialism and economic exploitation, they were able to significantly influence public opinion through their speeches, books, articles, and plays, making Haiti a matter of public controversy.[10] Later in the century, World War II further informed the African American sense of kinship with other oppressed peoples around the world. The

Council on African Affairs, led by actor and intellectual Paul Robeson, played a major role in increasing awareness of the exploitative conditions of capitalism in Africa and providing support for anticolonialist movements. In the 1950s, as African Americans fought for the expansion of their civil rights at home, they continued to envision black liberation as a global struggle for justice that included solidarity with the independence movements in Africa. Although by then anticolonialism was no longer a central issue on the agenda and was not a programmatic part of the civil rights movement, it continued to be present in the discourse of its most prominent figures, such as Martin Luther King Jr.[11] And while in the following decades, from the 1960s to the 1980s, African American political discourses may have overall lost its more radical edge, the critique to American capitalism and imperialism grew even stronger within specific African American organizations, such as the Black Panther Party, and via the active engagement of African Americans in the international campaign against Apartheid in South Africa.

African American transnational solidarity has also taken place in the contemporary context of roots tourism. Aware of their power as U.S. citizens and cognizant of the clout of their U.S. dollars, African American tourists in Brazil have actively "made use" of their identity to benefit Afro-Brazilians. In addition to the donations in cash and goods, such as books and school supplies, that are a common feature of their visits to Afro-Brazilian organizations, there has also been a constant demand on the part of African American tourists that more Afro-Brazilians benefit from the tourist dollars that they bring to the country. African American travel agencies and/or the groups that hire them frequently request that their tourist guides be black individuals, for example. There is also a general complaint about the fact that hotel employees in managerial and front desk positions are predominantly white (or light-skinned) Brazilians. African American tourists have also prioritized patronizing Afro-Brazilian-owned businesses whenever possible.

The lobbying made by African Americans on behalf of Afro-Brazilians is certainly well intended, and it has begun to generate results. At the same time, it is frequently accompanied by a discourse that establishes the leadership role that African Americans should occupy in the "advancement" of Afro-Brazilians. The notion that Afro-Brazilians are less developed socially, politically, and economically than African Americans can be located within a historically longer and geographically broader practice of African-American representations of other black communities in Africa and the African diaspora. The "evolved stage" of U.S. blacks vis-à-vis their diasporic counterparts has been a recurrent trope in these representations even within those contexts in which African Americans have sought to establish links of camaraderie due to common struggles and shared goals.

The coexistence between practices of solidarity and processes of hierarchization within transnational black relations has been examined by a number of researchers of the black diaspora, including several African American scholars. In *Forging Diaspora: Afro-Cubans and African-Americans in a World of Empire and Jim Crow*, Frank Andre Guridy employs the concept of "diaspora making" to describe the process through which African Americans and Afro-Cubans began to see themselves as part of a larger, transnational "black race." He analyzes both groups' attempts to forge commonality across difference and the development of common transnational strategies to fight racial exclusion. Yet, while examining how antiblack racism united these two black groups across national boundaries, Guridy pays close attention to how the ideology and material conditions of U.S. empire shaped these encounters. "The imperial assumptions in diasporic encounters were embedded in the postemancipation ideology of racial uplift, which resonated deeply with upwardly mobile blacks throughout the diaspora. As the historiography of the Pan-African movement showed long ago, diaspora projects emanating from blacks in the West were frequently based on the assumption that they were more 'civilized' than Africans in the continent of Africa. In short, the task of uplifting the 'race' from the vestiges of slavery fell on the shoulders of African descendants in the diaspora, particularly African-Americans, who often saw themselves as the leading lights of the global 'colored race.' This hierarchical understanding of the diaspora's relationship to the continent was replicated in African-Americans' perceptions of their relationship with Afro-Cubans."[12]

The hierarchical relationship among diasporic blacks has also been discussed in *Disparate Diasporas: Identity and Politics in an African-Nicaraguan Community*.[13] Before carrying out his ethnographic work among the Creoles in Bluefields, Nicaragua, Edmund Gordon had become very involved with the African People's Socialist Party in the 1970s. Therefore, he arrived in the field ready to "instruct" the Creoles that, as "blacks," they were supposed to ally themselves against the racist and imperialist U.S.-led capitalist forces, and therefore side with the Sandinistas. In addition to the shock of being called a "gringo" upon arriving there, Gordon was also surprised to find out that the racial and political situation was not as "black and white" as he had assumed it to be. The author's witty self-critique of the condescendence of his mission to "enlighten" the Creoles is in line with the book's recognition of the impossibility of imposing a singular form of blackness onto disparate Afro-descendant communities.

Also critical of an African American self-portrayal as the "global leaders" of the black race is Paulla Ebron's sharp analysis of the privileges, entitlements, and conspicuous consumption of the roots tourists with whom she traveled to the Senegambia region as part of a *McMemories* tour.[14] The author highlights the irony of a tour sponsored by the giant hamburger chain McDonalds, seen worldwide as a symbol of U.S. imperialist commercial domination, but which has become an enabler of minority cultural identities in the United States.[15] Among the unequal interactions that took place between the African American tourists and the Senegalese and Gambian hosts were the tourists' misconceptions about Africa grounded on a narrative of underdevelopment and on the idea that "Africans lacked business sense."[16] Ebron ironically remarks that the African American tourists "had a solution to the continent's 'problems.' As businessmen, with a consciousness of course, they would *develop* Africa."[17] Her fierce critique of the inauthenticity of the "homeland" tour is balanced, nonetheless, by her acknowledgement that this experience "at least had the advantages of reverent attention and heartfelt—if transient, privileged and awkward—solidarity."[18]

African Americans' entrepreneurial skills have often been cited as one of the features that they should share with their diasporic counterparts. This was evident, for example, in Booker T. Washington's Tuskegee Institute where, in the early twentieth century, Afro-Cubans and other members of the African diaspora were to be racially uplifted through learning industrial trades such as farming, construction, and the production of goods.[19] The idea that African Americans should spread their industrial and business skills across the diaspora has worked its way to the present time. For instance, an African American male tourist that I interviewed in 2004 argued that roots tourism should function as an opportunity for African Americans to establish economic relationships with Afro-Brazilians, which would, consequently, help the latter develop their country:

> There needs to be an economic relationship. There needs to be a step
> past the disposable income. This tourism to Brazil, and Bahia in particular,
> for African Americans is great, but there's more to be learned. I think one
> of the things from the point of view of Brazil for African Americans is not
> just the discovery of the preservation of African history, but what is the
> participation of Afro-Brazilians in *modern* Brazil? And how can African

Americans facilitate? Because of our participation in the modern United States, so to speak, what do we have to offer that could be helpful? And I see that as business.[20]

The leadership role that African Americans should play in the African continent and diaspora has been envisioned through the business lens, whereby they would economically develop and socially uplift their black peers, but it has also been conceived through the employment of their modern and Western positionality to help preserve threatened cultural and religious traditions. The latter is exemplified in Clarke's analysis of African American Yoruba revivalists in Nigeria and their decision to "rescue" Yoruba religion. Clarke argues that, disappointed with the dominance of Christianity and Islam and the impact of colonialism in diminishing Yoruba religion and culture, a group of African American Yoruba revivalists decided that "the future of retaining Yoruba cultural and religious traditions was no longer in the hands of Yoruba in West Africa but in the future of black people in the African diaspora.... Otherwise interpreted, the future of Africa was in the hands of blacks in the Americas."[21]

The coorganizer of the 1978 New World Festival of the African Diaspora who is, in fact, a businessman, also made the case that African Americans are supposed to share their entrepreneurial skills with Afro-Brazilians. He explained that one of the consequences of the festival was that black Brazilians then discovered that African Americans had access to specific goods, such as hair products and makeup designed specifically for black people, and which were not available for them in Brazil. So they started to ask him to bring some of these products and, as a result, he became a sales representative in Brazil for an African American line of hair products. Realizing the niche's potential, he brought not just the hair products but also the hair styling techniques. He established an agreement between Soft Sheen and SENAC that ended up training a total of 5,000 hairdressers in the states of Bahia, São Paulo, and Rio de Janeiro.[22] He spoke very proudly about how this process benefited Afro-Brazilians not only financially but also socially as it contributed to elevate their self-esteem through the care of their bodies. Reiterating the trope of black evolution, he explained that Afro-Brazilians were following in the footsteps of African Americans not only in political terms but also in the aesthetic realm since, at the time (late 1970s), "Brazil was twenty to thirty years behind the U.S. in beauty care products and services [for black people]."[23]

The idea that African Americans are more advanced than their diasporic counterparts and should therefore play a leadership role in the black diaspora can also be found in African American reports on Brazil from as early as the late nineteenth century. Challenging the then dominant notion that Brazil was a racial Eldorado, African American historian William T. Alexander, in his book *History of the Colored Race in America*, published in 1887, vehemently criticized the slow pace of the Brazilian abolition process, and urged U.S. blacks to organize for the release of their Brazilian "brothers."[24] A few decades later, upon facing discrimination in Brazil, which included being barred at hotels and rejected by Brazilian women, African American journalist Ollie Stewart proposed that the solution for Brazil's color line would be for a large number of African Americans to invest economically in the country and occupy positions of power such as owning banks, farms, and newspapers. "The trip convinced me that the American colored man is ahead of any other colored group I have seen. Brazilians have the greatest opportunity because they are so far behind."[25]

Past and present African American visitors to Brazil have proposed that, in order to challenge racism and discrimination, black people should not only pursue positions of power but they should also physically occupy places that have been traditionally marked by racial segregation, such as the secluded space of upscale hotels, to which African Americans, as black yet foreigners, have greater access. Similar to Stewart's suggestion in the 1940s that a large number of African Americans should tour Brazil and make their presence visible in exclusive spaces, the African American coorganizer of the 1978 New World Festival of the African Diaspora explained that one of the positive outcomes of this event was that it served as an eye-opening experience for Afro-Brazilians for whom African Americans, by occupying spaces that were off-limits for black people in Brazil, were serving as role models: "To see these people who looked like them going into the Meridien, and Othon, and Hotel da Bahia started a whole process where Brazilians, who did not see themselves as being able to go into these areas, began to do so, began to dialogue, began to discuss."[26]

One of the peculiarities of the leadership role that African Americans are supposed to play in the black diaspora is that it is conceived in relationship to people that are envisioned much more as "same" than as "other." In that sense, my study shares with the analyses of these various African American scholars referenced above a critique of how the "badge" of U.S. nationality affects the relationships of African Americans with other black communities in the African diaspora. Like my own, these studies scrutinize how efforts of solidarity toward those who are deemed the "same" do not necessarily do away with processes of hierarchization, thus creating a language and practice of solidarity that are, nonetheless, permeated by the notion of Western authority. Mary Louise Pratt argues that part of being a Westerner is to identify the Other as in need of one's intervention and uplifting.[27] This goes hand in hand with the notion that one's vantage point is the only one or the best one available, a conviction that leads Westerners to claim authoritativeness for their vision despite being on foreign land.[28] This self-entitlement, continues Pratt, is not exclusively a white male trait: Western women, hyphenated white men, and postcolonial writers, like Albert Camus and Richard Wright, have also occupied that space as they too have reworked the inherited tropology of estheticization, density of meaning, and domination.[29]

It is important to highlight, however, that African Americans have not been the only historically oppressed group to practice the Western "othering" of those with whom they share sameness. We could add to Pratt's list of subjugated-at-home-while-dominant-abroad actors, Western feminists, and U.S. gay men. North-American gay sex tourists, for example, while attracted to "exotic" and "different" local models of same-sex desire, often view themselves as promoters of modernity and gay rights in Brazil.[30] Although the economic uplift of Brazilian impoverished male sex workers is not the primary motivation for U.S. gay travel, "there is an element of paternalism . . . which, at its most visible, involved gay Northerners assuming a global gay identity and prefiguring a global gay community that they are obligated to protect, defend, and foster."[31] Also looking at tours that seek to promote "queer solidarity," Jasbir Puar argues that Western gay tourists in the Global South "operate within a missionary framework of sameness and difference, assuming some rubric of queerness that is similar enough to create solidarity around but is different from and, as such, not quite on par with metropolitan queerness."[32] M. Jacqui Alexander had already critiqued the "Orientalizing discourses" formed within the context of gay sex tourism in the Caribbean and their similarity with the scripts formed in heterosexual sex tourism, arguing that both draw on the same imperial geography and analogous epistemic frames.[33]

White feminists from the Global North have also often engaged in the Western othering of women from the Global South. A similar process of hierarchization had taken place in the making of transnational links of solidarity among women in the late nineteenth century when European and North-American feminists set out with "missionary zeal" to promote women's rights and social reform in the rest of the world. "The protagonists of these early organizing efforts were inspired by a 'spirit' of internationalism. But from early from, the divisions of class, nation, and empire were deeply embedded in feminist discourses and practices."[34] These hierarchies continue to be reproduced in current projects of transnational feminism. Although globalization has contributed to bring women together, it simultaneously makes more visible the inequalities that set them apart due to their different geopolitical locations.[35]

Arguing that national identity is integral to First World subjectivity, even when First World subjects deploy their privilege to act as claimant on behalf of others, Gada Mahrouse contends that Western white women, while oppressed at home, often enjoy masculine privilege when they find themselves practicing international solidarity activism in developing countries.[36] It seems that a comparable process happens race-wise in the context of African American sex tourism in Brazil. According to Woods, who interviewed several African American male sex tourists in Rio de Janeiro, Brazil allows black American men to experience a type of power that they do not experience in the United States.[37] Despite its sensationalist and moralist approach and its lack of a deeper critical analysis, Wood's book contains a wealth of research data on how African American sex tourists envision their newly found privileged positionality in Brazil. Especially revealing are their comments on how their American subjectivities approximates them to whiteness. This was expressed, for example, by an interviewee who was delighted because, after touring Brazil, he could finally say, "I [now] know what it feels like to be white,"[38] and another who explained that, as an American in Brazil, "I didn't feel like I had the nigger label on my back. . . . You're treated like you're almost a star."[39]

Whether traveling as sex tourists or roots seekers, Western consciousness and selfhood permeate African American relationships with Afro-Brazilians. Conversely, while African Americans constitute the wealthiest and most influential group in the black diaspora, their status as an oppressed group within the United States is crucial for their identification with Afro-Brazilians and other diasporic communities. As argued by an African American tourism agent operating in Brazil since the 1980s, "Everywhere blacks are on the bottom." I therefore do not downplay the subjugated condition of African Americans within the context of the United States. In addition to that, I too reject the cliché that diasporization is merely "imperialism in blackface."[40] African Americans in general have genuinely sought to establish camaraderie with other Afro-descendants; and African American tourists, in particular, are earnestly interested in building transnational links of solidarity with Afro-Brazilians.

At the same time, in order to understand identity as a principle of solidarity, it is necessary to "comprehend identity as an effect mediated by historical and economic structures, instantiated in the signifying practices through which they operate and arising in contingent institutional settings that both regulate and express the coming together of individuals in patterned social processes."[41] I thus examine roots tourism and the roots tourists' attempts at building solidarity through a perspective that takes into account the elements of continuity and rupture in the creation of modern hierarchies of power, wealth, and recognition and the different effects of these elements on black peoples depending on where they live. The study of transnational black relations must consider how the "power geometry of time-space compression,"[42] that is, the different positioning of social groups vis-à-vis global flows, affect the relations among black communities in the diaspora. My analysis, therefore, takes into account the dominance of the United States as a center, especially in terms of cultural and academic production, and the unequal access to global currents of power for those located in the core and in the semiperiphery of the world-system.

Constructing Transnational Black Solidarity via Roots Tourism

The turn of the twentieth to the twenty-first century has witnessed a boom of new forms of travel whereby Westerners have sought to employ their privilege, knowledge, resources, and even the status of their nationality for the benefit of their disadvantaged peripheral Others. The attempts to challenge the more often than not unequal international tourism encounters have gained life through a wide range of new genres of tourism that include, for example, "fair trade tourism," where the aim is to funnel tourism dollars to support indigenous and/or marginalized communities, and "volunteer tourism" (also called "voluntourism"), where Western youth go to African and Central American countries on service learning trips in which they engage in hands-on activities such as building cisterns and rebuilding schools. Perhaps the most controversial, and certainly the most radical, of these forms of travel are the so-called solidarity tours, where activists from the Global North travel to the Global South with the goal of deploying their Western citizenships in the defense of oppressed peoples. In many cases, Westerners go as far as positioning their prized bodies as "human shields" in such places as Iraq, Chiapas in Mexico, and in the Palestinian territory occupied by Israel.[43]

Although African American tourism in Brazil is not nearly as politically drastic or physically taxing as these solidarity tours, it shares with this as well as with the alternative forms of tourism described above the important concern over how one's international travel can contribute to the well-being of disenfranchised communities abroad. Aware of their power as U.S. citizens, African American tourists in Brazil have actively "made use" of their identity, as both tourists and Americans, to benefit Afro-Brazilians. There has been a constant demand on the part of African American tourists that more Afro-Brazilians benefit from the tourist dollars that they bring to the country. They have done this in a variety of ways that can be classified into general and recurrent solidarity *practices*, and specific solidarity *projects*, some of which have been completed while others are ongoing.

General and Recurrent Solidarity Practices

In my view, the most impactful examples of the general and recurrent practices of solidarity carried out by African American tourists in Brazil have included the donations in cash and goods that they make during their visits to Afro-Brazilian organizations; their financial support for Afro-Brazilian business owners, entrepreneurs, and artists; and their requests for black tour guides. Lionel Washington explained that for African Americans it is crucial to support Afro-Brazilians economically and politically, and that this is part of a broader transnational practice of solidarity among black communities. He sees these solidarity practices as being based on Kwame Nkrumah's "philosophy of African self-reliance": "What we need to do as people of African descent is come together to work on our behalf. We have to look at our interests as a people, because no one else is going to do it for us. We have to create our own model, for us, as a people."[44]

The visits to organizations that seek to empower Afro-Brazilians are a crucial component of African American roots tourism in Brazil, and they are always included in the itineraries of the tour groups. I observed this in every single group that I accompanied and in all the itineraries to which I had access. The organizations range from neighborhood associations to *blocos afro*, from Candomblé *terreiros* to educational institutions, and from independent schools to NGOs. Although initially the donations to these organizations were made spontaneously and without much previous arrangement, gradually, as roots tourism became more established and the visits to specific Afro-Brazilian organizations became more regular, the donations also became more systematic, and they are now often included in the total cost of the trip. Sylvia Marie, for instance, explained that when she first started to bring her own tour groups in 2004, she used to collect a contribution from each tour member "on the spot," that is, during the visit to an organization. But then she realized that it would make more sense to collect these contributions beforehand, not because her tourists are not generous donors, but because most of them prefer to have all their expenses planned ahead of time. The amount of the donation has ranged from US$20 per person to a total of US$700 that one of her groups collected "on the spot." She said that the donations were meant not only to support these organizations and the fantastic work they do, but also as a way of paying them for their time: "If an organization is going to spend time lectur-ing for us, it is only fair that we pay them. Besides, we are contributing for a cause."[45]

In tandem with Sylvia's observation, the coordinator of one of the most vis-ited black organizations in Salvador, explained that, for a very long time, he and other leaders of the institute had gladly carried out meetings with the Af-rican American tourists, welcoming them to the organization and lecturing sometimes for two or three hours in a row, without charging anything for it. He said that they had internally debated the ethical question of whether they should charge a fee for these visits, especially because, as he put it, "We are not a museum to be charging an entrance fee; we are an organization so we always asked ourselves 'how can we charge to talk about who we are and what we do?' On the other hand, however, the two or three hours that I or some-one else from the institute spend meeting and talking with the African Amer-icans is a time that we carve out of our work schedule. So we then decided that charging a fee, which in my view is still pretty minimal, would make sense."[46]

Payment is also made to the speakers, many of whom are Afro-Brazilian intellectuals and activists that are asked to lecture for the tour groups. These talks usually occur at the hotels that are patronized by the groups or in the headquarters of the Afro-Brazilian organizations. Longtime tour guide Lidia Matos explained that the choice of the lecturers has a lot to do with the spe-cific interests of specific groups, for example, some groups were more inter-ested in black women's rights, others in Afro-Brazilian religion, etc., but it also depends on whether the group is willing to pay for the more expensive ser-vices of some well-known academics. Over the years, as the tour leaders have made recurrent visits to Brazil, a handful of activists and academics have grad-ually become the preferred speakers for their tour groups. A similar process has happened with the Afro-Brazilian organizations: although there are plenty to choose from, only a few of them have become regular "stops" in the itiner-aries of the African American tourists. If, on the one hand, this selection pro-cess reflects the successful work carried out by these specific Afro-Brazilian organizations, thus transforming them into important attractions for the roots tourists, it is also the result of networking processes where the tour guides, as cultural brokers, have played a very important role in selecting the organizations and the lecturers.

In my view, although these visits to Afro-Brazilian organizations might be rather repetitive for, and even somewhat scripted by, the tour guides and the leaders of the organizations, the most important feature of these visits for the tourists is their sheer dynamism. Despite being scheduled and programmed in advance, these visits offer the opportunity for the materialization of inspirational transnational black encounters, sometimes with unexpected results. I witnessed situations in which these encounters resulted in enthusiastic discussions about the meanings of blackness and the different, but all too common, ways in which racism and white supremacy play out in Brazil and the United States. In some cases, the discussions led to an interrogation of the very idea of the "advancement" of African Americans vis-à-vis their diasporic counterparts. In August 2012, for example, I accompanied Sylvia Marie's group to an educational institute that prepares black youth for the competitive college entrance exams. Because of the successful work that it carries out, this institute has become a major attraction in the itineraries of the roots tour groups. I participated in the whole visit, which lasted for about two and a half hours, and I offered to serve as translator between the members of the tour group and the institute's director. Although the visit was originally supposed to consist of a lecture offered by the director, followed by a Q&A session, two young female students who were present when the visit happened were asked to provide the visitors with brief accounts about the role of the institute in their lives. Despite being caught off-guard, the young women delivered very moving testimonies about how their lives had changed after they joined the institute. They said that before becoming students there, they did not believe in themselves, and could not even envision attending college, but now they are confident that they can ascend socially by attaining a university degree. These testimonies brought several of the African American visitors to tears, and some of them emphasized the *sameness* that these young Afro-Brazilian women share with the African American youth back home.

Several of the tourists began to tell stories of youths they knew in the United States that face similar conditions of poverty, low self-esteem, and limited horizons. This conversation then led to a heated discussion regarding the differences and the similarities between racism in Brazil and the United States. The overall conclusion among the visitors was that there are many more similarities than differences between the ways in which racism operates in both countries, but that black youth in the United States do not find a way out while these black youths in Bahia were making a future for themselves. This was the first time that I heard African American tourists referring to Afro-Brazilians as a reference for the *future*, instead of depicting them as connected to the *past*. In sum, although these visits might be originally conceived of as a form of top-down and North-South solidarity, where a wealthier and supposedly more advanced group sets out to help their poorer and less developed counterparts, they open up the opportunity for transnational conversations that end up being not just about antiblack racism and racial oppression but also about how asymmetrically situated communities can learn from one another via horizontal dialogues.

Another major practice of solidarity employed by African American roots tourists in Brazil is their unequivocal and unapologetic support for Afro-Brazilian-owned businesses and Afro-Brazilian entrepreneurs and artists. The artists include painters, artisans, and jewelry designers. In the case of the artists, the African American support has entailed not only purchasing their products, but in some cases promoting their art through exhibiting their work and inserting them in networks of artists and galleries in the United States. On a cold Sunday afternoon in December 2007, I had the opportunity of visiting a gallery in New York City that was exhibiting and selling the work of an Afro-Brazilian painter from Salvador. Sylvia Marie had fallen in love with his Candomblé-themed art, which led her to connect him to an African American gallery owner with whom she was acquainted. The small crowd of predominantly African American art aficionados packed the gallery to admire the paintings of the Afro-Brazilian artist. The flyer that Sylvia Marie made to publicize his work describes his paintings as vibrant acrylics and watercolors that "boldly capture the essence of the Yoruba-based religion, Candomblé, widely practiced throughout Brazil and particularly in Salvador, Bahia, often called Brazil's 'African Heart.'"

The "Africanness" reflected in the artwork of Afro-Brazilian painters and sculptors is a major draw for African American consumers and tourists who seek out their cultural heritage. During the Festival of the Good Death, the streets of Cachoeira are filled with artists exhibiting and selling their paintings, sculptures, jewelry and handcrafts, all informed by Afro-Brazilian themes. These objects include t-shirts portraying the *Orixás* (Yoruba deities), bead necklaces with the corresponding colors of the different *Orixás*, wooden carvings depicting the Sisters of the Good Death, and paintings of "typical icons" of Bahianness such as the *baianas*, *capoeiristas*, and the colonial architecture of Cachoeira. Of course the Sisterhood and scenes of the Festival are the dominant representations portrayed also in the paintings. Revealingly, as consumers and patrons, African American tourists have also informed the content of the artwork produced in Cachoeira, especially when they make specific requests to the artists. A striking example of the influence of the tourists over the artwork is that one of the painters based in Cachoeira has begun to portray an unambiguously black image of Our Lady of Glory, which is how Our Lady of the Good Death is named after the ritual of ascension.

Virtually all the images in the heavily Eurocentric context of Brazilian Catholicism depict Mary and Jesus as white, when not blond and blue-eyed. The
Sisterhood of the Good Death, despite its historical ties to the liberation of
enslaved Afro-Brazilians, does not escape the practice of venerating white images of saints. The worshipping of a *white* saint by a *black* sisterhood that they
travel from so far away to visit has generated a good amount of frustration for
many African American tourists. As a consequence, if the tourists cannot replace the effigy of the white saint that is carried by the Sisters during the procession and then displayed in the Sisterhood's chapel, they can at least request
that the saint's image be blackened in the paintings that they take home as a
memento of their trip to the "closer Africa." While this poses an important
challenge to Brazilian Eurocentrism and its practices of whitening, it also
confirms that, because the tourist gaze is shaped mostly in anticipation to
travel, and therefore in the tourist's country of origin, it cannot easily be
disrupted by representations produced in the tourist destination. Ultimately,
this process reveals that while accessing Afro-Brazilian culture through tourism, African American tourists are also leaving their own imprint on the very
ways in which heritage, both at local and global scales, is constructed and
defined.

The affiliation of the Sisters to both Candomblé and Catholicism is also con-
fusing and disappointing for many tourists, and it is often understood as a
lack of "purity" and "authenticity." For the Sisterhood, however, the cult of Our
Lady of Glory is located in a context of religious syncretism that in itself represents a strategy of struggle and continuity of African beliefs. As Thornton
argues, the relationship between Christianity and African religions was not
necessarily hostile, and the lack of orthodoxy among African religions allowed
for a convergence with Christian philosophical interpretations.[47]

The Afro-Brazilian painter does not see a problem in painting a black
image of Our Lady of Glory and he has gladly complied with his clients' requests.
Along with all the other Afro-Brazilians that work with the tourists and who I
had the chance to interview, he spoke very favorably of the African American
support for black-owned businesses in Brazil. The black businesses that African
American tourists make it a point to patronize include a few restaurants, some
shops that sell Afro-Brazilian themed clothes and crafts, and a small number of
art galleries in Salvador and Cachoeira. Caetano, the Afro-Brazilian guide
who was in charge of guiding Sylvia Marie's group in 2012, also expressed appreciation for the African American support for Afro-Brazilians and he drew a
straight line between this kind of racial solidarity and the strength of black
identities in the United States: "Black identities are stronger there because they

sponsor each other! [*Eles se patrocinam!*] They believe that their money should circulate within their own community. We don't have that here. When they bring this [practice] here, they bring protection for the black community!"[48]

Rafael, a tour guide that I had interviewed in 2005, also expressed appreciation for the support that the African American tourists offer to Afro-Brazilians: "They always contribute, they always donate. The best tourist that comes to Brazil today is the African American tourist. No doubt! No one respects more the Brazilian people and the Brazilian culture than the African American tourist. Of course they prefer to patronize restaurants and businesses owned by Afro-Brazilians. Whenever there is Afro-Brazilian culture and Afro-Brazilian people, they support us. They are always very generous." Rafael also argued that the mere presence of African Americans in Brazil, as powerful, First World proud blacks, functions as a positive example for Afro-Brazilians: "From the moment they arrive at the airport, and the cleaning ladies, who are usually black, see that group of classy black women, all well-dressed, many wearing jewelry, and with whites having to bow to them, a message is being put forward right then and there. I am sure that that cleaning lady asks herself, 'who are these sophisticated, proud blacks?' So this message is really important and it is being sent all the time while the African Americans are here. Afro-Brazilians see the economic power and the pride of African Americans and they also see that African Americans patronize black businesses in Brazil."[49]

Generosity is undoubtedly one of the characteristics most often commented on by people who interact with the African American tourists in Brazil. David, a white American who had been living in Brazil for over twenty years and working as a tour guide for fifteen years when I interviewed him in 2003, highlighted as the two major features of the African American tourists, especially when compared with white American and European tourists, their open-heartedness and their open-handedness: "They are a very generous people, in general. I have never guided a group [of African Americans] where they did not want to make donations." He said that most of the tourists were aware of the fact that local people would, in fact, sometimes try to take advantage of their diasporic sensibility by exploiting their sense of shared Africanness: "This use of Africanness, like calling them 'brothers' and 'sisters' as a way of making a buck out of their generosity is pretty common, it's even understandable. It is because European tourists are a lot more guarded, but African American tourists are so open in their interactions with the *baiano* people that some people try to exploit that."[50]

There is a consensus about the generosity of the African American tourists among the tour guides and other Brazilians who work directly with the tourists. Denise, an Afro-Brazilian tour guide that I interviewed in 2011, and who has been working with African American tourists since 1992, also spoke very fondly of the African American tourists and stated that they are the best tourists to work with. She said that, in addition to being eager to learn, which makes the work of the guide a lot more rewarding, they sincerely appreciate their interaction with Afro-Brazilian people and culture. These features, according to Denise, result in the African American financial support for Afro-Brazilian artisans and entrepreneurs: "They have this concern for spending their money on people who look like them, who they consider to be their black brothers and sisters."[51]

Among the various practices of solidarity of African American roots tourists in Brazil perhaps the most bewildering for the majority of the white and/or light-skinned Brazilians working in the tourism industry is their specific request for black travel guides. African American travel agencies and/or the groups that hire them frequently demand that their tourist guides in Bahia be black individuals. Lionel Washington explained the importance for him, as an African American tourism agent, of putting his leverage at the service of people of African descent: "It would be an issue for me if the guide was not black. We only work with people of African descent. Of course I cannot define who anyone is. That is God's work. But if someone comes to me and says 'I am of African descent,' fine, that's all I need to know. I am not going to question them. But then I will not do business with someone just because they are of African descent; there are certain principles and certain contributions that they have to bring along with them."[52] Anthropologist Marcelo Ferreira identified similar practices in Rio de Janeiro, where he carried out his MA fieldwork on African American tourism. As a black tourist guide, Ferreira was constantly hired by local travel agencies to guide African American groups. The predominantly white owners of Brazilian tourism agencies complained that these groups made "racialized demands" to a tourism sector unaccustomed to such practices.[53]

In the case of Bahia, where there is a larger, although still insufficient, number of black guides than in Rio, some *mestiço* (mixed-race) guides who would not normally be considered black in Brazil have *blackened* their identity in order to portray themselves as Afro-Brazilians. In some cases, there are guides who are perceived by the tourists as black even though they are light-skinned enough to be considered white in Brazil. Others have blackened their identity not based on their phenotype but on their knowledge of Afro-Brazilian culture. Lidia Matos, for instance, who would probably be considered white even in the United States, stated that the African American tourists recognize her as a fellow black person: "They see me as black, more for how I think than for how I look. Some ask me [about my racial identity], but the majority simply assume that I am black because I have an Afrocentric view of culture." She explained that she understands the reasons why many African American tour groups specifically request black tour guides, but that a lot of people in Bahia were unaware of the rationale for that, which results in some owners of tour agencies referring to the African American tourists as "racist," which is a mistake on their part. It was also a mistake for them to neglect her whenever a group requested a black guide since there is, in her view, the recognition of her blackness among the African American tourists. "This has happened a lot here: some agencies started saying that the black American tourists are racists. Some owners of agencies tell me that all the time. They receive requests for black guides, and then they choose somebody else over me. But some groups specifically request me."[54]

David, the white American tour guide mentioned above, knew that there were situations when he was not hired to guide a group because the group had explicitly requested a black guide. He said that, as a white yet American person, he understood and respected the reasons for this request. He explained that this was easier for Americans to understand than it was for most Brazilians because of how these two societies have been organized racially. Furthermore, he said, he had never been mistreated by any of the black tourists for not being a person of African ancestry. I witnessed his interaction with Sylvia Marie's group, who he was in charge of guiding during their stay in 2004, and the rapport established was indeed very courteous and friendly.

In my view, one of the most positive consequences of the African American demand for black guides is that it has obliged the mainstream commercial realm of the Brazilian tourism industry, led mostly by white and light-skinned Brazilians, to recognize that there is indeed a scarcity of black guides. While many owners of Brazilian travel agencies have reacted defensively at the African American demand for black guides, sometimes even referring to African Americans as committing "inverted racism,"[55] they have had to prioritize hiring black guides over white ones. They have also been put in a position in which they have had to contribute to change a reality that predominantly favors whiteness, by seeking out and training specifically black individuals to work as tour guides, even if they have done this reluctantly, and mostly for the sake of "pleasing the tourist."

Specific Solidarity Projects

The general and recurrent solidarity *practices* described above have happened alongside a number of specific but very important solidarity *projects*, some of which have been discontinued and some of which are ongoing. I highlight two of these projects that, in my assessment, have been among the most impactful. The first case was the purchase by three African American artists of a house in 1985 that they then donated to the Sisterhood of the Good Death. The second case is a partnership that was established between an African American educational foundation and the aforementioned Afro-Brazilian educational institute that prepares black students for the competitive college entrance exams. This institute, as I mentioned above, has become an important attraction for African American visitors and it has been very successful at establishing transnational links of solidarity.

CASE 1: DONATION OF A HOUSE TO THE
SISTERHOOD OF THE GOOD DEATH

The purchase and donation of a house in Cachoeira to the Sisterhood of the Good Death is one of the most remarkable examples of the African American support for Afro-Brazilians. In addition to its important financial aspect, the donation of this house generated a significant ripple effect of both symbolic and material importance in the tourism sector of Cachoeira and, ultimately, on the state government of Bahia. The Sisterhood did not own a house where they could gather to prepare for the festival that happens every August, and which is the major reason why African American tourists visit the historic town of Cachoeira. Moved by the Sisterhood's hardship, three African American artists, Paul Goodnight, E. H. Sorrells-Adewale and Robin M. Chandler, decided to purchase a house in one of the central streets of Cachoeira and donate it to the Sisters in 1985.[56] According to the Bahiatursa employee who witnessed this process, the cost of the house at the time was US$3,000, an expense that was split among these three African American visitors. The Sisterhood celebrated the donation, which was quite publicized in the local and state media outlets. Following this, the municipal government of Cachoeira bought the house located next door, and which at that point belonged to the Lyons Club of Cachoeira, and offered that house to the Sisterhood. A few years later, the Sisterhood's lawyer, a resident of Cachoeira, bought the house located behind these two houses and also donated it to the Sisters. As a result of these donations, the Sisterhood then owned three buildings, all located next to one another, but they were very old and in dire need of restoration.

In January 1995, Jorge Amado, Bahia's most famous novelist, wrote an open letter where he "begged" the Brazilian authorities for help for the Sisterhood. He titled the letter "Tomo da Cuia de Esmoler" or, in a rough translation, "I Borrow the Beggar's Tin Can," which was published in *Folha de S. Paulo*, one of Brazil's most influential newspapers.[57] "Begging" in this case is a ritual practiced annually by the Sisters of the Good Death, where they dress up in full attire and roam the streets of Cachoeira requesting contributions and thus raising funds for the festival. Amado's letter "begged" for the Sisterhood's conjoined houses to be fully restored in time for the following festival. In his letter, Amado sought to embarrass Brazilian politicians by arguing that even foreigners have done a better job at supporting the Sisterhood. Instead of explaining that *African* American visitors had purchased of one the three houses, he opted instead to highlight their *foreignness*: "The little sisters tell me with joy about the donations—the bigger house, offered by a rich American, the smaller donated by one of Cachoeira's former mayors—and they relay the vicissitudes of the struggle to obtain the restoration of the two gifts, with beautiful façades, but both in ruins."[58] Amado's mistakenly reducing the three African American benefactors to just one is not really what is at stake here. What is revealing is the fact that he stripped them from their black identity—which is what connects them to the Sisterhood—to emphasize their generic *Americanness*. Their Americanness, in turn, leads him to assume that they would be necessarily *rich*. Interestingly, the black identity of the African American donors was also left out from the huge banner that the Sisterhood hanged outside the walls of the building, which read in Portuguese: "The Good Death thanks the American friends that bought this building for the Good Death. May God repay you."[59]

Amado's letter is addressed, in its first few paragraphs, to the Minister of Culture, but then it gradually broadens its recipients to include, more generally, the "men in the government" (*homens do governo*), as well as the "powerful" and the "rich." Naming a long list of potential donors, Amado implores that they direct their attention and charity to the Sisters of the Good Death, stating, "They are queens and yet they do not ask for a palace, only for a place where they can shelter the Virgin of the Good Death, their religious attires and adornments. The rich American understood this, and gave them a house; the local politician did his part, and donated the house next to it."[60] Amado's letter pressured the State government into ultimately restoring the three buildings and merging them into a unit, which was presented to the public on August 12 of that same year as the "Sisterhood's headquarters." Since then, the buildings have been used to accommodate the Sisterhood's chapel, museum, dormitory, and kitchen.

The Sisters and other Cachoeirans, such as several local sculptors and painters, speak very fondly of the African American appreciation for the culture that they produce. Selka argues that although the state of Bahia contributed much more than the African American donors to the reconstruction of these buildings, many people in Cachoeira credit the African Americans first. "Most sisters are quick to mention, for example, that African Americans helped to save the sisterhood with the money that they donated and the media attention they drew to the sisters' cause during the conflict with the Catholic Church."[61]

In my view, among the reasons why the African American support is more recognized than the state support is the sheer admiration, sometimes bordering on fascination, that the tourists express for the Sisterhood. I witnessed several encounters between the Sisters and African American tourists both inside the Sisterhood's headquarters and on the streets of Cachoeira. Although in some cases a tour guide translated the conversation between the tourists and the Sisters, in most of the meetings that I attended there was not a large amount of verbal exchange. The encounters are, above all, visually oriented. The tourists gaze in awe and admiration at the Sisters, and see them as living proof of the survival of African culture in the diaspora. These encounters reveal the extent to which the tourists' appreciation for the Sisters contributes to enhance the local respect for both the Sisterhood as an institution and the Sisters as individuals. The African American high regard for the Sisterhood contributes significantly to elevate the self-esteem of these elderly, impoverished, black women who are, more often than not, looked down by the Cachoeiran elite.

I interviewed several of the Sisters during the Festival of the Good Death in 2013, and there was a consensus among them that the African American tourists are the major supporters of their institution, both because of the donations they make and because of the reverence with which they approach the Sisters. At the same time, the Sisters predominantly view the African American visitors as tourists, and refer to them as *Americanos*, and not as *Americanos negros*. Answering my question about what was her view of the African American tourists, one of the Sisters explained: "The Americans that come to honor us here during our festival are our most important visitors. They come here every year, they visit us, they have the utmost respect for us, they bow in front of us and ask for our blessings. They contribute as much as they can to the *bolsa* [literally, "the purse" where the donations are collected]. They walk by our side in the procession, and they attend the mass. But they usually don't eat with us because, you know, they get an upset stomach, so they eat at the hotel because they are used to the food in the hotel."[62]

The Sisters also seemed amused and somewhat perplexed by all the attention that they receive from the tourists, as much as they undeniably appreciate it. One of the Sisters put it this way: "They ask us questions about the

Sisterhood, about when it was created. They ask us about our lives. And they take lots of pictures of us! And when they see a Sister that's really old, such as that one over there," she said pointing to a ninety-two-year-old Sister, "they love it so much that if they could they would take her home with them!"[63] This comment generated a lot of laughter among the Sisters, including the one that was the butt of the joke.

As the tourists and the Sisters gaze at one another during these encounters, quite different interpretations and expectations are produced. While the tourists mostly see the Sisterhood's blackness, Africanness, and their history of triumph over slavery, the Sisters see the tourists predominantly as Americans, without emphasizing their blackness or their shared commonality as slave-descendants. When I asked the Sisters what they thought about the *Americanos negros,* several of the Sisters explained that it did not matter that they were black. Among chuckles, one of the Sisters replied: "To me it is the same whether they [the tourists] are black, or white, or yellow, or blue. What matters is the respect that they have for us. They almost tread on each other to take pictures of us!"[64] Other Sisters responded in a similar way, and in addition to downplaying the tourists' blackness, they explained that the reason why the tourists came was because they too probably worship the Virgin Mary: "For me, there's no difference if the tourist is black or white. For me, to divide them would be prejudiced on my part. They come here searching for *Nossa Senhora.* I see all the tourists as the same."[65]

Another important example of the African American support for the Sisterhood that many people in Cachoeira speak appreciatively about is the relationship with Reverend Barbara King from Atlanta, a connection that began in the late 1980s. Because of her support for the Sisters, she was named an honorary member of the Sisterhood in 1990. Although this symbolic gesture does not make her an actual member of the Good Death, it is certainly an important recognition of her membership in the black diaspora. "Reverend King's honorary membership reflects her status as betwixt and between, a status that she arguably shares to some degree with African American visitors in Bahia in general. That is, it is as much a reflection of her role as patron as it is of her bond with the sisters. She is both close and far away, insider and outsider; she is a well-known stranger."[66]

The establishment of relationships that conflate the role of patron with that of a community member or even a relative is not uncommon in diaspora tourism. In Chinese diaspora tourism, for example, the overseas Chinese often become philanthropic benefactors and economic investors at the same time that they are strengthening their social and familial ties in China. As they build social capital through the strengthening of collective and cooperative networks revolving around relationships of trust, the institutional frameworks developed from diaspora tourism can allow members to act together to pursue common objectives while simultaneously reinforcing their common identification.[67] This process occurs in the tourism encounters of other diaspora communities as well, for example when Indian-Americans travel to India with the purpose of strengthening their Indian identities both by reconnecting with members of their extended family and by making investments in small businesses. These travel experiences enhance, simultaneously their ethnic/religious identities as well as their Indianness.[68]

The projects of racial solidarity developed through diaspora tourism have allowed roots tourists, African American or otherwise, to strengthen their diasporic identities. Furthermore, these projects have also resulted in challenges to the very meanings of Americanness, both because they have defied the conflation between Americanness and whiteness and because they have afforded African Americans (as well as members of other diasporas) the opportunity to see themselves as part of a global majority instead of a national minority.[69] Sylvia Marie explained that the heritage tours that she conducts are of crucial importance for raising the self-esteem of African Americans exactly because they become more aware of the existence of their diasporic counterparts: "I think it's an excellent way to see that we have people that we don't know who share our history, and that's important. It strengthens our pride, our understanding of our own history, and that we that we're not alone."[70]

CASE 2: PARTNERSHIP BETWEEN AFRICAN AMERICAN AND
AFRO-BRAZILIAN EDUCATIONAL ORGANIZATIONS
Another major example of a transnational solidarity project developed in Bahia was the partnership established between an African American educational foundation and the afore-mentioned Afro-Brazilian educational institute that prepares black students for the competitive college entrance exams. In 1999, Lionel Washington founded the African American educational foundation because, he said, he was receiving so many donations from the tourists to the Afro-Brazilian organizations, and especially so for this specific educational institute, that he needed to find a way to legally direct this money to them: "We were bringing our tours here, they were visiting the institute, and they were so moved by the work that they were doing that they would send us donations even after they returned to the States. But as a for-profit company incorporated in the United States, we could not accept donations. So we founded the nonprofit educational foundation and that way we have been able to funnel the

donations."[71] In the early 2000s, for example, the members of "a major African American church" were so impressed with the work of the Afro-Brazilian educational institute that they fundraised US$25,000 on their behalf. This was, according to Washington, the largest lump sum donation ever made in this context of transnational African American support for Afro-Brazilians.

In addition to making it possible to direct resources to the Afro-Brazilian institute, the African American educational foundation also began to organize study tours to Brazil, thus bringing several groups of students from the United States in educational tours. Most important, however, was the foundation's goal of inverting the dominant North-South direction of the transnational black travel routes: upon listening to the requests made by the leaders of the Afro-Brazilian institute, they collectively decided that they should also make possible for Afro-Brazilians to travel to the United States. When I interviewed Lionel Washington in 2003, he explained that the first cohort of Afro-Brazilian students was getting ready to travel to the United States the following year, where they would spend thirty days of full immersion in African American history and culture. Besides serving as an educational opportunity, the visit would also allow the students to fund-raise for the institute and seek out scholarships for themselves or their peers.

Eleven years later, I interviewed Angela, one of the four female students who visited the United States in 2004 as the result of this partnership.[72] She confirmed that the goals of the visit were to increase, among the Afro-Brazilian youth, awareness of the African American experience in the United States, and to raise funds for the Afro-Brazilian institute. The students made several presentations during their one-month stay in the United States where they were portrayed as concrete examples of the success of the institute as they had then just recently entered college: "We were the fruits of the institute," she explained. It is important to highlight that most of the students trained in this Afro-Brazilian educational institute, are or become activists since, beyond merely preparing them for the college entrance exam, the institute is very dedicated to raising the racial consciousness of their constituents.[73] The effects of the partnership, whether directly or indirectly, are palpable in Angela's life. After the month-long trip in 2004, she returned to the United States in 2006 where she attended Howard University on a full scholarship. At the time of the interview, she was a visiting graduate student at a U.S. university while pursuing her doctoral degree in Brazil. She spoke very enthusiastically about the experience of visiting the United States in 2004, of later living in the country in 2006 as a visiting undergraduate student, and about her current experience as a visiting graduate student in 2015–2016. She described seeing black people occupying positions of power—as politicians, administrators, and college professors, for example—as one of the most inspirational aspects of the black experience in the United States, which is especially striking when contrasted to the lack of black empowerment in Brazil. She pointed out, as an example, the fact that she is one of the very few black students in her Brazilian graduate program, where not only there is a scarcity of black students but also where all of her professors are white.

Angela's insights on the asymmetries of the black diaspora are of crucial importance for the understanding of transnational black relationships. This Afro-Brazilian intellectual and activist explained that the different levels of black empowerment between Afro-Brazilians and African Americans need to be understood in light of their countries' respective national projects, in other words, how the one-drop rule in the United States contributed to construct a strong black identity while the myth of *mestiçagem* in Brazil weakened blackness by creating a wide array of color categories. Responding to why many African Americans describe their condition as "more advanced" than Afro-Brazilians she emphasized the need to acknowledge the fact that the United States is an economic superpower, which serves as an engine that sustains African Americans. "Yes, they are more organized than we are. There's no denying that. But they have a *máquina* [machine/engine] behind them! Look at Spike Lee, for example. He makes fantastic movies, but he has this *máquina*, which is the United States, that supports him." She then went on to criticize what I have been calling here the "Western othering" that African Americans often engage in in their relationship with other blacks as well as the U.S.-centrism so often present in these interactions: "Most of the syllabi of the courses that I am taking here, in a department of African diaspora studies [at a U.S. university], focus on African countries and the black experience in the United States, but they exclude Latin American countries. I don't see myself reflected in these courses! . . . They tell the stories of the world's peripheries from the point of view of the center!"[74]

Afro-Brazilian actors, in general, have responded very positively to the practices and projects of solidarity of the African American tourists, even if most of them expressed awareness of the hierarchies within the black diaspora, and are sometimes critical of what they see as the "Americanness" of the tourists. A longtime Afro-Brazilian activist that works closely with the African American tourists in the partnership between the educational organizations stated: "African Americans are black, but they are also American (*americanos, estadunidenses!*)." I asked him to explain what that meant, to which he replied: "If you are born and raised in a place, you are influenced by the culture of that place. So, for instance, we have a way of dealing with things, with resources, as Brazilians, independently of being black or white, that we say, often: 'ok, I'll see,' instead of giving them a direct answer. And that generated a lot of clashes in our relationship with them. Because, for them, it is either 'yes' or 'no.' They are very Cartesian in that sense."[75]

At the same time, he also expressed great appreciation for the more objective way in which African Americans deal with resources and, more broadly, for how they have been able to obtain such resources and occupy important social positions within the United States. His remarks replace the trope of black evolution with a call for processes of mutual learning as he insightfully highlighted the intersections between racial and national identities, emphasizing that the different ways in which blackness is conceived of and lived should be understood in connection to what Angela referred to above as the distinct national projects:

> Whether we like it or not, we are Brazilians. There is a Brazilian identity that forms us, so we are formed and informed by the myth of racial democracy, no matter how high is our level of consciousness, which is why you can't just transplant to Brazil the strategies that have worked there [in the United States]. When you live inside the myth of racial democracy, the discourse of making the money circulate within the [black] community, for instance, is not as easy here as it is there. And this requires a process of consciousness raising among us, and in that sense we have to learn from African Americans. But they too need to learn why we are the way we are.[76]

Another Afro-Brazilian activist, who has also worked closely with African American tourists, was more critical of the privileged position and sense of entitlement of the tourists and, without any prompting, seemed keenly aware of the trope of the happy native, discussed in the previous chapter. Chatting animatedly while we accompanied the procession of the Boa Morte Festival on August 15, 2012, she firmly expressed her views on the African American tourists. Although she spoke fondly of a few specific African American individuals who have become her personal friends, she was very critical of African American tourists in general. "They see us as backwards and primitive! They should learn Portuguese so that they can understand who we really are." She then spoke highly of one African American individual in particular who did make the effort of learning Portuguese, which she saw as the result of her demanding respect and equality. "We're good friends today. But when we first met, he was walking around town taking pictures of people that were passing by! When he tried to take a picture of me, I said 'Wait a minute! Do you really think you can take pictures of people you don't even know, without even asking?' And that's how our friendship started. And I kept buzzing in his head for him to learn Portuguese. And he did."[77]

These statements indicate that, although conflicts and asymmetries do exist in these diasporic relations, they can be reciprocally worked out in the interest of building and sustaining solidarity practices and projects. Furthermore, these statements shed light on the crucial question of the dependence of solidarity on identity, that is, the question of whether solidarity requires the existence of a shared identity. As a dynamic of identification where "one subject or agent may come to see itself in others, to be itself through its mediated relationships with others and to see others in itself," sameness has worked as a base for social action and solidarity.[78] While most of the Afro-Brazilian intellectuals and activists that I interviewed nonchalantly recognized the existence of inequality in transnational black relations as an obvious result of geopolitical unevenness, most of the African American tourists seemed less comfortable to discuss asymmetries and were more eager to emphasize sameness over difference. The goal of underscoring sameness among diasporic black communities is, however, further challenged by the fact that the transnational black encounters discussed here are promoted through the inherently unequal structure of international tourism.

Emphasizing Sameness and Confronting Difference in Transnational Black Encounters

Lionel Washington, the owner of one of the largest African American travel agencies operating in Brazil, and one of the pioneers in this industry, stated in an interview that Afro-Brazilians and African Americans are "at different stages of advancement" due to the position occupied by the United States in the global economic order, but what matters is that both groups occupy similar subaltern positions within their respective nations.

> What African-Americans from the United States have to be very clear about with *African-Americans* from Brazil is that that [the economic advances of African Americans] was a byproduct—what we have achieved in many cases—was a *byproduct of being in America*. [However,] African-Americans in America are still on the bottom, and in Brazil the African-Americans are still on the bottom, and that's what we have to look at, and *not what we have achieved when we compare ourselves with the African-Americans from Brazil*. That is a non-issue for us. When we look at it, *we* are on the bottom.

What we have to do is look at ways that we can advance ourselves as a people in both structures, and in all levels, politically, economically, what we can do in our own interest, jointly.[79]

This statement greatly illustrates some of my arguments in this chapter as it highlights the complexities and challenges of establishing a common racial identity for peoples living in countries that are not just *different* but which occupy *unequal* positions within global hierarchies of power. These difficulties are evident, first but not foremost, in the identity categories employed by the interviewee to refer to African Americans and Afro-Brazilians. He uses the terms "we" and "us" at times to refer to U.S. blacks only, and at other times to refer to both groups jointly. His use of the terms *African-Brazilians* (certainly not in use in Brazil) and, even more striking, *African-Americans from Brazil*, adds another layer of complexity to the claim of transnational racial affiliation. It is meant to indicate that U.S. black identity should not be defined by its national boundaries or by its comparisons to the identity and life conditions of blacks in Brazil or elsewhere. U.S. black identity should be, instead, the same identity of blacks in the diaspora (or the Americas) where blacks are "still on the bottom." Yet, despite his attempt at unifying a black experience in the Americas and his emphasis on a common, transnational, black identity, his statement acknowledges that being from the United States qualifies blackness in a very specific way that attaches to it privilege, especially within the broader context of the black diaspora.

The paradox of the coexistence of *sameness* and *privilege* within the transnational black encounters promoted by roots tourism came across in several interviews. Louise, a lawyer in her mid-sixties, heartily emphasized how *similar* she was to the black people that she met in Brazil and in the African countries she has visited. She said that she was embarrassed that she had not known earlier about these important diasporic commonalities: "When I came to Brazil, and I am embarrassed to say this, I was stunned to see women who looked like me! . . . The media in America do not portray that. Brazil is just bossa nova and *The Girl from Ipanema.*" For Louise, traveling to other countries in the diaspora is a way of challenging this unawareness, but the downside of international travel is that it also confirms the worldwide extent of racism and white privilege. Other African American tourists also commented on the disappointment of encountering antiblack racism in Africa and around the black diaspora, where the similarities shared by Afro-descendants unfortunately do not prevent the mistreatment of blacks by other blacks. Sylvia Marie exemplified this in a story that she told me about a racist incident that she experienced in Ghana:

I have witnessed interactions between Africans, from various parts of the continent, and Europeans, and they are far more responsive to Europeans. Far more! I can give you an example. One year I took a group of about thirty people to Ghana, West Africa. We did a lot of shopping. You know, Americans love to shop! [Chuckles.] And actually they love to shop for African artifacts. So we, this group, bought twenty-seven Asante stools. So we thought: "How are we going to ship that home? The airline is going to charge a fortune for overweight." So my tour operator in Ghana suggested: "Why don't you all ship them together?" So I reserved the hotel's vehicle to take us to the airport so that we could ship the merchandise. And the day that we were waiting for the car to come, here comes a Ghanaian who was working for the hotel with a white European and he took my car! So I said: "Wait a second! I ordered this car, I reserved it." He said: "No, no, no he has to get to airport." So I had to be very, very demanding: "This is *my* vehicle. If you like to get him to the airport, that's great. There are taxis there, get him a taxi. I ordered this car in advance." His concern was for the European rather than for me, an African American that looked like him. That mindset is still there. They still perceive the Europeans as more important.[80]

The awareness of the existence of racism in the various sites of the map of Africanness coexists, however, with the recognition among African American tourists of their position of power as U.S. citizens when abroad. This acknowledgement came to life in the interviews when respondents expressed surprise with the warmth of Brazilians *despite* the fact that they were Americans.[81] For example, in answering the question "What did you expect to find in Bahia?" one of the tourists responded: "I expected to find the people very hostile toward Americans. I did not find that, they were very friendly, warm, and courteous."[82] The discomfort experienced by African Americans as foreign tourists was also often expressed in their being perceived locally as money-loaded. When I asked Sylvia Marie if she had ever encountered any kind of resentment, either in Brazil or in the African continent, for the fact that African Americans come from a powerful country, she replied that she had not, but she was puzzled by the common belief that American tourists are necessarily affluent: "The perception is that we're all rich because 'how can you to go Africa unless you are rich?' which is far from the truth. We are all working class people! [Chuckles.] We make a salary, and that's it! Some of us are living from paycheck to paycheck, some of us have to take a whole year before we can pay for a tour. The perception is that we have money, and because we have money, 'you'd better buy from me!' I have experienced some of that in certain African countries, but not in Brazil."[83]

The notion that African American tourists are wealthy has often hampered the attempts at promoting closer connections between the tourists and members of the communities that they visit. The divisions engendered by class, nationality, and the tourist condition undercut the blackness that is shared across the board. Even though they are black, as national citizens of the world's superpower, African American tourists are often perceived locally as privileged and prosperous, thus hindering the desired process of bonding. This frustration was painfully expressed by an African American female tourist who, although seeing tourism as an opportunity to potentially reconnect with other members of the black diaspora, also criticized it as a structure that further promotes inequality:

> I've had this impression when I've been to Africa as well. Sometimes, people in other countries don't really see us as human beings. You know, we work, we work hard in America, and we save our money to come and visit other countries, and I think that in some areas where there is economic deficiency, people sort of see us not as human beings but as a dollar sign. They look at us with dollar signs in their eyes, like: "They're coming, so let's get as much as we can from them." But then on the other hand I feel sort of ashamed of being a tourist. What am I leaving to this country, what am I doing to maybe make a difference or something? Because being a tourist is sometimes like being in a zoo . . . I was trying to make a connection, by looking people in the eye, and establish some kind of kinship between us, but it seems as if they are looking and saying, "Get away from us." And this makes me feel kind of ashamed of being a tourist. But that's all I can be.[84]

The idea that African Americans are privileged when compared to black communities in Africa and the diaspora is not only disconcerting for the tourists; it has also caused discomfort among scholars. Pierre, for example, critiques the belief that she encountered among Ghanaians that African Americans are "lucky" because they supposedly benefitted politically and economically from their ancestors having been enslaved. She argues that the state-sponsored Joseph Project, although encouraging the idea of kinship between African and diaspora blacks, also establishes a set of unique expectations, including the notion that African Americans are financially responsible for their less fortunate African brothers and sisters, a demand that is not placed on the shoulders of white tourists.[85]

Analyzing the same perception of African American tourists as privileged in the Ghanaian context, Holsey directs her critique not at the Ghanaian state or at the Ghanaian common-sense depictions of African Americans. She highlights, instead, the unevenness of the geopolitics of the black diaspora and Ghanaians' reaction to it. While carrying out her field research, she heard several versions of the following story: "If a slave ship were to dock off the coast of Ghana today, bound for America, and Ghanaians were told that they could get on but that they would have to endure the same conditions that the slaves did, the boat would still be full of volunteers."[86] Holsey insightfully analyzes this story as "a mockery of diaspora tourists' romantic visions of Ghana" and as a Ghanaian critique of their abject position within the global economy.

Ebron makes a similar observation in the context of African American tourism in The Gambia, also highlighting the local response to the asymmetries of the black diaspora. While visiting the famous village of Juffrey, a group of African American roots tourists were welcomed by one of the village's officials with a statement that brings to mind Jamaica Kincaid's critique of the tourist's mobility versus the immobility of the native.[87] Speaking in Mandinka and translated into English by an interpreter, the official said: "It is very nice of you to visit us here and to travel this far to get here. We want to welcome you home. We hope your stay will be very pleasant. But you must remember that we would like to visit you, too. You must make it possible for us to travel to the United States to visit you."[88] Ebron interprets this statement as a reminder that belonging to a family, in this case the black diaspora, brings with it demands and responsibilities.

Although I never came across a similar expectation in Brazil—that is, that African Americans should be responsible for the well-being of Afro-Brazilians—I certainly heard critiques to the privileged position occupied by African American tourists. Caetano, the Afro-Brazilian tour guide that worked for Sylvia Marie's group in 2012, for example, often commented on the material disparities between the tourists and the Afro-Brazilian communities they visited. During a tour around Salvador's Cidade Baixa—an impoverished area of the city which, despite its historical importance, has been disregarded by the municipal and state governments—he sarcastically exclaimed, as we gazed at the beggars through the bus window: "This is the *real* Bahia. This is very different from the area where your hotel is located." Also pointing to the privileged position that African American tourists enjoy in Brazil, a longtime Afro-Brazilian activist who has worked closely with them since the early 1980s commented on what he views as their demanding character as consumers: "African Americans like to purchase a lot, but they are quite exigent about the products they buy. They like to buy crafts and handmade goods, but if they buy a leather sandal, for example, it has to look rustic but it must have a First World finish."[89]

The privilege of African American tourists is also the object of an intense self-scrutiny, as expressed in some of the statements cited above that allude to the disconcerting nature of international tourism, such as the one that defines tourism as "like being in a zoo." A longtime African American visitor to Brazil spoke critically about the sense of entitlement that he has encountered among fellow travelers:

> By going to Brazil I began to understand that in many ways Americans are Americans whatever color they are. Because Americans have a sort of egocentric sense that the world rises and sets in the United States of America, and whatever issues that we have with ourselves are the most important things that everybody else has to pay attention to. . . . English-speaking people are so arrogant! They think that everybody is supposed to speak English! . . . African Americans are not rude necessarily or whatever, but they have the same kinds of tall vision expectations that white Americans have when they travel: they expect things to be just perfectly clean and antiseptic and whatever, and they complain, and I tell them "you are *not* in the United States!"[90]

Louise's objection to what she viewed as an unsatisfactory degree of professionalism among her hotel's staff is a good illustration of the critique outlined above. She expected the blue-collar hotel workers to be able to speak English and be up to date on international currency conversion, and was frustrated that her expectations were not met:

> English is a pretty international language—but I find that there's a lot of people in Brazil who do not speak English, seriously, people who work in tourist hotels, even in this hotel, but do not speak English, which I find shocking. . . . Like, for example, I bought water at breakfast and I gave the lady a five-dollar bill and she didn't know what to do with it! I don't think it is just a matter of training. I think she was thoroughly perplexed that someone gave her American money. And they had three American groups in the hotel that day![91]

The classifications of African American tourists in West African countries often conflate their foreignness with the privileges attached to whiteness. In Benin, for example, African American tourists are frequently called *yovo*, a term that stands simultaneously for "white" and "foreigner."[92] In Ghana, African American tourists are often referred to locally as *oburoni*, an Akan word, or *buronyi* in Fante. Usage of these terms have created contention between Ghanaians and African Americans who, according to Holsey, are dismayed to find out that they are labeled "white man" when they are, paradoxically, attempting to reconnect with whom they view as fellow Africans. She explains, however, that *oburoni* is not a racial label, and that it would be more accurately translated as "those who come from over the horizon." "This is not a racial label then but rather a demonstration of the ways in which Ghanaians often identify people by the places from which they come, in quite literal terms. Indeed, the Americanness of African Americans is quite significant from the point of view of Ghanaians. For them, African American and white tourists sometimes occupy the same mental space; they are all privileged foreigners."[93]

In a similar vein, Ebron argues that, while in the United States she is perceived as an embodiment of racial subordination, in West Africa she carried the status and mobility of her U.S. nationality. This status is classified locally through the designation *toubob*, which was used to label her and the roots tourists that she accompanied to the Gambian village of Juffrey, made famous by Alex Haley's *Roots* as the place from where his ancestors came and to where he later returned. She explains that no one translated *toubob* into English, "and thus most of the tourists remained blissfully ignorant of what might have been a point of deep confusion and alienation: that they as African Americans were being called 'white person' or 'European.'"[94]

Capone and Clarke have pointed to a similar process occurring in Nigeria where African American visitors, many of whom visit the country in order to deepen their religious connection to the Yoruba religion, are frequently referred to by traditionalist Yoruba priests as *oyinbo*, a term that also conflates the meanings of foreignness with whiteness, as it is often used as a designation for whites and Europeans.[95] Paradoxically, these transatlantic visitors are barred from an inclusive African identity because they are, simultaneously, privileged foreigners and slave-descendants. And in the eyes of the traditionalist Yoruba people, the condition of slave (and, as a result, of the descendant of slave) is incompatible with claims to noble genealogy.[96]

Painfully aware of these designations of difference, yet emphasizing that it continues to be necessary for African Americans to search for their origins, Saidiya Hartman opts to classify herself and her fellow roots seekers as *strangers*. In the agonizing account of her experience as both a "returned" slave-descendant and a privileged American citizen in Ghana, Hartman contends that the slave is a *stranger*, slave descendants are *strangers* within the nations they currently live, and they are still *strangers* when they visit Africa in search of a connection to the people and the land.[97] Hartman's insightful analysis of the privileged positionality of African Americans within the broader context of the black diaspora and their painful condition as strangers ties in with my argument that too much emphasis on sameness might obfuscate the goal of constructing more even diasporic relations.

· Similar to the concepts of *obruni* in Ghana, *toubob* in The Gambia, and *oyinbo* in Nigeria, terms that are indisputably applied to African Americans in these countries, the label "gringo/a" emphasizes the condition and identity of the outsider, the nonnative that comes from the dominating centers of the world and who is, therefore, associated with privilege and power. Although not frequently labeled "gringos" by Brazilians, African American tourists may also occupy a comparable position of power as their white counterparts, thus challenging the notion that privilege stems exclusively from white skin color.

It is necessary to examine whether and how gringos, with all the power associated with this identity, can help promote peripheral others. As one of the first scholars to take seriously the concept of gringo/a and to carefully scrutinize the meanings of this identity in Latin America, Diane Nelson is optimistic about the potential of solidarity projects, but she warns that it is crucial to rigorously explore the ways these interventions "may maintain colonialist-style relations."[98] I would add that, like all identities, being a gringo/a is contextual and relational, and it requires its Others in order to come into play. At the same time, it is not the mere presence of the Other that automatically triggers some kind of latent gringoness. Neither does being an American citizen, in itself, make one a gringo/a. More important than place of birth, legal status, skin color, and even gender, what defines a gringo/a, in my view, is the practice of Western othering, which is in turn grounded on the belief on Western authority and leadership.

In order to analyze the transformative power of solidarity, it is necessary to examine it not as a one-way transmission belt, where a more powerful group helps a less privileged one, and therefore detains all the power and agency. If we define solidarities as "transformative political relations," we can then see them as interconnected processes that are constructed by actors that are located in different places and who occupy uneven positions of power.[99] The different Brazilian social actors that are engaged in African American roots tourism have responded in distinct ways to the African American practices of racial solidarity. As discussed above, the predominantly white Brazilians who own and/or manage travel agencies have mostly reacted to the so-called racialized demands of the African American tourists by hiring black travel guides, or by giving them priority to work with African American groups, even if many of them have done so grudgingly.

Afro-Brazilian intellectuals and activists, on the other hand, have responded to and participated in these transnational black solidarity processes with a great degree of appreciation for the ongoing support provided by the African American tourists, even while remaining critical of the unevenness of the black diaspora and the privileged Americanness of African Americans. Most important, however, Afro-Brazilian social actors have not been passive beneficiaries of African American initiatives. They have also proactively set the terms of engagement in these interactions, and they have positioned themselves as important agents in the processes of construction of transnational black solidarity. Furthermore, Afro-Brazilian intellectuals and activists have also made, in some cases, their own expedient deployment of the Americanness of U.S. blacks. They have done so in the contemporary context of roots tourism, but this had already been a successful strategy in the case of Katherine Dunham's discrimination way back in the 1940s. Abdias do Nascimento viewed the Afonso Arinos Law as the culmination of a process that had been initiated and led by Afro-Brazilian activists who skillfully seized the attention that Dunham received in order to pressure Brazilian politicians. In an article published several decades after Dunham's incident, Nascimento made clear that it took the Americanness of a black person to stop the denial of racism in Brazil. While the discrimination of Afro-Brazilians was "so normal and common that it did not merit comments in the press," the discrimination of the North American choreographer Katherine Dunham obliged the country's leadership to recognize the existence of antiblack discrimination.[100]

Carl Hart's visit to Brazil in 2015 is the most recent example of the proactive participation of Afro-Brazilians in the construction of transnational black solidarity. In this case too, Afro-Brazilian activists and intellectuals seized the attention that was afforded to this renowned African American scientist to shed light on their own antiracist struggle. Although Hart was originally invited to visit Brazil by the prestigious, São Paulo-based, Brazilian Institute of Criminal Sciences, he was also asked to participate in a meeting of the Bahia-based network of grassroots organizations Iniciativa Negra por Uma Nova Política Sobre Drogas (INNPD; Black Initiative for a New Policy on Drugs), where he spoke about the intimate connections between racialization and criminalization. Hart's participation in this gathering attracted a lot of media attention and contributed to validate the INNPD's fight against the racism that is imbedded in the patterns of drug use and in the state repression to drug users in Brazil. Hart's position as a prominent neuroscientist who specializes in drug use was certainly the major reason for his invitation to visit with the INNPD. But the considerable media attention that his Americanness received when he was allegedly discriminated against in São Paulo made him an even more significant resource for Afro-Brazilian activists and intellectuals.

Conclusion

In his first trip to the African continent as president of the United States, Barack Obama paid a visit to Cape Coast castle in Ghana. Although the inclusion of this slave site in the president's itinerary was rather predictable, Obama's comment on the effects of slavery and forced departure on African American identity was quite surprising. Instead of reiterating African Americans' connection to Africa, his statement emphasized African Americans' *Americanness*: "I know an awful lot of African Americans who come to Africa and are profoundly moved, but also realize how American they are when they are here, and, you know, recognize that they could never live here. And that is part of the African American experience: you are in some ways connected to this distant land, but on the other hand you are about as American as it gets. In some ways, African Americans are more fundamentally rooted in the American experience because they don't have a recent immigrant experience to draw on."[101]

Many scholars in the United States have debated whether the alleged Africanness of African Americans has affected their belongingness to the United States, but my focus in this chapter was on how the Americanness of U.S. blacks has affected their membership in the African diaspora. I have shown that, within the specific context of roots tourism, the Americanness of U.S. blacks is comprised of three highly intersected dimensions. First, there is a discursive dimension that revolves around the idea that African Americans are the world's most "advanced blacks," and should therefore act as the "leaders" of the black world. Second, there is a material dimension, which is comprised mostly of the tourists' purchasing power and their access to material comfort, such as staying in expensive hotels and being protected from dangers that lay outside the "tourist bubble," although this material dimension is not exclusive to African American tourists, but is, instead, part of the international tourism experience in general. A third dimension of the Americanness of U.S. blacks in the context of roots tourism is the conscious and active political use that many African American tourists make of their power as U.S. citizens and consumers carrying U.S. dollars in order to establish links of solidarity with Afro-Brazilians. The discursive, material, and political dimensions are, undeniably, intertwined, and as they mutually constitute one another, they simultaneously construct the identity of the black gringo in Brazil.

Economic oppression, racism, and discrimination commonly affect the life conditions of black peoples throughout the Americas, thus contributing to produce the structures of feelings of a shared black particularity. Nonetheless other crucial components also build blackness. Studies of transnational black connections benefit from a greater examination of the role played by nation in the construction of racial identities, not only in regards to the legal status conferred on the citizens of a nation, but more important in terms of how Western subjectivities are enacted in transnational encounters. As Goldberg famously argued, citizenship is a subject-making practice where citizen-subjects interiorize state discourses.[102] And subjectivities are, in turn, formed through mobility and spatiality.[103] Transnational and diasporic connections do not necessarily supersede national identities and subjectivities, nor do they automatically eliminate economic, social, and cultural differences.

Differences, however, need not be perceived as an impediment for the practices and projects of solidarity. After all, instead of occurring as the automatic result of communities that are already formed, solidarities in fact *produce identifications*. I align myself here with those who propose that we move beyond the notion that solidarity is or should be built on similarity.[104] Instead of simply preceding political activity, solidarity is a transformative process that makes and remakes identifications, including the ability to forge commonality across difference.[105] In my view, what the solidarity practices and projects of the African roots tourists in Brazil have shown is that their success depends a lot less on the ability to forge *sameness* than on the goal of attaining greater *equality* within diasporic relations.

Furthermore, while both male and female tourists have reiterated the binary concept of a traditional African past versus a modern black future, men have overwhelmingly expressed the idea that African Americans should exercise the leadership of the black diaspora. Focusing more closely on the differences and similarities between the experiences of male and female roots tourists and examining the ways in which they differently represent Brazil and Afro-Brazilians as well as how they understand their own roles as members of the African diaspora, the following chapter analyzes how gender identities further complicate the linear and unidirectional trope of black evolution, and the consequences that distinct gendered gazes pose for black solidarity at home and abroad.

CHAPTER FOUR

We Bring Home the Roots

African American Women Touring the Diaspora and Bearing the Nation

The healing process brings us to Brazil and to Africa and to other
countries throughout the diaspora so that we can heal not only as
individuals but as a people.

—Gabrielle, African American tourist, Cachoeira, August 2000

"I knew that there were a lot of blacks here, but I didn't know that there were
big whole black areas like Bahia! . . . And I am really glad to go back and
share with folks back home what I have seen, and to explain to them the
connection. . . . I think that as time goes by and people hear of Bahia, that it is
a black Brazil, as word gets out, tourism will pick up. There will be a real pull
toward this country and toward this area to share the black culture." This
was how Maryanne enthusiastically described the significance of her trip to
Bahia. A retired educator in her late sixties, and who was visiting Brazil for
the first time when I met her in 2004, she underscored how crucial it was to
share with other members of her community in the United States the knowledge obtained during her trip. Like so many of the African American women
that I interviewed, Maryanne explained that to make others aware of the existence of Bahia and its impressive African culture is as important as personally
experiencing it firsthand.

For most of the women with whom I spoke, altruistic reasons, besides personal ones, were among the major motivations for their trips to the various
sites of the map of Africanness. Whether they travel in pursuit of the history
of slavery in West Africa, the great civilizations of Egypt and Ethiopia, or the
preserved Africanness of Bahia, they conceive of their travels as a means of recovering a lost heritage that they deem crucial for the cultivation of a strong
and dignified black identity in the United States. Many African American
female tourists articulated variations of the phrase "We bring home the roots"
when explaining the significance of their travels to Brazil and the African
continent. I argue that these women have taken on the role of cultural
bearers, where they consider themselves responsible for nourishing the cultural components of their ethnic group. Seeking to understand why they

conceive of their travels in this way, and why women make up the majority of the African American roots tourists in Brazil, this chapter analyzes some of the gendered dimensions of travel.

In previous chapters I focused on the effects of the asymmetries of class and, above all, national identities on the connections among black diaspora communities. In this chapter I analyze how gender impacts these transnational relations while it simultaneously differentiates the experiences of female and male travelers. There is now consensus around the need to deconstruct the implicitly masculinist abstract tourist subject.[1] Analyzing why and how women travel is thus important in the project of challenging the supposed neutrality of "the tourist." At the same time, by focusing on women travelers, it is crucial not to confirm men as the norm that goes on unexamined and unquestioned. I thus seek to map out the differences between women and men without further othering women. Even though the chapter looks more closely at women, it does so in order to examine gender more broadly, including the power relations between women and men, travel and tourism as fundamentally embodied and gendered practices, and the gendering of the diaspora though the feminization and masculinization of space, place, and time.

Tourism, Gender, and Embodiment

Most of the studies of women in the scholarly literature on tourism have focused more on female tourism workers than on female tourists.[2] This most likely reflects the concern of progressive scholars with the effects of tourism development on the lives of the disenfranchised, who are overrepresented by women. While these studies are undeniably important, the analysis of the gendered nature of tourism can also benefit from a careful examination of female tourists and their respective representations of the places and peoples with whom they engage during their trips. Furthermore, it is necessary to investigate how women and men conceive of their own travels. What are their specific motivations to go abroad? And what do their trips mean to them? Although I certainly do not contend that *all women* or *all men* attribute the same meanings to their trips, it is undeniable that gender impacts, in multiple ways, how and why women and men travel.

Analyses of female tourists, in turn, have revolved significantly around white women.[3] From the quintessential Victorian travelers, who are typically portrayed as having challenged the traditional gender expectation that femininity should be defined by "staying home," to the present-time European and North American female sex tourists, who are also seen as defying gender and sexual norms, white women have received most of the attention in the studies of the gendered nature of travel and tourism. Some of these analyses have scrutinized the white and/or Western subjectivities of women travelers, especially when women recognize that there may be parallels between their gender oppression at home and the racial and colonial domination of nonwhite populations abroad.

Some authors have questioned "what difference does gender make" in the travel narratives and representations of otherness of, for example, imperial subjects traveling in Africa during the Victorian era.[4] Women's and men's representation of otherness to a great extent reflect their gendered relationships to their own society.[5] "In acknowledging themselves to have been 'colonized' by gender, at least some women travelers recognized their own embodiment of the power and prestige of the ruling group and opposed colonization based on race."[6] This raises the question of how the recognition of the power of one's Western subjectivity applies to women travelers when they are members of a racially oppressed minority in their home country. In order to tackle this question, it is necessary to analyze how embodiment differently impacts the experience of traveling and touring for women and men more generally as well as its effects on African American female roots tourists in particular.

Like all other social and cultural realms, tourism is fundamentally gendered. One of the obvious reasons is because overall society and tourists themselves are gendered. As Enloe, Massey, and other feminist scholars have shown, historically, in the West, women have always had more restricted access to travel than men. Home was defined as the realm of femininity while traveling and soldiering were not only reserved for men, but were, in fact, the confirmation of masculinity. "The attempt to confine women to the domestic sphere was both a specifically spatial control and, through that, a social control on identity."[7] Travel in general has thus been empowering for women since it has allowed them to exert autonomy and challenge traditional gender roles.[8] While this is accurate to a great extent, it is also undeniable that women, even in this day and age, do not travel as freely as men. The fear of harassment, sexual or otherwise, and rape, while permanent threats to women "at home," may be intensified when women travel abroad and are exposed to the unknown. Although these risks more often materialize for women who travel involuntarily, as is the case of refugees, migrant workers in the hands of coyotes, and the victims of trafficking, women who have the privilege to travel for leisure, and thus voluntarily, are not necessarily spared. In many countries, the misogynist stereotype of Western women as "sexually liberated" exacerbates the dangers of traveling to unfamiliar foreign contexts.

Male tourists can wander around less preoccupied about attacks to their physical and psychological integrity, whereas female tourists are expected to learn at least some basic gender rules regarding what is considered to be culturally acceptable. The female tourist must "absorb minimal knowledge about when to wear what length sleeves and skirts and when to cover her hair. Whole websites are now devoted to offering guidance to women tourists on proper feminine attire in specific countries."[9] There are several guidebooks designed specifically for female solo travelers, where they can find more specific information on the destinations, the local customs, and other tips for traveling safely. A recent example of this trend is Flávia Julius's *Os Destinos das Comissárias de Voo: Guia com 50 Viagens Só para Mulheres* (or, in a loose translation, The destinations of the female flight attendants: A guide to 50 trips for women only), a compilation of travel tips based on interviews with female flight attendants from around the world. The advice ranges from memorizing the number of one's embassy in the country visited, always carrying one's passport, and respecting the local dress code: "Never break the protocol regarding local customs. Don't even think of wearing an unabashed bikini in the beaches of countries where women use veils." Another important recommendation for women traveling alone is to take advantage of guided tours.[10] The bottom-line of this book, as well as that of so many other guidebooks intended for women traveling alone, is that female tourists can remain safe as long as they comply with the sexist rules of the locations they visit.

In most places around the world, traveling solo or without a male companion is still a hurdle for women. The case of the two young Argentinian tourists who were brutally murdered while backpacking in Ecuador in February 2016 made headlines worldwide and generated the international campaign #Viajo-Sola (Spanish for #SoloTraveler, #ViajoSozinha in Portuguese). The campaign called attention to the dangers posed to women who travel alone or in the company of other women. It also fiercely criticized the misogynist condemnation that victims of sexual violence commonly receive in mainstream and social media. In an open letter titled "Yesterday They Killed Me," Paraguayan student Guadalupe Acosta put herself in the shoes of the murdered women claiming that as long as misogyny prevails, *all* women will be unsafe in *all* places, regardless of their age, social status, or how they dress and behave. The forceful letter was translated into many languages and shared more than 700,000 times on Facebook.[11] Just a few years earlier, in 2012, the horrific gang rape and murder of an Indian woman inside a bus had also galvanized international attention. Reports of the incident in newspapers worldwide portrayed India as "unsafe for women."[12] Once this negative publicity severely impacted international tourism the Indian government decided to intervene in the country's long-standing practices of sexual abuse of women, even though Indian feminist activists had been calling attention to the issue for decades. "It was when sexual harassment and sexual assaults appeared to jeopardize foreign women tourists' safety that the media and officials started to pay attention."[13]

Inadvertently, the power attached to the Western identities of foreign women may have constructive results for women living in tourism destinations, independently of whether or not these identities are strategically deployed. And even in those situations in which officials do not take action, at least the media attention that tourists receive when their lives are threatened may in itself serve as a resource that can then be mobilized by local activists. After all, governments around the world must prevent their destinations from becoming labeled unsafe for women travelers as this affects their overall tourism industry. The International Women's Travel Center, a website dedicated to providing safety tips for women travelers, ranks Brazil as the third worse country for a woman to visit, after India and Mexico. Their website describes Brazil as "very dangerous and obnoxious" and the "home of 'quicknapping' where a tourist is kidnapped briefly for a stop to the ATM to get cash and then released. . . . Tourists are specific targets in Brazil, with a rising amount of crimes by children and teenagers. . . . Even at popular tourist areas like beaches, tourists are vulnerable to crime."[14]

Women's greater need to protect their physical and psychological integrity is therefore one of the reasons why traveling solo is not as available an option for women as it is for men. This explains to a great extent the popularity among women of traveling in tour groups. While providing protection, safety, and comfort, the "bubble" of package tours allow women to travel to places that would very likely be out of reach for them otherwise. One of the purposes of a package tour is the guarantee that its members will be guided and sheltered from the beginning to the end of a trip. In addition to the *tourism professionals*—such as travel agents, tour guides, drivers, and security guards—*tourism spaces* need to be bounded and managed in order to secure the bubble of a package tour. Members of a tour group move from the hotel to the tour buses and vans and back to the hotel. And even the walking component of, say, a city tour is usually restricted to specific and safeguarded perimeters.

This bubble poses a particular paradox for diaspora travelers since it affects the prospect of establishing the much-desired connection with the diasporic counterparts. At the same time, however, it is the closer one can get to a guarantee of physical integrity while abroad. One of the most insightful analyses of the contradictions of the tourist bubble for racially oppressed women can be found in June Jordan's biographical account of her trip to the Bahamas. She describes the painfully ironic situation in which, in order to remain safe while abroad, she had to resort to a capitalist corporation: "I did not want to be harassed by the middle-aged waiter, or his nephew. I did not want to be raped by anybody (white or Black) at all and I calculated that my safety as a Black woman alone would best be assured by a multinational hotel corporation."[15]

Whether in the Bahamas, India, or Brazil, female tourists who can afford to pay for the tourist bubble are certainly able to enjoy greater safety and protection against various forms of sexism. In Brazil, women are constantly subjected to being catcalled and verbally harassed in the streets. While this sexist practice affects all women, regardless of age, race, and national identity, it does so in different ways. Having lived in Brazil for most of my life, I witnessed numerous situations in which foreign women were very specifically targeted, especially if they could be phenotypically "read" as non-Brazilian. One of the most striking incidents happened in the early 2000s when I was enjoying an evening out in Salvador with a group of friends from São Paulo. We were at a bar in the touristy area of Pelourinho when a "local" man decided to hit on a Brazilian woman of Japanese descent, mistaking her for a foreigner. Furious because she did not correspond to his wooing, the man became aggressive and started yelling "How come this Japanese gringa is snubbing me when I pick up blonde gringas all the time?!" The man's verbal attack against our friend shocked us not only because of its utter violence; it was astounding because of his racial and misogynist ranking of female tourists.

In her book *Sex Tourism in Bahia: Ambiguous Entanglements*, Erica Williams discusses the figure of the *caça-gringa* (gringa hunters), male hustlers who seek to pick up foreign women for the entangled purposes of making money, enjoying the pleasures of their home city in the same way as a foreign tourist is able to (for example, by eating in fancy restaurants and frequenting expensive nightclubs), but also in order to access cosmopolitanism through establishing connections with foreigners and thus accessing international networks. Although their way of approaching foreign women is often "smoother" than that of the man in the episode described above, the frequency and oftentimes insistence of these attempts at interaction can also be interpreted, by many foreign women, as disrespectful and abusive. The expectation of sexual availability that many gringos/as and black Bahians (whether male or female, gay or straight) often mutually project onto one another is connected to the broader context where these interactions take place: Salvador da Bahia, a city whose dominant tourism image is that of a sexual-racial paradise, where the "specter of sex tourism" looms over its inhabitants and visitors in racialized and gendered ways.[16]

Overall, sexual abuse in Brazil, whether verbal or physical, is more often directed at younger women, whether Brazilian or foreign. Throughout my research I never witnessed or heard of any form of sexual harassment directed at the female African American tourists. Perhaps this is because, besides being protected by the tourist bubble, most of the roots tourists are seniors. The package tours provide them with not only safety and access, but also the comfort and convenience that their often elderly bodies require. When some of these expectations are not met, tourists may complain, demand the return of their investment, or even decide to no longer patronize the travel agency, hotel, or subsidiary companies that service the tour. The anticipation among many tourists that every little detail must run smoothly during their trips may contribute to create some tensions between tourists and tourism workers. For example, in one of Sylvia's tours that I accompanied in Salvador, some of the tourists were very upset about the height of the tour bus, which made it challenging for them to hop on and off the bus to visit the attractions along the way. As a result, they decided to just stay inside the bus during the whole tour, creating frustration for the driver who then had to give up his cigarette break so as to look after the tourists while arranging a place to park where it would be safe for them to stay inside the bus, given the threat of armed robberies, not uncommon in Brazil's largest cities.

Furthermore, because women are predominantly perceived as more docile or gullible, they are also more often approached by beggars and pickpockets. Again, in this case too, the tourist bubble usually shields women who travel on package tours, especially if they stick to the program and do not tend to wander around on their own, which was the case for most of the tourists that I observed. Yet the implied, albeit dominant, notion that women are not worthy of the same respect as men make them the target of other forms of disrespect that sometimes not even the package tour can prevent. Racial identity indisputably intersects with gender, and if women overall are less respected than men, black women in particular are not only more so, but in very specific ways. Discussing racism in the Brazilian context, Louise, the African American tourist quoted in the previous chapters, explained that her corporeal similarity with Afro-Brazilians places her at a disadvantage even as she enjoys the benefits of international travel. This is often exemplified when store clerks mistake her for a black Brazilian woman, and thus do not treat her as a potential costumer: "Even though we are American tourists, they [store clerks] have a distance. They don't embrace us, even when I go into the stores like H. Stern, Amsterdam [high-end jewelry stores], until we convince them by whatever means that we are Americans with middle-income or higher income, it's like: 'You can't afford what we have here.' It's always there, this low-level racism."[17]

Louise's statement reveals that if they succeed in making known their *American* identity, African American travelers can often shield themselves from racism. In fact, most of the African American tourists that I interviewed expressed awareness of the privilege attached to their condition as both tourists and U.S. citizens. Even among the tourists that did mention having experienced racism in Brazil, such as not receiving the attention they were expecting from vendors, there was a general consensus that once they were recognized as foreigners, the treatment immediately improved. For example, in answering my question "Was there anything about Bahia or Brazil that was different from your expectation?" one of the female tourists responded: "I experienced some racism—store clerks not being particularly welcoming, until I spoke English and they realized I was an American."[18] Another female tourist, member of the same tour group, voiced an opposite reaction to the same question: "I expected more discrimination as a black person. I did not experience much of that."[19]

While the treatment afforded by store clerks was often used to measure racism, it was also a way of gaging the tourists' overall reception in Brazil, especially as it pertains to notions of diasporic similarity. In other words, a strictly professional interaction with a vendor was sometimes read as "cold" and detached, thus revealing the desire to be recognized as a member of the diasporic community. Responding to the question "How was the connection to the local people?" a female tourist, member of Sylvia Marie's group, stated: "Connection was almost on a 'service' level with the exception of the planned visits to the schools. It would be wonderful if we were received as true brothers and sisters as opposed to 'American costumers' to purchase items. I have learned a tremendous amount in the short time that I have been here. I would hope that through more education and awareness that both blacks in the United States and in Brazil will understand their connection and become one with a true cultural and ancestral bond."[20] Another female tourist, responding to the same question, stated that the connection with Afro-Brazilians was: "Pretty good. Many people complimented me on my elaborate hairdo. So that was a point on which I was able to connect with a lot of Bahians. Other than that, unfortunately, it was limited to me speaking with service professionals."[21]

As the quote above implies, although female embodiment can have negative effects on black women's travels, it can also be the source of positive experiences. In fact, many, if not most, of the African American women I interviewed emphasized how delighted they were to observe the physical resemblance between themselves and so many Brazilian women. They highlighted the

similarities of their skin color, phenotype, and hair texture, and the importance of witnessing, when not in fact discovering for the first time, that other
women inhabiting other countries shared so many of their physical features.
Women tourists brought up the topic of physical similarity much more than
men did, suggesting that self-consciousness, at least as it pertains to our embodied existence, is more prevalent among women than it is among men, although there are most certainly exceptions.

In the revealingly titled documentary *That's My Face*, discussed in chapter 1,
Thomas Allen Harris also underscores the similarities, both cultural and
physical, that African Americans and Afro-Brazilians share. He shows that
searching for sameness is not only his own quest, but is instead part of a
broader African American pursuit. Harris explains how his documentaries are
as much about the wider African American community as they are about his
own life: "I make autobiographical films, but the way I define it is much more
inclusive than just me. It's about the community that I'm a part of, and the
people I meet along the journey. . . . All kinds of people have come up to me
and told me that this is their journey, because when I made the film, it wasn't
about me. It was about dreamscapes. I made it with enough holes in the narrative that you could add your own narrative to it."[22] Among the people that
Harris met "along the journey" was a young African American woman that,
like him, was also wandering around the streets of Salvador. She explained that
the reason for her visit to Bahia was the need to encounter sameness, very
much in tune with what the female African American tourists described to
me: "I needed to feel what it feels like to be part of the majority. I needed to
be in a place where everyone else looked like me."[23]

Several of the female tourists that I interviewed not only emphasized the
physical similarity that they share with other black women in Brazil and
throughout the African continent, but they also underscored the importance of
knowing that such resemblance exists. Again, Louise's words are emblematic:

> It's amazing how ignorant, I shouldn't say ignorant, how *unaware* many
> African Americans are of their own diaspora. What was presented to me
> as an American about Africa is completely different from what it is. Why
> is that hidden? Why is it hidden that there are people, women, in Brazil,
> who look just like me? You put them on 125th Street and if they don't
> open their mouths you think that they belong there. The same is true of
> Egypt. Why is that hidden? I don't believe that the typical African American
> understands that there are people who look like them and probably have
> the same origin, who are in Brazil.[24]

A female tourist, in her early sixties, whom I interviewed in Cachoeira in 2000, explained that knowing that there are black people living and thriving in other countries is crucial for the self-acceptance of African Americans. She commented on how surprised she was to find out that Brazilians use such a wide range of color categories to racially classify themselves, which she sees as a divisive strategy that black people everywhere should reject so as to unify as a people. But she was not only critical of Brazilians indulging in these color categories. She spoke of the need for a universal rejection of "colorism" so that black people can accept themselves as black no matter where they live: "Black people everywhere need to take on the psychology of accepting themselves as black up here," she said, pointing to her head. She also explained that the encounter with physical similarity abroad was crucial for the self-acceptance and healing of African Americans.[25]

These interviews reveal a tendency among female tourists to conceive of their journeys to the various points of the map of Africanness as educational opportunities. By traveling to different parts of the diaspora, it is possible to learn about the experiences of other black communities, including how they have been able to retain Africanness in their cultures. But the goal of *learning* serves the perhaps larger purpose of *teaching* since most of the women that I interviewed emphasized the importance of sharing with others what they had apprehended and experienced abroad. Furthermore, they conceive of the knowledge acquired in their trips as better equipping them to work toward the goal of healing themselves and their communities at large from the ails of racism and discrimination.

Cultivating the Roots and Healing the Diaspora

Tourism processes are gendered in both their production and consumption. However, studies of women in tourism have focused more on women as *producers* (sex workers, manual workers, crafts sellers, cultural performers, etc.) than as *consumers* of tourism. Nevertheless, if one of the recurrent questions in the literature is how tourism offers women opportunities to empower themselves and challenge subordination, then it is necessary to study female workers and female tourists alike. This seems even more significant when these female tourists are African Americans since their identities are shaped by the distinct, and sometimes conflicting, layers of class, gender, race, and nation. On the one hand, African American women, regardless of class, belong to a historically oppressed minority within their nation and have to deal with gender domination within and beyond their ethnic group. On the other hand, however, they are national citizens of the world's superpower and are therefore endowed with the privileges attached to this condition, at least when abroad. Class affiliation is then probably the most stable element in their identities, and is in fact what allows them to travel and be tourists. But, as I began to explore in chapter 1, there is yet another crucial element that shapes the identity of the African American roots tourists: their age group.

A female tourist in her early sixties explained that it is a specific generation of African Americans who is mostly seeking out their roots abroad. Compared to the previous generation, which was less influenced by the black power movement, her age group is the one doing most of the traveling to Africa and the African diaspora:

> We are thirsting for knowledge of the past, and that's why you see this heavy traveling of large senior groups, you find the senior members in the black American community doing a tremendous amount of travel all across the African continent and all throughout South America. But it's been a struggle to get to this point. Some of the older members, they, maybe, resisted longer. Our generation was part of the black consciousness movement, and we were shaped by one set of circumstances. For those members of the black community that are older than us, it was hard for them to let go of the word *colored* and *negro*, it was harder for them to begin to travel to Africa.[26]

This quote suggests that the most important feature that the roots tourists share is a cognitive map of the world that is significantly informed by the post-civil rights era. One of the essential paradoxes of post-civil rights American politics, as Tillet explains, is that although African Americans formally possess legal citizenship, they simultaneously suffer from a "civic estrangement" that results from their marginalization in the civic myths, monuments, and narratives of American national identity. This estrangement has led African American artists and intellectuals to reclaim "sites of slavery" located outside of the country in order to emphasize the belongingness of blacks to the nation. In that sense, African American roots tourism enables post-civil rights African Americans to replace, and to some extent reconcile, their feeling of exclusion from an American national narrative of legal citizenship for all.[27]

This argument certainly applies to the roots tourism that occurs in Brazil as well, although in this case recovering cultural roots prevails over the reclaiming of sites of slavery, as I have discussed in the previous chapters. Nevertheless, it is important to highlight that whether the motivation to travel is to reclaim sites of slavery or recover cultural roots, women make up the majority of diaspora tourists. In my research, I encountered an overwhelmingly greater amount of women than men among the African Americans who visit Brazil as roots tourists. Carrying out field research for his master's thesis, anthropologist Marcelo Ferreira noted that the predominance of women over men is also the case among the groups of African American tourists who visit Rio de Janeiro, corresponding to 75 percent of members of the tours that he observed. As in Bahia, the groups are composed mainly of women traveling alone or with a close relative, usually a daughter or niece, but sometimes their husbands.[28] The convergence between Ferreira's observations and my own can be explained by the fact that most of the groups that travel to Bahia include Rio de Janeiro in their itineraries.[29]

Ebron found the same gender imbalance among the African American roots tourists that she accompanied in the Senegambia.[30] In fact, most ethnographic studies of African American roots tourism in West Africa quote predominantly women tourists, suggesting that women quite likely make up the majority of these visitors.[31] The predominance of women seems to be the case also among other ethnic groups that carry out diaspora and heritage tourism around the world.[32] In addition to generally being older, more educated, and more affluent than mass tourists, most of the diaspora tourists are female, an issue that has yet to receive the attention it deserves. There is certainly a pragmatic, albeit no less gendered, explanation for why women make up the majority of roots and heritage tourists: as the ones who are usually in charge of reproductive labor and the maintenance of the overall well-being of the family, Western women are predominantly responsible for planning vacations.[33] When I asked Sylvia Marie why there were always so many more women than men in her groups, she responded that "women are just more proactive, more organized, and better at planning things ahead of time." The few men that participated in her tours were usually the husbands of some of the female tourists who had been the ones in their families to "plan the whole trip and drag the men along (chuckles)."[34] Research conducted on the topic of women acting as their family's main travel planners and dominating the travel decision-making process corroborate Sylvia's observation.[35]

Yet more conceptual reasons may also explain why women make up the majority of the participants in roots tourism. The interviews suggest that women take upon themselves the role of "healers" and "mentors" of their communities. Most of the women stressed that they need to educate other people in the United States about the broader African diaspora so as to make them aware of both the existence of other black communities across the world and of the Africanness of their culture. Sylvia Marie, for instance, often reiterated that she saw it as her mission to educate African Americans about their "counter-parts in the diaspora." And no better way to do this than to travel to meet these counterparts face to face and experience firsthand their life and culture in Brazil and beyond. For Louise, the lawyer in her mid-sixties, who was visiting Brazil for the fourth time when I met her in 2012, the reasons that had brought her to the country were very clear. She traveled to find her past and learn her history, but not only because this would bring her personal fulfillment; it equipped her to become a more valuable member of her community: "How can we be a professional or a teacher and have never set foot on African soil or have never set foot in South America or where your people are?"[36] Gaining this knowledge through travel to various sites of the black diaspora was therefore crucial for her. But it was just as vital to share the gained knowledge with others, especially younger African Americans who had not been exposed to the broader African diaspora.

The connection between Western women's travels and their role in serving their communities has a long history. White European women often traveled, for example, as nurses in charge of tending to wounded soldiers during international wars, or as teachers sent overseas as part of civilizing missions. The certainty that they would perform "womanly" tasks abroad served as a guarantee that women would remain feminine and not rupture gender boundaries despite traveling, which was dominantly perceived as a male prerogative. Historically, the association between traveling and tending to the well-being of others has also been part of the experience of many black women. Examining antebellum explorations of black women travelers in and from the United States, Cheryl Fish perceives a connection between women's travels and community uplifting. Nancy Prince's and Mary Seacole's voyages were constantly marked by the benevolent labors of healing and educating members of the societies to which they either belonged or were temporarily attached.[37] These examples are not meant to suggest that women's travels are or have always been necessarily tied to serving their communities. However, past practices do not simply vanish; they tend to leave "traces" in the present. As Gómez-Barris and Gray have argued, if we are to understand the ways in which ideas, memories, and imaginings contribute to produce subjects, conduct social relations, and make social worlds, it is crucial that our investigations prioritize traces as the "pivotal roles of absent presences."[38] Furthermore, the "structures of feelings"[39] shared by the members of an ethnic group are also fundamentally gendered, thus collectively informing one's motivations to travel.

Examples of the gendered conceptualizations of black female travel can be found in the literary works of Caribbean-American writers Paule Marshall and

Audre Lorde. Although they depict their travels to the homelands of their ancestors as motivated by a desire for spiritual recollection, they constantly tie their individual pursuits to the broader need to intervene on behalf on their transnational, diasporic communities. In her novel *Praisesong for the Widow*, Marshall is critical of what she sees as the neocolonialist characteristics of international tourism. Lorde too, in several of her writings, rejects all forms of neocolonialism and claims that peoples of African descent have a mutual responsibility to protect one another from old and new forms of oppression. Both authors advocate for diaspora tourists to better inform themselves about the peoples and cultures they visit so that they can become more ethical travelers and more responsible members of their transnational communities. "Both Marshall and Lorde are conscious of their mobility and privilege as United States citizens and status within literary circles, yet they understand the shared experiences and oppressions with being a part of the African diaspora."[40]

Raiford's analysis of Eslanda Robeson's memoir of her journey through Southern Africa in the 1930s also reveals the awareness of her privileged position in that context and an altruistic concern that her travel experience should serve the higher purpose of further interconnecting African Americans and Africans. Disrupting the "backward-looking" gaze, dominant within Anthropology but also among African American literary circles of the time, Robeson's text and photography portray Africans in their diversity and make a claim to Africans' *presentness*.[41] This is a powerful illustration of McKittrick's argument that black women, as geographic subjects, have often rewritten national narratives, respatialized feminism, and reconceptualized place, providing "spatial clues as to how more humanly workable geographies might be imagined."[42]

Also alert to the contradictions inherent to being, at the same time, black, female, a U.S. citizen, and a member of the African diaspora is June Jordan's aforementioned "Report from the Bahamas."[43] In this intersectional examination of her short vacation in the Caribbean, Jordan unpacks how her "consciousness of class," "consciousness of race," and "consciousness of gender" are triggered in her encounters with Caribbean black people. Although she does not refer to a specific "consciousness of nation," Jordan is well aware of how her privileged positionality as an American tourist sets her apart from, for example, the black woman who works as the chambermaid in her hotel, or the black women whose crafts she will either haggle or refuse to purchase: "We are not particularly women anymore; we are parties to a transaction designed to set us against each other."[44] The "transaction" that disconnects her from other black women, or black people more broadly in this context, stems not only from the inequalities of power of international tourism, but also from the geopolitics of the black diaspora.

By emphasizing women's mindfulness of the potential privileges attached to specific elements of their identities, I am cautious not to generalize or essentialize *all women* as necessarily self-aware. Yet, when reflecting on the question "What difference does gender make?" in the transnational relations established between citizens of a superpower and members of the world's peripheries, it is safe to argue that although "a woman's point of view does not guarantee a reciprocal relationship with an Other, . . . it accommodates a crack in the concept of Self that can be widened to shed light on the concept of Other."[45] Although originally developed to deconstruct the privilege of whiteness in the North American context, Adrienne Rich's oft-cited concept of the politics of location is helpful here as it explains that ultimately all identities and the subject positions that they enable are linked to geopolitical and metaphorical locations. Locations, in turn, should be understood as places in relation to history, "used not to reify gender through nostalgia or authenticity but to unpack the notion of shared or common experience."[46]

In tandem with Robeson's, Marshall's, Lorde's, and Jordan's awareness of the differences and inequalities that set apart different diaspora communities, some of the female tourists that I interviewed emphasized the importance of not idealizing the people they would meet during their trips, or romanticizing the nature of such encounters. In a conversation with a group of African American women, all in their mid- to late-sixties, that I met in Cachoeira during the Festival of the Good Death in 2000, one of them stated very clearly that it was not a preformed image of Bahia that she planned on "bringing back" to the United States:

> We also come with notions about what we're going to find, so the struggle, I think, is not romanticizing Africa, or Brazil, or Cuba, because you're dealing with some of the same struggles that we are. When we went into the ceremony last night [of the Sisterhood of the Good Death] and there was the white Virgin Mary stretched out, and in my mind we're talking about a sisterhood of black women, and a tradition that extends all the way to colonial times, and African Americans come with the idea that we're going to see a black Jesus on the cross, and we're going to see all these black images, and so forth [chuckles], and then we get hit with the reality that colonialism has been just as much a part of your history as of our history! Even though you've been able to hang on to certain traditions and practices of African culture, the influence [of European colonialism] is

there. So we're trying to see that our young people also go through the healing process. . . . So there is a number of ways in which you're struggling just as we are. So just as the struggle brings us here to Brazil, it also sends some of us in our community to try to see how we can turn things around. And it makes us aware of what is going on in other countries in the diaspora, and what can we do, and it makes us more aware of the pitfalls. And sometimes all we can do is give a prayer that here in Brazil, as you go though some of this ground that we've covered already, you don't through the baby out with the bathwater.[47]

This complex statement, filled with a wealth of ideas, is worth quoting at length for several reasons. First, this female tourist makes clear that one of the reasons for her trips to Brazil as well as to Cuba and the African continent is to bring back elements that can heal the members of her community back home, especially the youth. Second, the struggle, as she calls it, is part of the life of black communities around the world, and not only her own. Analyzing black women's representations of place "in a world that has profited from black displacement," McKittrick argues that "black women's expressive acts spatialize the imperative of a perspective of struggle."[48] It is the commonality of this shared struggle that brings so many African American women to different sites of the map of Africanness in search of references that may contribute to increase the knowledge regarding how other black communities live and thrive. Third, the legacy of colonialism that they encounter in Brazil, although disappointing and disruptive of the Africanness that they hoped to experience, also serves to enhance sameness since it is a feature that African Americans and Afro-Brazilians share. Yet even as her insightful evaluation of the subtleties of transnational black relations calls for less preconceptions and more openness on the part of the tourists, it does not do away with the trope of black evolution. After all, black people in Brazil are still conceived of as supposedly going through ground that African Americans have already covered. While most of the female tourists expressed greater self-awareness of the differences that set them apart from their diasporic counterparts, many of them also confirmed the tropes that are dominant in the African American roots tourist gaze.

Many years later, in 2012, a visit of Sylvia Marie's group to the educational organization that prepares black youth for the college entrance exam, reiterated this paradox whereby African American tourists while open, and in fact eager, to learn about the specific struggles of Afro-Brazilians, still position these diasporic counterparts as trailing the ground that African Americans have already covered. During the visit, there were many questions about affirmative action in higher education, and the coordinator of the institute explained that some mixed-race Brazilians, who would not normally identify as black, have now begun to do so in order to benefit from the system of racial quotas. This created puzzlement among the tourists, and several of them asked why people who have black ancestry would not claim that ancestry or even be recognized as black by others. The coordinator replied that this was not the first time that a group of African American visitors had trouble understanding the specific ways in which racism operates in Brazil, including for example the many color categories that racism generated, and which do not exist in the United States. Because I was serving as the translator during this visit, I tried to further clarify the coordinator's point. I argued that having black ancestry alone does not define one as black in Brazil and that color gradations, hair texture, and overall phenotype significantly inform how one is read and reads oneself racially. I also stated that the so-called intermediary color categories (*moreno, pardo, café com leite*, etc.) position people outside of blackness, differently from the United States where such terms as "high yellow" or "redbone" might qualify one's phenotype, but still within the boundaries of blackness.

Sylvia Marie responded to the point we were making by underscoring that, despite the apparent differences, African Americans and Afro-Brazilians actually have much more in common than meets the eye: "This is not unlike we are in the United States. Perhaps with us *it is not as severe today as it used to be*. Race has had such a strong negative effect on us as people of African descent that we don't want to identify with it. And that is the root cause. We've been made to feel so inferior that we were made black. But once we can embrace the fact that our root is Africa, then we can begin to be proud of who we are, and then we don't feel the need to say 'I'm *pardo*.' How many of us in America don't say 'My grandmother is Indian'?"[49] The members of Sylvia's tour group received her comment with chuckles and many nods of agreement. In order to emphasize that important historical processes have equally affected disparate diasporic communities, Sylvia unintentionally reiterated the evolutionist trope that African Americans *today* are less affected by these processes than are Afro-Brazilians. In my view, this asymmetrical positioning is not done, however, with the goal of ascertaining the superiority of African Americans over other communities in the diaspora. It is, instead, the result of a desire to recognize the existence of features that black communities commonly share across national boundaries, thus establishing sameness over difference. In this case, the commonly shared features are the denial of black ancestry and the need to embrace Africanness.

Although many of the women I interviewed did in fact reiterate the trope of black evolution by taking for granted the notion that African Americans are "ahead" of Afro-Brazilians, they did not position themselves or the United States as occupying a leadership role for the African diaspora at large, as many of the men tended to do. The concern of most of these women was in finding common ground among diaspora groups so that one could learn from the other on how to best "heal" their communities and continue to move toward overcoming the struggle. This was very clearly stated in an interview with two African American women in their mid-sixties, and who were visiting Brazil for the first time in 2000, after having traveled to several African countries. Although they echoed the notion that some black groups are more or less advanced than others, they emphasized that the most important result of the transnational encounters that occur through tourism is that black communities can learn *about* and *from* each other: "Where individuals are in Brazil is at a different point in time as to where individuals in the United States are. But there is something that we can each learn from the other, and from the other's experience, and that we can share. And some of those experiences that took place in the United States are working their way down to Brazil, and they are going to have some influence, one way or the other, as we are influenced and impacted by other's experiences, and it's going to make a change."[50] They then enthusiastically described how impacted they were in encountering Bahia's African culture and how important it is for more African Americans to experience that.

The interviews above indicate that embracing "Africa" and the Africanness that exists in the diaspora is fundamentally important in the restoration of a dignified black identity. The centrality of African heritage in the process of healing is also noticeable in the increasingly popular phenomenon of DNA testing. Access to one's genetic ancestry has become ever more available for the public, especially in the United States, where by 2015 the industry had served close to two million customers.[51] In addition to carrying out diaspora tourism, roots seekers, African American or otherwise, have increasingly resorted to DNA tests in order to obtain more knowledge about the past. In tandem with my research findings that show that the majority of roots tourists are women, Nelson's research on DNA testing shows that African American women also make up the bulk of both conventional and genetic genealogists. Furthermore, these women too envision the restoration of lineages and knowledge of the past as crucial in the education of their relatives as well as members of their broader communities.[52] One of Nelson's informants, for example, who was interviewed in the BBC documentary *A Slave's Story*, expressed her hope that the revelation of her ancestor's genetic ancestry would "bring healing" to herself and her community.[53]

To explain the predominance of women in genealogical communities, Nelson draws on Carolyn Rosenthal's work on women as "kinkeepers."[54] Rosenthal had employed the term to describe the practice of maintaining family ties as a form of gendered labor. Normatively, kinkeeping tasks such as the activities of telephoning, writing letters, and engaging in mutual aid, have been assigned to women. Women have also served, traditionally, as bridges between generations.[55] Even though Rosenthal's research focused on women who take on the role of keeping contemporaneous family members in touch with one another, the argument is certainly applicable to the maintenance of ties to the ancestors, whether those known and close or those unknown and long gone. Because women have taken on the role of kinkeepers in the various but usually interconnected realms of roots seeking, such as genealogy building and diaspora tourism, it is important to analyze the motivations for these gendered practices. If gender is a meaningful organizing principle in family relations and kinship systems, it would not be much different in the context of tourism which, after all, is not a cut-off realm, but is instead permeated by the same codes that guide ordinary life.

Gendering Space, Place, and Time

In order to understand the gendering of tourism, and more specifically of roots tourism, it is necessary to listen to how women and men envisage their travels, represent the places and peoples that make up their desired destinations, and conceive of their own roles in the diaspora. But in addition to that, or better yet, entangled with it, it is as crucial to examine how the dominant travel discourses are themselves also fundamentally gendered. To comprehend how these processes function in the specific case of African American roots tourism in Brazil, it is important to unpack how the dominant tropes that sustain the roots tourist gaze are gendered. As explored in chapter 2, the three major intersecting tropes that inform and sustain this gaze are: the idea of Bahia as a "closer Africa" for African Americans; the trope of the "happy native," or the perception of Afro-Brazilians as more culturally fulfilled than African Americans; and the trope of "black evolution," which envisions a unidirectional path where African Americans have reached stages of political mobilization that are yet to be attained by Afro-Brazilians. As discussed above, the different ways through which women and men conceive of their travels and represent the places and peoples that make up their desired tourist destinations is connected to how they engage with the gendering of travel discourses.

As Doreen Massey explains, the categories place, local, and global are never neutral or objective. They are, instead, invoked and naturalized through gendered, sexualized, and racialized processes. "Spaces and places are not only themselves gendered but, in their being so, they both reflect and affect the ways in which gender is constructed and understood."[56] Furthermore, space is not disconnected from time, and neither should they be analyzed as binary opposites, with time taking precedence over space as, for example, in Marx's famous claim of "the annihilation of space by time" in capitalism. Massey is very critical of the masculinist understanding of time as having agency over space, where space is associated with stasis, simple reproduction, nostalgia, and passivity while time is associated with activity, change, and transformation: "With time are aligned History, Progress, Civilization, Science, Politics and Reason, portentous things with gravitas and capital letters."[57] This asymmetrical dualism, she explains, is intimately connected to the construction of the radical distinction between genders and the power relations maintained between them. As a result of this masculinist, binary, and mutually exclusive form of thinking, time has been coded masculine and space feminine.

Extending this critique to the analysis of the gendering of *place*—in the sense of specific location instead of the more abstract notion of *space*—I would add that the ways in which places have been gendered also reveals a gendering of time. The trope of Bahia as a closer Africa, that is so central for the African American roots tourist gaze, undeniably represents both Bahia and "Africa" in feminized terms. Both locations are conceived of as "homelands": Mama Africa as the obviously gendered "motherland" and Bahia as a more implicitly gendered shortcut to Africa. The characterization of a place as "home," that is, as "an unchanging stability to be looked back on, to be returned to, is itself masculine."[58] And it is so both because this form of thinking of home usually conflates place with a specific person (that is, the mother) and because this, in turn, represents the mother as an unchanging point of reference.[59] Thus, the gendering of place as female is also a process that *places*, in the sense that it *attaches*, gender and, more specifically, women to place.

Yet the feminization of a place is also intertwined with the feminization of the culture that is primarily associated with such place. The representations of an Africanized Bahia predominantly rely on images of black women as cultural markers, quintessentially exemplified in the *baianas de acarajé* (discussed in chapter 5) and, in the case of roots tourism, essentially embodied by the Sisters of the Good Death. A flyer that Sylvia Marie produced to distribute to her tour groups replicates both of these feminized representations to describe Bahia as a closer Africa. This flyer, which is part of the beautifully arranged folder that each of the tour's participants receive during the orientation session, contributes to represent Bahia as located in an imaginary past as it invites the tourists to step back in time to "dance in the streets at the Boa Morte Festival," and witness the Afro-Brazilian martial art form of Capoeira and Candomblé, "the Brazilian religion steeped in African heritage." The representations that illustrate Sylvia's flyer are, of course, similar to those found in many other flyers, websites, and the overall tourism promotional material, where the images of fully garbed *baianas* are meant to stand in for Bahia's Africanness.

If to look at women's place in travel and tourism requires looking at men's place in these realms, it also requires an examination of the contrast between women who travel and women who do not travel as well as the interactions between them. Revealingly, in African American roots tourism in Brazil, women are represented as the "guardians of culture," whether they are the "subjects" or "objects" of tourism, that is, respectively, the female tourists who "bring home the roots," and the Sisters of the Good Death who are portrayed as "living samples" of the preservation of African culture in the diaspora. The Bahiatursa employee who has played a major role in promoting African American roots tourism in Bahia explained the importance of the Sisterhood of the Good Death as embodying the links to the sought-after African past: "The African Americans see the Sisters as a living document of the black culture of the New World. They represent the links that have been broken for them. And here they are able to reencounter these links."[60]

Although several researchers have pointed to the effects of tourism in the empowerment of women, especially impoverished women who may become economically independent from men through selling crafts or performing their cultural identities, this process may also, on the other hand, reaffirm the role of women as the quintessential markers of culture.[61] This representation simultaneously portrays women as embodiments of the past. In Guatemala, for example, Mayan women artisans who parade in the marketplace in their traditional dress have been more successful at attracting tourists to buy their crafts. By actively deploying their female indigeneity, these women confirm their position as the repositories of cultural tradition.[62] In Chiapas, the iconic image of the Zapatista woman in braids and bandannas adorn a large number of t-shirts and posters while in the tourist areas of San Cristóbal de las Casas, "gendered indigeneity is on proud and public display" as indigenous women now deploy notions of traditional and authentic indigeneity to become more attractive to tourists.[63] For Florence Babb, tourism has become a productive realm to revisit Marisol de la Cadena's claim that "women are more Indian." In an earlier analysis of female indigeneity among Peruvian peasants, de la Cadena had shown that while men may acquire the identity of mestizo and thus ascend socially, women in the same community had significantly less access to ethnic mobility, thus maintaining their social subordination.[64] With the intensification of international tourism, Babb argues, what used to be a liability, in this case, being both female and indigenous, has become a form of cultural capital as women have deployed their dress and language as signs of a much-desired authentic otherness.

In that sense, by enabling women to become the breadwinners, tourism has transformed gender relations within and outside the home, thus triggering progressive social change, but paradoxically this has often times occurred because women have been portrayed, and have portrayed themselves as the "face of cultural continuity" and preservation. This certainly applies to the Sisterhood of the Good Death, although in this case the cultural authenticity that they perform corresponds to the tourists' desire for sameness instead of difference. As discussed in the chapter 3, roots tourism has undeniably benefited the Sisters. Even though it has not changed their economic status, since most of them continue to live in relative poverty, tourism has brought them much-deserved attention and recognition from the part of the municipal and state governments, not to mention the feelings of pride and higher self-esteem that the Sisters have been able to enjoy. But this has relied on a process that positions the Sisters, the culture that they guard and preserve, and the place with whom they are conflated, as frozen in the past. And if a place is represented as belonging to the past, it suggests that time, and its implicit masculinity, has not exercised agency over it, thus confirming that stasis lies at the core of the association between space and femininity.

Furthermore, the deployment of the image of the Sisters of the Good Death to represent an Africanized Bahia, while potentially empowering and certainly dignifying for the Sisters, does not prevent the strengthening of the trope of black evolution where African Americans perceive themselves as more advanced and/or more fortunate than other black diasporic communities. Despite marveling at the Africanness that the Sisters of the Good Death have supposedly been able to maintain and retain, some of the female tourists also commented on how physically deteriorated Afro-Brazilian women of their age, including some of the Sisters, appeared to be in contrast to themselves. Deborah, a retired probation officer, who visited Brazil for the first time in 2004 as a member of Sylvia Marie's group, expressed this very clearly. She had by then visited Cuba, Senegal, Ghana, South Africa, The Gambia, Zambia, Zimbabwe,

Kenya, Zanzibar, Tanzania, and Ethiopia. Although she was enthusiastic about the Africanness that she found in Bahia, and despite praising the fact that the poverty that she saw in Brazil was not as abject as the poverty she had seen in West Africa, she was surprised at how "worn out" senior Afro-Brazilian women appeared to be: "The women of age here are totally different from American women. I look at your women and I see weariness. I saw a woman the other day that I know was younger than I was but who seemed a lot older. I mean, look at us! I am a retired person but I am really in my golden years. I am sixty-seven. And most of the women in this group are in their late sixties and early seventies. I saw those ladies and I started praying, saying 'God, I am glad that I was raised in America, in North America.' Because it is a whole different look, a whole different attitude, a whole different purpose."[65]

This quote conveys several of the issues addressed in this chapter. First, it expresses a conflation of the gendering of people, place, and time. Second, it shows female embodiment as a reflection of the geopolitical position of the United States vis-à-vis Brazil and West African countries. Third, it reiterates the notion, discussed in previous chapters, that the enslavement and subsequent relocation of one's ancestors has led to one's contemporary status as a citizen of the United States. And being an American, as Deborah unequivocally states, is a blessing for which one should be grateful. This confirms that the trope of the "happy native" relies on rhetoric association and antithesis, that is, the enthusiasm for a specific aspect of the culture of the Other does not prevent that the Other's overall society may be perceived as inferior or at a disadvantage when compared to one's own, as I discussed in chapter 2.[66] Fourth, it shows that, while discourses are gendered, both women and men may reproduce these gendered notions. Subjectivities, whether of women or men, are formed through mobility and spatiality.[67] Although women may indeed accommodate a "crack" in the concept of Self that might make them more attuned to the Other, as I discussed above, they are not immune from reiterating the masculinist trope of black evolution that projects African Americans as "ahead" of their diasporic counterparts. In fact, when I asked Deborah if she felt the same way about the women she met in her trips to the African continent, she replied that she did so in West African countries, but did not in South Africa: "I felt the South Africans were right there in our corner; I didn't feel that they were far behind. They are a First World country."[68]

If the matured faces and fuller bodies of older black women have been deployed, albeit not exclusively, in tourism promotional material, to portray Bahia's Africanness, it is the youthful faces and leaner bodies of young mulatas that have predominantly adorned the tourism images of Rio de Janeiro. An

Afro-Bahian woman who worked as a stylized *baiana*, welcoming tourists in the airport and tourism information offices, comically remarked on how her physical features make her suitable for the job: "A real baiana has to be dark-skinned like me! And now that I am getting older and have gained weight, that makes me even more typical [to be a *baiana*]. *Já curti meus dias de sereia, agora curto meus dias de baleia*! I've enjoyed my time as a mermaid, now I enjoy my time as a whale! [Chuckles]."[69] In chapter 2, I discussed how Bahia and Rio, although usually included in most itineraries of African American roots tourists, are predominantly conceived of as very different and, to some extent, even opposite destinations. The tourists that I interviewed frequently compared Bahia with Rio de Janeiro, always preferring the former over the latter, and often alluding to binary conceptualizations of tradition versus modernity, and cultural purity versus cultural hybridity. While Bahia has been predominantly associated with tradition and Africanness, Rio de Janeiro, Brazil's second largest city, has been mostly connected to modernity and sexiness.

Thus, places are not only racialized and gendered; they are also sexualized or de-sexualized, which has undeniable implications for the forms of tourism that develop in different locations. This is not to deny Bahia's position as a sex tourism destination for white and black tourists alike. As mentioned in a previous chapter, African American sex tourism does indeed take place in Bahia, especially gay sex tourism, but it is simply not comparable to the scale of the African American heterosexual sex tourism that takes place in Rio. While analyses of African American sex tourism in Bahia are more recent,[70] African American sex tourism in Rio has become an increasingly observable fact ever since it was first widely publicized in an *Essence* article published in 2006,[71] and it has since become an extremely contentious topic of discussion in books, blogs, magazine articles, and in a YouTube video revealingly titled *Frustrated: Black American Men in Brazil*. According to the video as well as numerous other sources that have discussed this issue, those who are "frustrated" with African American men descending in Rio for sex are, supposedly, African American women.[72]

Although African American sex tourism in Brazil is not a focus of this book, it is important for my discussion insofar as it also shows how the gendering of place is connected to the gendering of time. And this is because the trope of black evolution, or the idea that Afro-Brazilians inhabit an "African American past," is prevalent also in the discourse of the African American men who carry out sex tourism in Rio. Similar to European and white North-American males who engage with sex tourism in peripheral countries, and in line with the roots tourists' nostalgia for the past, African American sex tourists also project a romanticized primitiveness onto the "natives" by constantly comparing Brazilian women's subordination and willingness to serve them, sexually and otherwise, to how black women back home allegedly used to be like in the "good old days" before they became so independent and self-sufficient.[73]

The trope of black evolution, as in fact any evolutionist reasoning, is inherently masculinist. Because it uses time to classify difference, presupposing that peoples evolve from less to more advanced stages, evolutionism relies on the naturalization of the masculine action of time over a static and feminine notion of space or place. The civilizing and/or uplifting logic present in Western discourses of evolution, as well as other epistemologies originated in the Enlightenment, are profoundly gendered and grounded on patriarchal presuppositions that have relied on the implicit assumption of the masculine self, usually but not necessarily white, as the neutral standard against which the feminized Other, usually but not necessarily women, should be measured.

In the specific case of roots tourism, the trope of black evolution is also the result of the "landscaping" of identities, that is, the projection of one's identity onto a specific place or, in a more diasporic fashion, *places*. The identities that are projected onto places are themselves gendered which, in turn, contribute to the gendering of their meanings. Although there now seems to be a consensus regarding how the tourist gaze builds on previous orientalist discourses that emphasized difference and reiterated otherness, the trope of black evolution shows how this process takes place also within discourses that seek to emphasize sameness. As Afro-Brazilians have been associated with past lifestyles, they are ultimately temporalized as Other. And as the masculinism of time becomes a marker of difference, it distinguishes the modern black self from the traditional black Other. Thus, if the map of Africanness is as much temporal as it is spatial, as I have shown in previous chapters, its temporality is, in turn, as I have shown here, gendered.

Conclusion

Several authors have argued that by prioritizing travel, scholars have contributed to privilege the mobility of masculine subjects, thus perpetuating the dominant masculinism in the study of diasporas.[74] Clifford, for example, explains that when diasporic experiences are viewed more in terms of displacement than placement, traveling rather than dwelling, men's experiences tend to dominate.[75] I argue, however, that to challenge male dominance and to understand how women function as agents of diaspora making, the focus does not necessarily need to be on home, placement, or dwelling. It should also include women's practices of traveling and experiencing their identities in different locations. Opting for a rather different angle, Jacqueline Nassy Brown claims that in order to expose and challenge the gendered hierarchy of diasporas it is important to attend more to the "politics of gender" than to "women's experience" since the former constitutes and normalizes the latter. Although I certainly agree that focusing on women's experience alone is not enough to either correct the dominant masculinism of diaspora studies or to examine the gendering of diasporas, I would argue for a more dialogic understanding of the politics of gender and women's (and men's) experiences. Instead of seeing one as unilaterally defining the other, it might be more productive to see these two processes as mutually constitutive. After all, the ways in which gendered individuals conform to or challenge the physical and social locations to which they have been assigned contribute to the gendering processes of their own communities and the diaspora at large.

Analyzing how women engage with normative gender roles, whether to challenge or enact them, is important for the understanding not only of how gender shapes diaspora identities but also, in turn, how belongingness to a diaspora affects, or not, gendered identities. Because they are multicentered, diasporas comprise several potential "homelands." If to reach these dispersedly located homelands, one must travel, this opens up the possibility of diasporas to unsettle traditional gender associations between "home" as feminine and travel as masculine, especially when women are the ones carrying out most of these travels. This is even more important in a context that has been historically marked by the mobility of masculine subjects, which made men, for a very long time, the main agents of black diaspora making.[76] Yet, despite the liberating promise of diasporas as multicentered, and thus potentially decentralizing configurations, there are in reality no guarantees as to how transnational affiliations and mobility ultimately inform gendered and racialized subjectivities. While it is true that the limitation imposed onto women's mobility has served as a tool of gender oppression, access to mobility is not automatically emancipating or transformative since, as we have seen here, women can gain access to travel but still assume traditional gender roles. Traveling internationally in order to, ultimately, cultivate the cultural roots of one's community suggests that women are taking on the role of bearers of the nation.

Yet, if "to bear," on the one hand, means to give birth to, carry, and sustain as well as to abide by; on the other hand, it can also mean to create and express. The many female roots tourists that I met throughout the course of my research have been enacting all of these multiple and sometimes disparate meanings of *bearing*. One of the most remarkable examples of women actively creating and expressing the African diaspora in novel ways can be found in Sylvia Marie's dynamic, entrepreneurial work as a travel agent, which I had the opportunity to observe for a little over ten years. Sylvia first visited Brazil in 2003, as a member of a tour group led by an African American man who had been by then bringing groups to Brazil for more than twenty years. Just one year later, when I met her and accompanied her group throughout their stay in Bahia, Sylvia was already leading a tour of her own. In 2012, when I accompanied her group throughout their entire eight-day stay in Bahia and three-day stay in Rio, this was then the ninth time that she was leading a tour group to Brazil. By the time of her first visit to Brazil, Sylvia had already traveled to more than fifteen African countries, many of which she had visited by taking tour groups through her solo-owned and operated travel agency since 1991. Upon first traveling to Brazil, she realized the importance of expanding her tours to include this black country, which she sees as one that is overflowing with Africanness.

It is important to examine how gender relations in tourism are constructed and how they inform issues of inequality and control, but without losing sight of the fact that these relations may change over time. Sylvia Marie along with a handful of female travel agents have been gradually occupying a market that, while dominated by women, has been largely managed by men. This indicates that a transformation is taking place as women are becoming more active in the production and not just in the consumption of tourism. Although not transformative a realm as some may have once imagined, tourism does indeed offer women opportunities for leadership and entrepreneurship, even if this does not necessarily mean overcoming more conventional gender rules and expectations. And while leadership and entrepreneurship, because of their ties to a capitalist framing of the world, may not be the best elements to measure progressive change, women's altruistic understanding of the links between Self and Other, and between individual and community, do indeed allow us to imagine "more humanly workable geographies."[77] The problem with preserving traditional gender roles is not that women continue to feel responsible for bearing the well-being of their communities, but that men overall have not expressed the same concern, or at least not as intensely.

The next and final chapter also examines the transformations and continuities in African American roots tourism in Bahia since its inception, but redirecting the focus to the role of state actors and agencies. The intersection of race, gender, and nation continues to guide the analytical thread as we now delve into the state's efforts to embrace the notion of a black diaspora and recognize the existence of distinct black identities amid the longstanding dominant narrative of harmonious racial mixture.

CHAPTER FIVE

The Awakening Giant
The State's Belated Acknowledgment of Roots Tourism

In a state such as Bahia it would be logical to assume that the most prevalent
type of tourism would be that based on African heritage. However, this is not yet
the case. In a state whose most outstanding artists, intellectuals and thinkers are
of African origin, a strategy to attract African and African Diaspora visitors
should have been implemented many years ago. Yet, it was not.

—Leonelli, *African Heritage Tourism in Bahia*

Brazil has been portrayed in African American tourism promotional material
as both an awakening and a sleeping giant, depictions that allude to the alleged
development stages of Afro-Brazilian racial consciousness.[1] The metaphor of
the giant has been employed not only to compare Afro-Brazilians to African
Americans and, more implicitly, Brazil to the United States, but also to contrast the "Brazil of the past" to the "Brazil of the future." Because there is now
an official acknowledgement on the part of the state regarding the African
American presence in Bahia, some might argue that the future has finally arrived. In 2007, the state of Bahia's Secretariat of Tourism (SETUR) founded
the Coordenação do Turismo Étnico Afro, the Coordination of African Heritage
Tourism (CAHT), in its official English designation—to cater specifically to the
African American roots tourism niche, finally breaking with the inertia and
indifference that had dominated the state's position since the inception of
African American tourism in Bahia in the late 1970s.

In this chapter, I analyze this shift in light of the significant, albeit insufficient, discursive and practical transformations that have occurred in Brazil regarding race and racial equality since the center-left PT took control of the
state government of Bahia in 2007.[2] I examine whether this transformation in
the state's overall political orientation as well as in its position regarding African American tourism specifically has contributed to challenge the long-
standing discourse of *baianidade* (or Bahianness) that has predominantly
represented blackness through domesticated and stereotypical images instead
of a force to be reckoned with. How differently, or similarly, is Afro-Bahian culture marketed for foreign tourists—who are predominantly white—vis-à-vis
its promotion for tourists who are not only black but also, for the most part,

critical of racialized forms of domination? I also look at how the state of Bahia's belated endorsement of African American roots tourism compares to other forms of governmental promotion of diaspora tourism around the world.

Bahia Awakens to Roots Tourism . . . Three Decades Later

Considering the ever-growing presence of African American tourists in Brazil, it is striking that the state has not paid them much attention. In my view, this attitude discloses the obliviousness on the part of the authorities of the importance of these black visitors, especially in the state of Bahia, where African American tourism has become steadier over the last three and a half decades. My critique is much less concerned with the possible economic benefits generated by strategies oriented toward African American tourists than with the social and cultural meanings of this lack of initiative. Elsewhere I argued that the absence of stratagems geared toward African American tourists exposes the peculiarities and intricacies of Brazilian racism. Instead of explicit, confrontational antiblack attitudes, the official tourism strategists reveal their disbelief in the power of black people even while they occupy the doubly valued position of being tourists and *americanos*.[3]

This context changed, somewhat, with the creation of the CAHT in 2007, an office established within the structure of SETUR to cater specifically to the African American roots tourism niche. CAHT emerged as the result of a partnership established between the Federal Government's Ministry of Tourism (MTUR) and the State Government of Bahia, whereby the former would transfer to the latter a total of R$22 million (approximately US$11 million per the conversion rate at the time) to support the development of various tourism segments. The then governor of Bahia, Jacques Wagner, and the then minister of tourism, Marta Suplicy, publicly signed the accords during the celebration of the Festival of the Good Death on August 15, 2007, in Cachoeira. One of these accords established the Programa de Ação do Turismo Étnico Afro da Bahia (PATEAB; Program of Action of African Heritage Tourism) which received an initial funding of R$1,245,000 (approximately US$622,500 per the conversion rate at the time).[4]

For the federal government, one of the major goals of this program was to "attract a greater number of tourists, especially North Americans of African descent, to Bahia, bringing them closer to the places and cultural manifestations that are linked to their origins. Exactly for this reason, the place chosen for the launching of the Program was the historic city of Cachoeira, where the traditional

Sisterhood of the Good Death is an international reference."[5] The idea that African Americans should travel to Brazil to find their origins can be found in a number of governmental documents as well as in the pronouncements of the then governor and minister of tourism. The latter declared that "Bahia is the heart of Brazil, in afro terms, and it is [therefore] important to work to develop the desire of the black tourists in knowing their roots." Also acknowledging the African American desire to finds their roots in Bahia, during the public signing of the accords, the governor asserted that SETUR would invest increasingly in this kind of tourism given that there was a strong demand already in place.[6]

A few months later, in March 2008, the U.S. secretary of state Condoleezza Rice visited Bahia as part of an official trip to Brazil. Reverberating the idea that African Americans can encounter their roots in Bahia, local newspaper reports described Rice's visit as an almost mystical experience. Some articles highlighted, for example, how emotional Rice became while attending a ceremony in the Church of our Lady of the Rosary of Blacks (Igreja de Nossa Senhora do Rosário dos Pretos), built by African and Afro-descendant slaves in the eighteenth century. More significantly, these reports depicted Rice's engagement with Afro-Brazilian culture as moments that supposedly "unleashed" her blackness, such as when she couldn't help but clap along to the music played in this church's religious ceremony, or when she "samba-danced with delight" and "played the tambourine with ease" during a performance by Afro-Brazilian singer and then minister of culture Gilberto Gil,[7] or when she couldn't resist tapping her feet and swaying her head as a group of Afro-Brazilian children played percussion.[8] Implicit in these accounts of Rice's enjoyment of Afro-Brazilian culture is a representation of Bahia as a magical place where one's contained, essential blackness can be let loose.

The government of Bahia capitalized on Rice's visit to further promote the Program of Action of Afro Ethnic Tourism, both by publicizing it as evidence of the African American passion for Bahia as well as in the governor's direct plea for Rice's support for the program. Resorting to the representation of Bahia's rich Afro-Brazilian culture and underscoring the state's sizeable black population, governor Jacques Wagner asked for Rice's assistance in order to "capture direct flights from many different cities in the United States to Salvador" and to attract investments in order to further develop ethnic tourism in Bahia.[9] It was also during that trip that Rice signed, in Brazil's capital Brasília, the US-Brazil Joint Action Plan to Eliminate Racial Discrimination (JAPER), a bilateral governmental agreement aimed at combating racism and addressing racial disparities in the realms of health, education, environmental justice, and economic opportunities. Tourism, however, was not included in the agreement as a potential area of action.

While recognizing that black ethnic tourism already existed, SETUR simultaneously and paradoxically represented it as a *new market, a new tourism segment* that was supposed to be part of the so-called third stage of Bahia's tourism development. The cataloging of Bahia's tourism in three historical stages was developed under the auspices of Domingos Leonelli, the state of Bahia's secretary of tourism from 2007 to 2013. According to this classification, the first stage, which lasted from the 1930s to the 1970s, was characterized by the construction of an *identidade turístico-cultural* that was consolidated mostly in the 1960s with the founding of Bahiatursa, the state of Bahia's tourism board. This "touristic-cultural identity" refers to the strengthening of the discourse of *baianidade*, which scholars have criticized as a dominant narrative that is grounded on the dissemination of domesticated and stereotypical representations of blackness, and which celebrates a supposedly harmonious racial coexistence that seeks to shut down dissent.[10] As discussed later in the chapter, it is quite striking that a left-leaning government, which sought to embrace and foster African American roots tourism in Bahia, has remained largely acritical of the hegemonic discourse of *baianidade*.

The second stage, according to Leonelli's classification, happened from the 1970s to 2006 with the implementation of tourism infrastructure, especially in terms of communication, transportation, and hotels. The controversial restoration of Pelourinho is part of this second stage.[11] The year 2006 is represented in this chronology as a game-changing moment because it was during that year that the Secretaria de Cultura e Turismo (Secretariat of Culture and Tourism) was split into two Secretariats, one dedicated to Culture (SECULT), and the other devoted to tourism (SETUR).[12] The creation of a stand-alone SETUR then inaugurates the third and current stage, which is represented as being marked by quality, innovation, economic integration, and sustainability. Thus, the creation of new *roteiros* (which can be translated as both *routes* and *segments*) is a crucial part of this third stage, where "tourism should be understood as a state policy and not only as a policy of [specific] governments."[13] Afro ethnic tourism was thus conceived of alongside other new segments that SETUR was then developing, including nautical (or maritime) tourism, rural tourism, and LGBT tourism.

By inserting "ethnic tourism" in this chronology of the development of tourism in Bahia, SETUR characterizes this tourism market as the result of its own plan to attract African American tourists, thus significantly downplaying the fact that this kind of tourism had already emerged and developed due to the initiative and effort of African Americans themselves, and that it was the state that was finally awakening to roots tourism. Accounts of how the CAHT was conceived varied widely in the interviews I carried out with staff members of SETUR, tour guides, and black activists. Several individuals nominated themselves as having been "the one" who had come up with the idea of creating the CAHT and suggesting it to the secretary of tourism. As a longtime Bahiatursa employee sarcastically observed when I mentioned these diverging narratives with him: "Now everybody wants to be the father of the child." Although it is impossible to pinpoint who had greater influence over whom, it is reasonable to speculate that the creation of the CAHT was not the result of one single person's idea, but rather of the intersection of several factors that were taking place locally, nationally, and internationally.

The black activists and tour guides who claim to have persuaded the white secretary of tourism to establish some form of state initiative to support roots tourism explained that their relationship with him stemmed from their mutual participation in political activism circles. Domingos Leonelli is in fact a longtime leftwing activist and established politician. And black political activism in Brazil has developed predominantly within the realm of, or at least in a dialogue with, left-wing political parties. Thus, it is not surprising that conversations about the need for the state to devote greater attention to African American tourism would have emerged from the interface of the black and leftist political militancies.

If, at the local level, the overlap between black and left-wing activisms and the election in 2007 of the Workers' Party candidate, Jacques Wagner, to the government of Bahia created the conditions for the establishment of the CAHT, initiatives that were happening at the national and international levels further bolstered this process. It was during that same year that MTUR adopted the concept of "ethnic tourism" of the United Nations World Tourism Organization (UNWTO), which stimulated the segmentation of the Brazilian tourism market by providing the states with guidelines to create new itineraries focusing on the heritage of indigenous groups and *quilombolas* (communities formed of descendants of runaway slaves). Bahia was then the first state to establish a program revolving around these guidelines: the aforementioned PATEAB in 2007, under the auspices of SETUR.

Implementing the UNWTO guidelines, MTUR defined ethnic tourism under the broader umbrella concept of "cultural tourism," and alongside the rubrics of "religious tourism," "mystic and esoteric tourism," and "civic tourism." Thus, for MTUR,

Ethnic tourism is composed of touristic activities where one experiences an authentic engagement with the modes of life and the identities of ethnic groups. The purpose is to establish a close contact with the host community, to participate in its traditional activities, to observe and learn about their cultural expressions, lifestyles, and unique customs. Very often, these activities can be articulated as a search for the tourist's own origins, through a return to the traditions of one's ancestors. Ethnic tourism involves the communities that represent the European and Asian immigration processes, the indigenous communities, and the maroon communities, and other social groups that have preserved their ethnic legacies as values that orient their ways of life, knowledges, and doings.[14]

It is quite striking that MTUR's definition does not reiterate the conventional notion that ethnic tourism is motivated exclusively by the search for the "other." It highlights that ethnic tourism can also take the form of roots tourism where the search for one's cultural origins features as the motivation for travel. It also indicates, as potential ethnic tourism attractions, several of Brazil's immigrant communities, thus not restricting this tourism segment to the country's black and indigenous populations. At the same time, however, MTUR's definition confirms the idea that ethnic tourism revolves around the "preservation" of culture and tradition. Although SETUR played a much more direct role in promoting black ethnic tourism in Bahia than MTUR, this definition is certainly an element of convergence between both governmental agencies.

The state of Bahia's self-portrayal of its role in developing African American tourism in Bahia allows us to analyze how the state's position, subsequent to the founding of the CAHT, compares to its position in the previous decades since the late 1970s, when African American roots tourism to Brazil began. In order to reflect on this transformation, I examined the stated objectives of the Coordination, both to analyze their content and to assess to what degree they have been achieved. I also consider the resonance, or lack thereof, among African American tourists and tourism agents based in Brazil and the United States, of the CAHT's effort to achieve these objectives. According to information spread across several official documents, the CAHT's main objectives were: a) To disseminate the concept of African ethnic tourism; b) To research and collect data that could contribute to improve this segment; c) To train tourism workers; and d) To promote the inclusion of the Afro-Brazilian community in ethnic tourism so that Afro-Brazilians could benefit directly from it.[15]

The CAHT's objective of disseminating the concept of African ethnic tourism rested on two premises, which were repeatedly mentioned by politicians and tourism officials. The first premise is the state's promotion of the idea that African Americans can indeed find their cultural origins or roots in Bahia. The second premise is the challenge of developing a segmented tourism niche that revolves around Afro-Bahian culture in a context where tourism *overall* has revolved around Afro-Bahian culture. This last point was made evident in the very words of the secretary of tourism: "Here [in Bahia], all tourism is ethnic, our culture has African elements in all its manifested forms."[16]

One of SETUR's strategies to disseminate African ethnic tourism was the production of a calendar of African heritage events, called Dia-a-Dia da Negra Bahia, or "Day-to-Day in Black Bahia." Although this calendar was meant to "serve as a guide for those visiting Bahia who wish to consult a comprehensive daily schedule with useful information throughout the year,"[17] none of the members or leaders of the tour groups that I interviewed mentioned relying on this calendar to organize their itineraries. Most of them, in fact, did not even know about or had ever seen this brochure, thus pointing to its very limited effectiveness.

Another strategy used to promote the concept of African ethnic tourism was the participation of the office's coordinator in tourism-related events and promotional advertising campaigns in the United States. However, the overwhelming majority of these events were not geared specifically for African American tourism, such as the New York Times Travel Show, in New York City, which I attended in 2012 and 2013. On both occasions, Bahiatursa shared a booth with Embratur, and the head of CAHT was present, distributing brochures and talking to visitors. Despite the prominence of Afro-Brazilian culture in the promotional material, which included a live performance of New York-based capoeira players and samba dancers, there was no specific promotion of ethnic tourism as such. During the several hours that I spent at the event in both occasions, I did not witness any African American tour agent approach the booth.

It is important to recognize that the CAHT did also send its representative to promote Bahia as an ethnic tourism destination in events that are in fact mostly frequented by African Americans, such as the Festival of African Music and Heritage in New Orleans, and the National Black Arts Festival in Atlanta.[18] However, I never came across a tourist or tour agent who had attended any of these events. I do not mean to suggest that this type of promotion has necessarily been ineffective. I contend, instead, that more research, perhaps of a quantitative kind, would more accurately gage the success of this initiative. The CAHT itself has not carried out any kind of assessment of its activities to measure the effectiveness of its promotion of ethnic tourism.

Another major initiative that the state represented as having been intended to attract African American tourists was the establishment of a direct flight between Miami and Salvador in late 2009, with American Airlines. Even though this was the only direct flight between Salvador and a U.S. city, none of the tour groups that I interacted with had taken advantage of this flight, preferring instead to travel via Rio de Janeiro's Galeão airport or São Paulo's airport of Guarulhos, which are Brazil's major international hubs. As a frequent passenger on the Miami-Salvador flight for many years, including in the month of August, which is the peak period for African American roots tourism in Bahia, I never came across any group of African American tourists on board. Again, although my personal experience obviously cannot measure the success of this flight in attracting roots tourists, the state government does not collect this kind of data, and it is therefore not able to assess the effectiveness of this flight, even though it has portrayed the flight as one of the state's greatest achievements in the promotion of African American tourism.

In fact, the research and data collection on African American tourism in Bahia was possibly the least realized of the CAHT's objectives since very little was accomplished on this front. One of the "methods" of the CAHT's coordinator to estimate the number of African American tourists that were visiting Bahia each August was to make phone calls to the tour guides that he knew, asking them how many people were participating in the groups that they were guiding. On two different occasions, I witnessed guides responding to this phone call with a mix of annoyance and frustration. In one instance, upon ending the call, the tour guide complained that the work of CAHT was ineffective and that SETUR, as a state institution, should be able to keep track of how many African American tourists visited Bahia annually, without needing to resort to this *trabalhinho de formiga*, or the constricted, small-scale work of an ant.

Furthermore, not only did SETUR not efficiently collect the data or carry out the research it committed itself to do, but, perhaps even more awkwardly, it conflated the existing data on *American tourists overall* with *African American tourists specifically* to argue that the Program of Action of Afro Ethnic Tourism was yielding positive results. Overall, there seems to have been a disjunction between the insufficient realization of the CAHT's objectives and the official depiction of its work. In a section called "Ethnic Tourism Charms the U.S.," which is part of a document titled "Bahia Life: State of Bahia Guide Golden Book," SETUR states:

The investments made since the launching of the program [of Action of Afro Ethnic Tourism] are beginning to bear fruit. In 2008, Bahia was literally invaded by the Americans, who jumped from tenth place in the ranking of foreigners who come to the state to fifth place, ahead of Argentina. According to EMBRATUR, 15,085 people living in the United States arrived in Salvador in 2008. The number is 333% higher than in the previous year, when just over 3 thousand people from the United States came to Salvador. Between 2003 and 2007, the average was even lower with a flow of 2,600 visitors.[19]

Another problematic conflation of SETUR's description of its achievements can be found in its stated goal of qualifying tourism workers for the heritage/ethnic tourism sector. Although the official documents and press releases describe this goal as if tourism workers would be trained to meet the specific needs of roots tourism, in reality, what I witnessed when I attended one of the editions of the "Seminários do Turismo Étnico Afro" (forums of ethnic tourism), and based on the interviews I conducted, there is no content specific to heritage or culture, black or otherwise, in these training programs. They are predominantly grounded on the usual norms of the hospitality industry, which trains individuals to work as waiters, cooks, housekeepers, and to learn the basic rules of hygiene, courtesy, and good manners. This was also made evident in the registration form meant to be filled out by the participants of the "Seminário Regional do Turismo Étnico Afro" that I attended in São Francisco do Conde in 2011. A section in the form asked attendants to check the box next to the course they would like to attend. The options were: "entrepreneur; cook; waiter; receptionist; housekeeper; other (specify)."

When I asked the head of the CAHT why there was no content specific to heritage tourism in the training of the tourism workers, he responded, defensively, that tourism workers should be instructed to warmly welcome the tourists, independently of whether the tourists were black or white: "When you prepare a destination, you prepare it on a general basis. The difference in this case is that we are training workers in an area, the Recôncavo, where African heritage prevails, you see? But when you train the workers, it is a professional training, so when these tourism professionals (whether it is a waiter, a receptionist, etc.) learn about the kinds of care that a tourist needs, it doesn't matter if the tourist is African American or not."[20] Consistent with the coordinator's statement, the small town of São Francisco do Conde, where I attended the tourism workers training event, although located in the Recôncavo region, is not frequented by African American tourists. More troubling, however, is that there is virtually no international tourism there to begin with, which raises the question of how and where these workers would be inserted in the tourism market subsequent to their training.

Interestingly, the goal of preparing tourism workers for the heritage/ethnic tourism sector has also been associated with the more noble objective of integrating the Afro-Brazilian community in roots tourism so that a greater number of Afro-Brazilians can benefit directly from it. In one of the several documents where it discusses heritage/ethnic tourism, SETUR states, "It is relevant to develop qualifying projects so as to insert the Afro-Brazilian community in the tourism labor market, generating the increase of employability and income of the population, in addition to stimulating entrepreneurship among the members of this community."[21] It is important to recognize that, for the first time in its history, the state government of Bahia acknowledged the need to make tourism beneficial for those whose image and cultural production sustain the tourism industry. Even more significant is that SETUR went as far as affirming that tourism should be directed at "repairing racial injustice." On the first page of the book *African Heritage Tourism in Bahia*, the governor of Bahia stated that tourism, especially a type of tourism that is centered on African heritage, should be promoted as an "instrument of reparations" for black people: "Although we still have a long way to go, the investments made in developing African Heritage Tourism reinforce political and economic commitments to communities of African descent, which have historically been excluded from the economic benefits generated by tourism, and to which they have contributed so greatly."[22]

A few pages later, however, as the book sketches a "profile" of the African American tourists, the reader starts to wonder if the economic integration of Afro-Brazilians in ethnic tourism is *a goal of the state* or an *attempt to meet the wishes of the tourists*. It lists some of the key characteristics of African American tourists, such as their main ports of entry (São Paulo, Rio de Janeiro), the duration of their stay in Bahia (average of four to ten days), and the amount they spend in Brazil (average US$1,100). The book also emphasizes the preoccupation of African American tourists with the well-being of the local black population, and their desire that their tourism dollars be used to generate greater racial equality: "Besides the subjective and identity-based links that African American tourists wish to establish, there is concern with regard to the distribution of tourism-generated income. It has been established that tourists of African descent are concerned about the participation of the Afro-Bahian community in the management of tourism-related profits."[23] The book then explains that one of the CAHT's aims was to meet the specific needs of this market. Therefore, if the black tourists coming from the United States wish to see their dollars being used to promote the advancement of Afro-Brazilians, then the CAHT should work to promote the economic integration of Afro-descendants through training them for employment in the tourism sector.

Governmental Promotion of Diaspora Tourism around the World and How the State of Bahia Compares

According to SETUR, the Program of Action of Afro Ethnic Tourism implemented in Bahia was so successful that it would serve as a model for similar initiatives across Brazil.[24] In fact, at least one Brazilian city did send representatives to Bahia in order to learn about the program. In March 2011, representatives from the Special Coordination for the Promotion of Racial Equality,[25] an office of the municipal government of Campinas, in the state of São Paulo, visited with the head of CAHT to learn about the experience so that it could also be implemented there.[26] Bragging about its pioneering role, SETUR contended that the federal government had very little participation in the governance of heritage tourism, and that it was the state of Bahia that was at the forefront of the implementation of actions to promote this type of tourism.[27]

Granted, in most countries where diaspora tourism has been promoted—including Ghana, Benin, Ireland, Scotland, Wales, China, Lebanon, Syria, and Israel—it has usually been managed by their national governments, and with little participation of local administrations, such as those of the cities, provinces, and states, as it occurs in Bahia. At the same time, despite the recent shift in the state of Bahia's position and its more proactive role in promoting diaspora tourism, SETUR's overall participation is very limited when viewed within the larger context of roots tourism in Bahia, which continues to develop largely as the result of tourist demand and under the auspices of the private sector. Furthermore, when compared to other countries' government-led initiatives of promotion of diaspora tourism, the work of Bahia's CAHT also fares rather poorly. Viewed within this bigger picture, the state of Bahia's awakening to roots tourism could perhaps be described as too little, too late.

Diaspora tourism only became a matter of state interest in Bahia in 2007, whereas other governments around the world have been promoting variations of it since as early as the 1990s. Ghana's fifteen-year National Tourism Development Plan (1996–2010), for example, was established on the basis of the recognition of diaspora tourism as a niche market waiting to be explored. Ghana's government had identified the UN's Slave Route Project's potential

to attract a greater number of African American heritage tourists, thus decid-
ing to invest in this sector: "the number of African-Americans returning to
West Africa and Ghana in particular to explore their cultural roots is increasing. Their demand for facilities and assistance in exploring their heritage must
be a major factor in the product development such as the slave route project."[28]
In fact, no other African government has been as actively involved in promoting diaspora tourism as Ghana's. The importance of cultivating Ghana's connections with its diaspora for the country's tourism development was further
made evident in 2005, when the Ministry of Tourism was renamed Ministry
of Tourism and Diasporan Relations.[29]

In 1999, albeit in a much smaller scale, the Scottish Tourist Board also began to target members of its diaspora as potential tourists. The Scottish par-
liament identified the roots tourism of diaspora Scots, carried out mostly via
genealogy and family history travel, as a key niche market to be pursued.[30] Just
a year before, in 1998, Wales had begun targeting its own diaspora through the
promotion of specific tourism initiatives. Because many members of both of
these nations' respective diasporas have distant relatives who live in these
"homelands," the promotion of VFR (visiting friends and relatives) tourism
has figured as a central strategy to attract them. Among the initiatives deployed
by both Wales and Scotland to attract diaspora tourists was the publication and
dissemination of promotional material among potential tourists, aiming to
entice their feelings of identification with these respective lands and their
peoples.

It was also in the 1990s that the governments of Lebanon and Syria began
promoting roots tourism initiatives with the goal of attracting their respective
diasporas. The Syrian state cosponsored excursions, labeled "Roots Encounter," from the early 1990s through the mid-2000s, to bring together Syrian-
descendant youth and adults living in the Americas. Among these were many
Brazilians, who also made up the largest delegation attending the tours organized by the Lebanese state. In addition to seeking to improve the image of
their countries around the world, these state-led tourism initiatives sought to
foster a sense of national attachment and political allegiance among members
of their diasporas. A major way of doing so was through promoting excursions
to sites that are visibly marked by Israeli aggression.[31]

Yet the tactical and political use of diaspora tourism by the Syrian and Lebanese states pales in comparison to the scale and intensity of Israel's deployment of tourism to politically mobilize its own diaspora. As Cohen explains
in his analysis of the "Exodus Program," the state of Israel is actively engaged in
promoting tourism among its diaspora with the major goal of stimulating

identification with Judaism and strengthening the ties of diaspora Jews with Israel.[32] Research on state-led or state-supported initiatives such as the famous "Birthright Israel" has shown that, as a result of participating in these programs, individuals deeply strengthen their loyalty to Israel and feel more confident about explaining Israel's position in the Middle East. Since its creation in 1999, approximately 350,000 Jewish young adults from all over the world, with the majority from the United States, have participated in "Birthright Israel," which offers a ten-day, entirely paid for trip to Israel with the goal of nurturing Jewish identity and fostering political solidarity with Israel.[33]

Another feature that unites different forms of diaspora tourism, but which is also heightened in the Israeli context, is that, despite governmental efforts to attract diaspora members in order to strengthen their ties to their respective "homelands," the "homecoming" is essentially symbolic and hardly ever translates into tourists becoming "natives" or moving to these countries. This is especially paradoxical in the case of Jewish diaspora tourism to Israel because, although the creation of the modern state of Israel, in theory, should mean the eventual end of the Jewish diaspora, the majority of Jews living in Western countries do not relocate there. Guaranteeing powerful allies abroad then supersedes the need for their relocation.

Despite their specificities and political consequences for each country, governments around the world have employed diaspora tourism to bolster connections between their nation-states and members of their diasporas, especially those that are considered to be geopolitically favored. Diaspora members abroad have been conceived of as assets that can be deployed to lobby on behalf of the nation-state, to make investments in the country's development, and as sources of income generation. The Indian government, for example, has actively engaged with the Indian diaspora since the late 1990s, when the diaspora began to be seen as a "hidden asset."[34] Although India's relationship with its diaspora is ambivalent, for reasons that include the complexity of religious, regional, and language division among Indians in the diaspora and their reluctance to engage in tourism activities promoted by the state when most of their travels to India has been based on family networks, the Indian government has established tourism policies to attract its diaspora.[35] Among these policies is the promotion of an annual, international festival called "Family of India Day" to help overcome negative perceptions that diaspora members have of India so as to potentially attract their economic investment in the country's development.

In the context of the African continent, again the Ghanaian government not only has been the most proactive but it was also the pioneer in strengthening links with members of its diaspora. As early as the 1950s then president Kwame Nkrumah invited several African Americans, especially professionals in the fields of health and education, to move to Ghana to help develop the country. Nkrumah believed that, because African Americans had had access to privileged educational opportunities, they should be committed to developing African countries. Although Ghana did not witness a "back-to-Africa" movement similar to what happened in Liberia and Sierra Leone, it received the greatest number of African American expatriates of any African nation.[36] Other West African countries, such as Benin and Senegal, have also promoted roots tourism geared specifically at attracting African American tourists and, potentially, their investments in these nation-states' economy.

Conversely, neither the Bahian nor the Brazilian state conceive of African American roots tourists as "hidden assets" who are somehow obliged to support their diasporic counterparts. In part this can be explained by the fact that African American roots tourism in Brazil reflects a lateral diasporic connection, that is, a relationship that occurs between communities that are located beyond the diaspora's "center," which in the case of the African diaspora has been conventionally and symbolically conceived of as the African continent. African Americans do not descend from Afro-Brazilians, so the problematic notion that they are the "lucky" offspring of enslaved Africans, born in the privileged United States, does not apply to their connection to Afro-Brazilians, and even less so to Brazil as a country.[37] However, the CAHT's unawareness of the various African American efforts at establishing solidarity projects with Afro-Brazilians not only confirms the state's overall ignorance of a segment they purported to stimulate and support, but it is also revealing of how official Brazilian authorities, in the tourism segment or otherwise, do not easily recognize the power of black people even when they are endowed with the status of geopolitically favored nationalities.

Among the major strategies that governments around the world have used to promote diaspora tourism are the publication and distribution of tourism promotional material geared specifically for diaspora tourists and the support for events such as cultural and religious festivals that often attract these tourists. Again, the Ghanaian government has been at the forefront in both of these types of initiatives, as their promotion of the annual celebration of Emancipation Day and their production of glossy brochures and pamphlets exemplify. The production and dissemination of specific tourism promotional material to attract potential diaspora tourists has been an initiative of other governments as well. In 2000, for example, the Wales Tourist Board mailed copies of a letter, accompanied by a video, to Welsh diaspora descendants living in the United States inviting them to visit Wales.[38] Similarly, in the early 2000s, the German National Tourist Board produced and mailed a guidebook titled "Germany for the Jewish Traveller" to 3,600 New York-based rabbis with the intent of attracting Jewish-American and Jewish-German-American tourists.[39]

The state of Bahia's CAHT has also invested in these two strategies, that is, the production and dissemination of tourism promotional material and support for festivals, although in a much smaller scale if compared to the examples described above. The state's support of the Festival of the Good Death in Cachoeira has undeniably improved over the years, and especially since the campaign led by Jorge Amado and other intellectuals and artists, analyzed in chapter 3, and which predated the creation of the CAHT. Nonetheless, the Sisterhood itself as well as other black cultural organizations have noted that this support is still insufficient both in that it does not cover all the expenses of the festival and because it does not promote the event more widely. The unsatisfactory investment in Cachoeira's tourism infrastructure, more broadly, is evident in the insufficient number of hotels and in the noticeably deteriorated state of many of the town's historical buildings. These structural problems have contributed to restricting African American tourism to Cachoeira predominantly to a one-day visit, when, given the almost week-long Festival of the Good Death, the town could benefit from a much longer stay of these tourists, who are evidently eager to engage a lot more with Cachoeira's history and culture, and especially so with the Sisterhood.

As for the investment in promotional material, the CAHT produced two major publications and a few brochures geared specifically toward African American roots tourists, practically creating them from scratch. These publications are discussed in more detail below. The same level of innovation, however, has not applied to the routes and itineraries purportedly created for this tourism segment. To be fair, the CAHT did not have much say in the development of the itineraries offered to African American visitors as these had already been consolidated throughout the last three and a half decades, and are therefore previous to the creation of the CAHT. The tourism agencies that cater to this segment, relying heavily on the expertise of a handful of tour guides, have been the major producers of the itineraries of the African American roots tourists, and they are, in reality, not so different from the conventional itineraries of white North American and European tourists. Black and white tourists alike visit predominantly the same places and engage with the same attractions, which in the case of Salvador includes the historic sites of Pelourinho, Praça da Sé, Mercado Modelo, and Elevador Lacerda, and the beaches along the northern coast, with Praia do Forte featuring as the most visited. The different experiences result above all from how the roots tourists' gaze imbues the places, events, and cultural expressions with meanings that highlight Bahia's Africanness.

The relabeling of existing tourism products to cater to diaspora tourists is not exclusive to Bahia, though, and it has been identified in other regions of the world. In Germany, there has been a process that some have referred to as a "careless repackaging" for Jewish tourists of already existing tourism attractions: "Though the temptation may be to capitalize on economies of scale and scope by adapting existing formulae to address such niches, tourism producers must avoid repackaging extant products, events and experiences with a diaspora façade. Otherwise, they risk just adding to the increasing congestion in heritage and cultural tourism markets."[40] In my view, another detrimental impact of this repackaging might be the dissonance between the diaspora tourist's search for sameness and their treatment as "ordinary" tourists. As discussed in previous chapters, African American roots tourists—and this can be applied to diaspora tourists more broadly—are often disappointed when they are not recognized as members, albeit honorary, of the communities with which they seek to (re)connect.

Overall, there are many blind spots in the CAHT's work. Although in its official documents and press releases, the CAHT has highlighted its connection to the major social actors involved in roots tourism, this information was constantly contradicted by these very actors. In its major publication, the CAHT stated that in order to achieve its objectives, it had "carried out a series of meetings, debates and seminars with communities of African descent, entities representative of Bahia's African cultural legacy, as well as with intellectuals, anthropologists and ethnologists, researchers and scholars of what has come to be known as African ancestrality."[41] Refuting this claim, however, virtually everyone that I interviewed, including U.S.- and Bahia-based tourism agents, tour guides, and cultural producers, expressed frustration with the CAHT, and most of them stated that either they had not been invited to attend meetings or that their input was not valued.

In addition to the wide-ranging disapproval of the coordinator's performance, the question surrounding the official status of the CAHT also challenged this office's legitimacy and, as a result, its overall success. There was no decree or resolution to officially institute the creation of the CAHT, and this office was never formally listed in SETUR's or Bahiatursa's organograms. As a consequence, the informal nature of the CAHT allowed for significant changes to be made to the coordinator's role. In 2012, instead of focusing specifically on the African American segment, he was put in charge of the entire U.S.

tourism market. When I questioned the reasons for this shift, several SETUR employees responded that this was due to a lack of commitment of those positioned higher up in the chain of command. A recurrent complaint that I heard was that many positions in state offices were occupied by friends or relatives of politicians, and not by qualified individuals. This shift in the coordinator's role coincided with the moment in which Leonelli was getting ready to leave SETUR, which happened the following year.

Furthermore, the stated objectives of the CAHT were either not fully comprehended or perhaps not quite accepted among other important members of Bahiatursa and SETUR. An interview with Bahiatursa's director of international relations, for example, contradicted several of the CAHT's claims regarding its purposes and goals. She explained, for example, that the American Airlines direct flight (Miami-Salvador), was meant to attract a larger number of Americans in general, and not specifically African American tourists. She also stated, to my great surprise, that the CAHT's overall work was not meant to be restricted to promoting Bahia solely among African Americans as that would establish a "form of discrimination."[42] I interpret her comments, however, less as an indication of the CAHT's flaws than as an expression of her own positionality, as a white, middle-class Brazilian who has worked in the state's tourism promotional sector for many years and who seems to be entrenched in a conventional way of doing the tourism promotion of Bahia, one that is grounded on a discourse of *baianidade*, as is revealed also in other excerpts of her interview, quoted later in the chapter.

In a rare and small-scale academic analysis of the PATEAB, tourism researchers Carvalho and Avila noted that, five years after the program's launch, no quantitative research on the profile of ethnic tourists had been carried out. In tandem with my own observations, the authors argue that, instead of promoting ethnic tourism specifically in U.S. cities that have larger black populations, the CAHT piggybacks on the already established international tourism promotion initiatives of Bahiatursa, thus restricting its activities mostly to Miami and Washington, D.C.[43] I also heard this critique from a Bahiatursa member, when I was invited to present my research to a group of SETUR and Bahiatursa employees in August 2013. One of them, who also works as a history teacher and who seemed skeptical about the CAHT's work, had asked me to share my research findings with some of his colleagues, so that they could, in his own words, "improve their knowledge about the African American tourists." Approximately twelve people showed up, and they all listened attentively to my presentation and engaged enthusiastically in the Q&A session that followed. Some of them observed that the CAHT did not seem aware of the information I was relaying, even in regards to the more basic knowledge about the African American visitors, such as their dominant age group and that the majority are female. They blamed this unawareness on the fact that the CAHT had never bothered to carry out an assessment of their promotional work among African Americans, therefore there was no way to know whether any of the goals had actually been achieved. It is important to highlight that the head of the CAHT did not attend my presentation and, although he was aware of my research, he never expressed any interest in getting to know more about it, even though I had emphasized several times that I was willing to contribute, pro bono of course, to the CAHT's work.

Expressing frustration, one of the Bahiatursa employees vented: "The Coordination has, all along, been carrying out a very misguided promotion. The market in the United States is very segmented. Society there is very segmented! There are [specific] black groups there for everything, so the Coordination should be targeting these black groups." This same person also criticized the promotional material that the CAHT distributed to African American tourists, which, he stated, "always portrays the tourists as whites, and where blacks appear as waiters, baianas, capoeristas, or simply opening a coconut for the tourist on the beach."[44]

The critique of the lack of specificity of the promotional work of the CAHT is, in my view, well founded. The deployment of the images of Bahia that continuously reiterate the discourse of *baianidade* is, undeniably, yet another way in which the CAHT's work overlaps with the generic work of Bahiatursa. This is noticeable even in the publications that have been produced to target specifically the African American tourism niche, including the brochures, the book *African Heritage Tourism in Bahia*, and several articles included in editions of the magazine *Viver Bahia*. In order to scrutinize how a supposedly left-wing government has represented blackness and *baianidade* in this new context, following the CAHT creation, I examined if and how the three dominant tropes that sustain the African American roots tourist gaze feature in these representations.

Blackness Represented Anew?

One of the most tangible results of the CAHT's creation was a hardcover, 152-pages-long book, published in 2010, simultaneously in two editions: one in Portuguese, titled *Turismo Étnico Afro na Bahia*, and the other as its English-language translation, titled *African Heritage Tourism in Bahia*. The reason why the book's title in English is not the literal translation of the Portuguese title

("Afro Ethnic Tourism in Bahia") is due to the fact that a U.S. interpreter had been hired to do all the translations for the CAHT, and she determined that "African Heritage Tourism" would more fittingly capture the kind of tourism that it was trying to develop. I had been intrigued as to why the name of the CAHT itself referred to "ethnic tourism" in Portuguese while its official label in English referred to "heritage tourism." Besides, in the former, the adjective employed to characterize the kind of tourism being proposed was "Afro" while in the latter it was "African." Certainly, in English, the term "heritage tourism" better represents diaspora tourism, while "ethnic tourism" continues to be associated with the search for otherness. But the question remains as to why the term *turismo étnico* dominates this industry in Brazil. In any case, although one might think that there would have been a thorough discussion in order to select the CAHT's name in both languages, ultimately this was the decision of a temporary external consultant.

According to the CAHT's coordinator, the main purpose of the book *African Heritage Tourism in Bahia* was to function as a "conceptual framework" (*marco conceitual*), a kind of handbook for the expansion of African Heritage tourism in Bahia. Tourism professionals, both in Brazil and in the United States, make up its intended audience. At a first glance, the book's abundant and colorful photographs and a good amount of its textual content seem to refer, in some way or another, to the major tropes that sustain the African American tourist gaze on Brazil: Bahia as a closer Africa, the happy native, and black evolution. The book acknowledges, for example, the important role played by African American movements and leaders in inspiring Afro-Brazilian mobilization, especially in the 1970s. Nonetheless, in contrast to the trope of black evolution that is present in the roots tourism discourse, the book not only recognizes that there are differences between these two groups but it also establishes that they have distinct goals and aspirations within the context of their respective nations:

> Contrary to the direction of the racial movement in the United States, where people of African descent strove to be recognized as Americans, the movement that arose in Bahia took on a new feature, based on the reaffirmation of ancestrality. An emphasis was placed on the strength of traditions brought from Africa by forefathers, which in Brazil was maintained with great difficulty, undercover, and often times veiled from public sight. In Brazil, Black Awareness social movements aspired to promote Afro-Brazilian pride and dignity by redeeming ancestral history, defending fundamental rights and exacting reparations for injustices suffered since the time of

slavery. Broader than a political and cultural movement, the organized struggles always maintained a social component and a common focal point: providing opportunities for the new generations.[45]

Challenging the idea that Africanness is a previous, and thus lower, stage in the path toward blackness, the text explains that it is *by means of their Africanness* that Afro-Brazilians have and will continue to be the agents of their history. Furthermore, Bahia's abundant African heritage is represented as the result of a long and difficult process of resistance, and not because the circumstances made it "easy" for Afro-Brazilians to preserve their African culture. Diverging from the notion that in Brazil the ubiquity of cultural roots coexists with a lack of political mobilization, the book poses that Afro-Brazilian political mobilization has been grounded on and inspired by its cultural heritage. Although in the book's portrayal Afro-Brazilians are inviting African Americans to come to Brazil in ever-greater numbers, they are not proposing to trade in their tradition/Africanness for the modernity/blackness of their rich cousins from the North. At the same time, however, the book does confirm the trope of Bahia as a closer Africa. The overwhelming emphasis on the African heritage of Afro-Brazilians—and its detailed description of the different African ethnicities brought to Brazil as well as the African traditions that have been preserved in the realms of religion, cuisine, language, music, dance—confirms the notion that Bahia is the place to find roots.

In fact, the notion that Bahia is the "Africa of the Americas" is reiterated also in the other publications that SETUR has produced to disseminate among African American tourists. This is certainly the case in the many articles published in the magazine *Viver Bahia*, analyzed below, and it is also made evident in a bilingual brochure, titled "Bahia: The Deepest Expression of African Culture in Brazil." It is important to highlight that the Portuguese title of the brochure, which is positioned right above its English title is: "Bahia: A Maior Expressão da Cultura Afro no Brasil." The term *cultura afro* has been translated into English as "African culture" because of the decision of an external consultant hired to do the translation, as explained above. Nonetheless, it contributes to reiterate the trope of Bahia as a closer Africa as it points to a culture that is supposedly African, and therefore preserved, instead of a culture that is Afro-Brazilian and therefore necessarily hybrid because of its multiple historical transformations. But if the title were not enough, the photographs that illustrate the brochure further emphasize Bahia's Africanness (figure 5.1). Of the four photographs on the cover, two are of statues of Orixás, and the other two depict people: a black female percussionist smiling at the camera/gazer;

Bahia

A maior expressão da cultura afro no Brasil.

The deepest expression of African culture in Brazil.

BRASIL
Sensational!

Bahia!
it is much more

Turismo Étnico | African Heritage Tourism

FIGURE 5.1 Cover of the bilingual brochure "Bahia: The Deepest Expression of African Culture in Brazil," produced by the state of Bahia's Secretariat of Tourism as promotional material for the Coordination of African Heritage Tourism.

Faith and festivals mix races and religions in Bahia.

African culture is flourishing in Bahia. The state's African legacy is present in the day-to-day lives of the Bahian people, whether in religion, music, cuisine or art. Brought from all over Africa between the 16th and 19th centuries, Africans arrived to Bahia as slaves, bringing their culture and customs with them. Eighty percent of Salvador's population is of African descent, making it the most African city outside of Africa. Here, African culture has fused with other cultural elements to create a truly Afro-Brazilian identity. In Bahia, visitors can get to know and experience firsthand the state's deep African legacy in its most beautiful manifestations and in the daily lives of its people.

CAPOEIRA *Capoeira*

A capoeira é outra expressão da história e cultura negra na Bahia. Mistura de luta e dança, seus movimentos e cantos cadenciados são a memória viva da busca de um povo pela liberdade. Hoje a capoeira rompe fronteiras e preconceitos, conquistando o mundo com sua identidade afro-baiana.

Capoeira is another expression of African history and culture in Bahia. A mixture of martial art and dance, its movements and cadenced chants are a living memory of a people's struggle for freedom. Today, capoeira has overcome prejudice and moved beyond Brazil's borders to conquer the world with its Afro-Bahian identity.

FESTAS RELIGIOSAS *Religious Festivals*

Na Bahia, ao longo do ano, os orixás são homenageados com música, dança e comidas sagradas. Muitas dessas comemorações se misturam às homenagens e devoção aos santos católicos, num sincretismo religioso que une, por exemplo, Iemanjá à Nossa Senhora da Conceição, Iansã a Santa Bárbara e Senhor do Bonfim a Oxalá. Os terreiros de candomblé possuem calendários próprios, herança da cultura africana, com algumas festas abertas aos visitantes. Em Santo Amaro da Purificação, no mês de maio, a festa do "Bembé do Mercado" celebra o fim da escravidão no Brasil em 1888. É a única cerimônia do candomblé realizada ao ar livre.

Throughout the year in Bahia, the orixás are honored with music, dance and sacred foods. Many of these festivals have become integrated into celebrations in honor of Catholic saints in a mixing of religions known as syncretism. Thus, the sea goddess Yemanjá is associated with Our Lady of Conceição, Iansã, the goddess of storms and winds with Santa Bárbara, and Oxalá, the father of the universe, with Our Lord of Bonfim. Each Candomblé house of worship has its own calendar of events, inherited from the practitioners' African ancestors, with some ceremonies open to visitors. In Santo Amaro da Purificação, during the month of May, the "Bembé do Mercado" festival celebrates the end of slavery in Brazil, which occurred in 1888. It is one of the only Candomblé ceremonies that take place in an open public setting.

FESTA DA BOA MORTE *The Good Death Festival*

Uma das mais importantes comemorações litúrgicas da fé brasileira acontece no mês de agosto, na cidade de Cachoeira, no Recôncavo Baiano. É a Festa da Boa Morte. Senhoras negras, com mais de 50 anos, saem em cortejo pelo centro da cidade, vestidas como verdadeiras rainhas, em devoção à Boa Morte, ou Dormição de Maria, como é chamada a Assunção da Virgem aos Céus. São mães-de-santo que se vincularam à Igreja Católica para continuar cultuando, sem perseguição, seus orixás, divindades do candomblé. Assim, seculares tradições africanas encontraram no sincretismo religioso uma forma de preservar sua história.

One of the most important liturgical celebrations of Brazilian faith takes place in the month of August in the City of Cachoeira, located near All Saints' Bay. During the Boa Morte or Good Death Festival, women of African descent of at least 50 years of age participate in a procession through city streets dressed as true queens, in devotion to the Good Death, or Dormitio Virginis, as the Assumption of the Virgin Mary to heaven is known. Most of these women are Candomblé high priestesses whose ancestors adopted Catholicism as a means to continue worshipping their African deities or orixás, without fear of persecution. Thus, centuries-old African traditions found sanctuary in religious syncretism as a means of preservation.

FIGURE 5.2 Page 3 of the bilingual brochure "Bahia: The Deepest Expression of African Culture in Brazil," produced by the state of Bahia's Secretariat of Tourism as promotional material for the Coordination of African Heritage Tourism.

and a young, white, tourist couple pecking the cheeks of an older, black, Baiana, who is smiling and holding an *acarajé* with her extended hand in an offering gesture, against the background of the colorful Pelourinho architecture. Of the other eight photographs that adorn the brochure, seven depict black people posing as: *baiana de acarajé*; bare-chested male musicians vigorously playing percussive instruments; muscled capoeiristas; an artist painting a portrait of Pelourinho; religious pilgrims attending the Bonfim church festival; and Sisters of the Good Death parading on the streets of Cachoeira. Some of these pictures can be seen in figure 5.2.

When I asked Bahiatursa's director of international relations about the state's longtime deployment of Afro-Bahian cultural elements, such as the image of the *baiana de acarajé*, the icons of Candomblé, and so on, to promote the destination for tourism, she immediately rectified my question by emphasizing that there was no "use" of Afro-Bahian culture since this was a "natural" part of the region's heritage: "Bahia has a very strong African heritage. There was never the *need* to work with these elements. This is something *natural* to Bahia. So, to promote Bahia we *naturally* rely on Bahia's natural elements."[46] Pressing her further, I asked if the new conception of tourism that the state was developing, which sought to direct tourism to promote the economic integration of Afro-Brazilians, had in any way interrogated the deployment of Afro-Brazilian cultural expressions. Once again she reasserted the "natural" character of Bahianness, and its implicit reliance on a joyful and domesticated notion of blackness:

> The icons of our culture are eternal. Governments can come and go, but there are cultural elements—our syncretism, our *musicalidade*, our capoeira, our cuisine—this is what Bahia is, it is this cultural cradle. This is who we are. We are not making this up, this is *natural* here. I never travel abroad [to promote Bahia] without a baiana! They are able to transmit the energy, the smile, the whole *baianidade*. People go crazy with the baianas! With capoeira it's different because capoeira exists all over the world, but the baianas, we really have to bring them with us.[47]

There is, of course, nothing "natural" about Bahianness and its reliance on a very specific understanding of blackness that reduces it to a set of stereotypical representations. This is the result of a historical development that started in the 1930s and gradually defined Bahia as "Brazil's Africa," as I discussed in chapter 2. In the 1970s, in its attempt to promote Bahia as an attractive destination, the state-backed tourism industry invented the notion of a "Bahian way of life" (*viver baiano*), characterized by "affection," "magic," and "infectiousness," all seen as "typically black characteristics."[48] The delightful

"Bahian way of life" was captured in the official slogan of Bahia as rendered by Bahiatursa, the state tourism board: "*Bahia: Terra da Felicidade*" (Bahia: Land of Happiness). An important part of this campaign was the creation of the magazine *Viver Bahia* also in the 1970s. The magazine's title was intended as an invitation for tourists to live the "Bahian way of life."[49]

There are two distinct moments in the magazine's interrupted trajectory. The first was in the 1970s when the tourists targeted by Bahiatursa were predominantly white, middle class, Southeastern Brazilians, for whom the magazine promoted Bahia as a typical sun-sea-and-sex tropical paradise. During this phase, pictures of the Bahian coast, sprinkled with seminaked, bronzed, female bodies were abundant, with Afro-Brazilian culture occupying a secondary albeit important role in promoting the tourism image of Bahia. Analyzing the counterculture movement that flourished in Brazil during that same time, Christopher Dunn shows that some of the staff writers of *Viver Bahia* also wrote for the underground almanac *Verbo Encantado*. This helps explain why both publications represented Bahia as "a magical place of ludic pleasure and mysticism where one could have an encounter with an alternative, non-Western culture."[50]

By the end of that decade, *Viver Bahia* faded away until it was no longer published. The second distinct moment of the magazine started in 2007 when SETUR decided to bring the magazine back to life and in tune with the state government's new tourism initiatives, especially the segment of African Heritage Tourism.[51] No longer promoting Bahia exclusively as a beach-centered tropical paradise, the magazine has since then focused primarily on Afro-Bahian culture. Published in bilingual editions (Portuguese and English), *Viver Bahia* now mainly targets foreign tourists, among them African American roots tourists.[52]

Despite its new focus on Afro-Bahian culture and on the centrality of black people in the definition of Bahia's public image, as well as its concern in catering to African American tourists, *Viver Bahia* continues to reproduce several of the previous tropes that have been promoted by the official discourse of *baianidade* since the 1930s, including the frequent allusion to *mestiçagem* as a sign of racial harmony, and the idea that Bahia is Brazil's Africa. All the editions of the magazine are filled with articles, photographs, and drawings depicting black people and Afro-Brazilian cultural expressions such as religion, cuisine, art, music, dance, and capoeira. Above all, the magazine's dominant narrative is firmly anchored on a narrative of racial democracy, where slavery is either erased or portrayed as having played the benign role of transplanting African culture to Brazil.

The article "Herança Viva da Escravidão" (Live heritage of slavery), published in 2007, is a clear example of this discourse.[53] It describes the Afro-Catholic sisterhoods and brotherhoods as an initiative carried out by slaves in order to continue worshipping their African gods and goddesses, the Orixás, and for the purpose of establishing mutual aid. Although these institutions did end up serving these purposes, they had been originally created by the Catholic Church with the goal of forcefully converting slaves into Catholicism. Religious syncretism was an unintended consequence of the creation of the sisterhoods and brotherhoods and not one of its preestablished goals, as the article implies.

The same argument that slavery allowed for the transplantation of African culture to Brazil can be found in another article published in the same edition of *Viver Bahia*, "O Pai do Prazer, Filho da Dor" (The father of pleasure, the son of pain), which describes samba as a "blessed African heritage originated from the batucajés of terreiros, and the drum beating of the slave quarters and planted fields where the Recôncavo slaves lived and worked, [and that is now] echoed in Brazil and beyond into the world."[54] References to slavery throughout the magazine are immediately followed by descriptions of cultural mixture and racial harmony. An article describing the origin of the city of Salvador, for instance, reads, "It was here, in this magic place, where the sun shines almost for the whole year, that, from 1550 through 1850, the largest ever known contingent of African slaves arrived. . . . The mixture of races, colors, creeds and cultures of three or more continents happened here, and still happens, and created the people unique in their own way of doing things and celebrating life."[55] In addition to sustaining the dominant national discourse of racial harmony and *mestiçagem*, *Viver Bahia* portrays slavery through the narratives of cultural preservation and continuity.

In tandem with the African American tourism discourse that celebrates the element of cultural survival, that I analyzed in chapter 2, Bahia's official tourism discourse also prefers to focus on how the enslaved and their descendants managed to "preserve" their original African culture, *despite* slavery. The cover of the first issue of the new version of the magazine *Viver Bahia* illustrates this well as it portrays a colorful picture of the Sisters of the Good Death, followed by the caption "Sisterhood of the Good Death celebrates life." Inside the magazine, an article describes the Sisters as "black women, descendants of African slaves, who preserve the traditions and the religious and cultural teachings of their ancestors."[56] Despite briefly mentioning the origin of the Sisterhood within the history of slavery, the article emphasizes the organization's victory over slavery. It explains that the first Sisters were originally obliged to convert to Catholicism, but that this generated a rich syncretic practice that allowed for the preservation of Africanisms.

The representation of slavery as a means for cultural transplantation and preservation is also visible in a flyer-cum-postcard that one of the major African American travel agencies produced in 2006. The eight-by-six inch card is illustrated with ten small and strikingly beautiful photographs of the Sisterhood of the Good Death. The text on the back of the card explains that although the Sisterhood "began as a group of freed black women who joined forces in the 1820s to raise funds to purchase the freedom of slaves" they have managed to preserve the culture of their ancestors even after slavery was over: "Though slavery was abolished in 1888, generations of sisters have faithfully carried on the annual religious commemorations, thus keeping alive ancient traditions and elements of the African belief system of their ancestors."[57] This is one of the many examples of the paradoxical convergence of narratives between, on the one hand, the race-conscious African American roots tourist gaze and, on the other hand, the narrative of racial harmony implicit in the state's discourse of Bahianness.

Ironically, although Bahia's Africanness is a central component of its image as a tourism destination, it is more often than not dissociated from the history of slavery, the very reason why an African heritage exists there. Although this paradox is more accentuated in Bahia, it applies to the Brazilian nation as a whole. Proof of which is that, despite having received the largest number of enslaved Africans in the entire world, Brazil has very few slavery-related heritage tourism sites. And the few that do exist are, in fact, the result of very recent enterprise. The Historical Circuit of African Heritage (Circuito Histórico e Arqueológico da Herança Africana), established by the municipal government of Rio de Janeiro in the Valongo Wharf, a slave port and cemetery discovered in 2010 during the city's preparation for the 2016 Olympics, is one of the few examples of the still rare Brazilian initiatives to commemorate slavery in the public sphere.[58]

In Bahia, where there are plenty of potential slavery-related heritage tourism sites, none have been represented or memorialized as such. In fact, the absence of a public recognition of slavery coexists with the very ubiquity of its vestiges. The legacy of slavery is everywhere in Bahia: it can be seen in the colonial architecture, it can be smelled in the *acarajés* fried in palm oil by the *baianas* selling African delicacies in the streets, it can be heard in the drum beat of so many of the Afro-Bahian rhythms, and it can be felt in the daily social interactions among people of different skin tones and classes. Lacking amid this profusion of slave references is precisely the public recognition of Bahia's history of slavery.[59]

The absence of monuments, memorials, and other public markers of slavery in Bahia contrasts dramatically with the overpowering symbols that have been reclaimed and in some cases built from scratch to represent the history of the slave trade in West African countries. As they reveal the engagement of their respective states in either promoting or erasing the history of slavery, the existence and absence of these markers also contribute to position places in the map of Africanness by imbuing them with specific meanings. Expectedly, the dominant meanings of the different places in the map also inform the meanings attributed to the people who inhabit such places. If slavery is silenced and Africanness is amplified, the people who live in Bahia can only be imagined as enjoying the easygoing style of the *Viver Baiano*, the celebratory Bahian way of life, thus confirming the trope of Bahians as "happy natives," as discussed in chapter 2. It has been discouraging to witness how a supposedly left-leaning government, that is explicitly aware of the need to deploy tourism to promote the social and economic integration of Afro-Brazilians, has been at the same time so acritical of the discourse of Bahianness and its reliance on stereotypical representations of blackness, which have, in turn, contributed to the reproduction of racist practices.

Conclusion

One of the ironies of the state's belated acknowledgement and effort to promote roots tourism is that, in the span of less than a century, the Brazilian government went from *barring* to *attracting* African American visitors. As discussed in chapter 1, in the 1920s, Brazilian officials actively banned U.S. blacks from entering the country. And this was not just the result of the *branqueamento* (whitening) policy—whereby white immigrants were preferred so that they would racially mix with and ideally whiten the dark-skinned Brazilian population—but also because the government wanted to keep out "radical ideologies that sought to heighten race consciousness," especially in a context marked by the emergence of black political organizations in Brazil.[60] This resulted in the prohibition of issuing visas to virtually all black foreigners, including those who sought to visit the country for the purpose of leisure: "The Brazilian authorities' exclusion of black immigrants grew into a paranoid fear of black tourists by the mid-1920s."[61] Although the legislation that banned nonwhites was written in geographic terms (banning specifically the entrance of Africans and Asians) and not in strictly racial terms, its interpretation had to be adapted in order to prevent African Americans from coming to Brazil, especially in a context of rising black nationalism in the Americas.[62]

Five decades later, the anxiety surrounding the potential arrival of supposedly radical racial ideologies lingered on, leading the Brazilian Ministry of Foreign Relations to position itself against the 1978 New World Festival of the African Diaspora, which, as discussed in chapter 1, was a foundational event for the development of African American roots tourism in Bahia. The document that Brazil's Ministry of Foreign Relations submitted to the president to convince him to ban the festival was grounded on the rationale that the presence of African American visitors could potentially depict the situation of blacks in Brazil in a "false" manner and, even worse, it could introduce among Brazilian blacks "foreign ideologies" that could politically mobilize them in ways that would represent a danger to the nation. The term "diaspora" was depicted as especially threatening in the document: "This designation [diaspora] indicates that the Festival is inspired by a vision of the black problem that is not in line with the traditions of Brazilian society, nor with the Government's position. In fact, we do not consider applicable for Brazilians of the black race the concept of diaspora, which belongs, in its own sense, to a completely different cultural and religious tradition."[63] The Minister of Foreign Relations depicted the festival as a menace to Brazil's "societal principles of non-discrimination and racial integration" and therefore as not deserving of Itamaraty's support.[64] Furthermore, he recommended that all Brazilian tourism boards, namely Embratur, Bahiatursa, and Riotur, abstained from participating in or supporting this initiative given the possibility that the festival could raise "critiques to the Brazilian racial situation from the point of view of black cultural 'emancipation.'"

Three decades later, and in a seemingly complete reversal, *diaspora* and *black emancipation* have become central concepts in the state's effort to promote African American tourism. All of the CAHT's four major objectives, in one way or another, effectively engaged with these concepts, treating diaspora as a given and black emancipation as an ideal to be achieved. With the exception of the goal of training tourism workers, all the other objectives (that is, to disseminate the notion of heritage tourism; to collect data to support its development; and to promote the emancipation of Afro-Brazilians via African heritage tourism community) were undeniably novel in the context of the state's approach to tourism in Bahia. With the creation of the CAHT, the concept of African heritage tourism and the idea that the state should work to attract African American tourists were promoted for the first time ever. Most important was the recognition that the state must direct the fruits reaped in the tourism industry to promote the economic inclusion of Afro-Brazilians, revealing that the language of black activism has been incorporated into the discourse of the state.

However, as powerful as they are, discourses do not always materialize into action. Not only is the state a latecomer in the game, but also it has not been effective in creating synergy among the already existing stakeholders of African heritage (or roots) tourism in Bahia. One of the major reasons for the state's ineffectiveness is that the CAHT did not seek to identify and build on the work that these stakeholders have been doing for the last three and a half decades. Everyone I interviewed expressed a lack of confidence in the work carried out by the CAHT, which was overall not well received by the tourism agencies, tour leaders, and cultural producers. Furthermore, no actual policies or strategies were created to effectively funnel the tourism dollars from the African American tourism niche to Afro-Brazilian communities.

Most important, despite some important changes in the state's treatment of tourism in Bahia—including the belated acknowledgement of the presence of African American tourists and a greater participation of Afro-Brazilians in positions of power within SETUR and Bahiatursa—the official discourse of *baianidade* remains predominantly unchallenged. Reproducing the same old portrayals of Bahia as a mystic land of happiness, grounded on the harmonious mixture of races and cultures, the state government, even while led by a center-left political party, continues to feed the notion that Bahia is more a joyful state of the soul (*estado de alegria*) than a geographic state that is brutally marked with class asymmetries and racial inequalities. Furthermore, the same state that has, on the one hand, or better yet, *with* one hand, symbolically promoted black emancipation, has used the other hand to maintain its ruthless policing and oppression of the black poor. The police slaughtering of twelve black youth in Salvador's impoverished neighborhood of Cabula in February 2015, that became known as the "Cabula massacre" (Chacina do Cabula), is just one of the recent examples of the state's continued practices of violence against black lives.

A lot has been written about the so-called ambidextrous neoliberal state that uses its benevolent left hand to minimally maintain welfare while using its authoritarian right hand to deregulate its economy, marketize its society and punish its citizens.[65] It is important to not loose light of the fact that, beyond its complementary and strategic purposes, the state's ambidexterity as well as its overall ambiguity is also the result of how "past" representations linger on in the present. In the specific case of Bahia, the old, but regrettably not outmoded, notion of blackness as deviant and in need of containment coexists with the novel recognition that local (yet specific) versions of blackness should be expanded in order to attract its diasporic and geopolitically favored counterpart. This is yet another reason why linear understandings of history are flawed. Linearity implies that old ideas are superseded at each new stage, instead of identifying their power to linger on alongside newly formed representations within complex nodes of meanings. Thus, the metaphor of the sleeping, or the awakening giant, if ridden of its evolutionist underpinnings, can in fact be useful to represent the state's acknowledgement of roots tourism, because the giant may be indeed half-awake and half-asleep. Alternatively, however, the giant may have one eye open and one eye shut because he is sarcastically winking in mischief.

Epilogue

As I write the final pages of this book, Brazil is undergoing one of the worst political crises of its recent history. It is impossible to disregard the explosive condition in which the country finds itself, not only because of its profoundly detrimental consequences for the lives of most Brazilians, but also because of the evolutionist language that has been dominantly employed to account for the shocking turn of events. The political crisis has also affected, although indirectly and at a much smaller scale, African American roots tourism in Brazil as the numerous headlines featuring the Zika epidemics, the series of protests initiated in June 2013, and the overall political turmoil has made the country appear unsafe for tourists.

On January 1, 2010, Brazil had inaugurated Dilma Rousseff as its first female president. Despite facing fierce opposition from the corporate establishment and while confronting a deceitful and misogynist defamation campaign from the nation's major media outlets, Rousseff was reelected for a second term. The likelihood of Rousseff's reelection had been at stake both because of the economic downturn that was then beginning to affect the mood of voters, and because of the enormous protests that had erupted in Brazil's major cities in June 2013. Differently from previous political demonstrations throughout Brazilian history, which had predominantly attracted leftists, the June 2013 protests brought to the streets people from a wide range of ideological positions. The country's systemic and widespread corruption, the funneling of public money to fund the infrastructure of the 2014 World Cup and the 2016 Olympics, coupled with an orchestrated media slander campaign, seemed to have gathered individuals and groups from across the political spectrum. Later on, however, the left-right boundaries became once again clearly defined.

Several reasons account for the plunging of Rousseff's approval rate and the disarray that ensued these protests, but the most instructive explanation for the then mounting political crisis lies, in my view, in the power of representation. It is undeniable that the coalition of the most regressive and rightwing forces won the narrative battle and succeeded in making hegemonic their own version of what was going on in Brazil. Following the decline of the global commodities boom, which had made viable the Latin American "pink tide," the social and economic pact that had been established between President Luís

Inácio "Lula" da Silva's administration and Brazil's wealthiest sectors was no longer tenable. Elected in 2003, Lula was Brazil's first left-leaning president. Riding on the wave of the global commodities super cycle Lula not only was reelected for a second term in office (2007–2010), but he also secured the election and reelection of his Workers' Party candidate, Dilma Rousseff (2011–2014 and 2015–2016).

During the thirteen-year-period of the successive PT administrations, Brazil experienced the most significant social reforms of the country's history. Through a series of cash transfer programs, approximately thirty-six million Brazilians were lifted out of poverty, and Brazil was removed for the first time from the UN Hunger Map. Eighteen new federal universities were created from scratch, and they were strategically dispersed across the country so as to cater to students living in poorer and more peripheral areas. The substantial growth of Brazil's system of higher education was coupled with the expansion of programs of social and racial quotas. Although quotas had already been implemented unsystematically in several Brazilian universities since 2004, they were endorsed and expanded in 2012 when President Dilma Rousseff sanctioned new legislation that reserved 50 percent of all seats in federal universities for black, indigenous, and impoverished students (that is, students who had attended public schools). In 2011, Brazil became the world's sixth largest economy, and the country's Gini coefficient, the most commonly used measure of inequality, improved from 58.6 in 2002 to 52.9 in 2013. The country also achieved its lowest unemployment level (4.8 percent in December 2014), reaching the condition of full employment.

All these remarkable achievements, however, were obtained without major changes being made to the problematic political legacy inherited from the period of the military dictatorship (1964–1985), and therefore the PT governed in a context that continued to be marked by widespread corruption and a culture of impunity. Furthermore, the funding for the social welfare programs were mostly derived from an extractivist economy contingent on raw material exports. This neodevelopmentalist model and its dependence on natural resource extraction is not only devastating for the environment, but it also preserves the unequal relations of geopolitical subordination even if to new world centers, such as China. Internally, the fundamental structures of capitalism have also remained significantly unchallenged as the pro-poor welfare programs did not compromise the wealthiest sectors of Brazilian society, who continue to control not only the country's major economic resources but also the major mass media outlets.

Most important, however, is that the progressive social changes produced a deep discomfort among many middle- and upper-class Brazilians who were not happy to see such a vast number of poor and black people no longer "knowing their place." As the predominantly black members of the ascending social class begun to rub shoulders with the largely light-skinned constituents of the long-established elite in universities, airports, high-end shopping malls and other previously exclusive places, race and class boundaries became a little less rigid, generating a strident backlash. And while this factor alone does not explain the institutional coup that demoted our democratically elected president in 2016, it certainly played an important role in the narratives dispute. Among those who had participated in the June 2013 marches to protest corruption were many of these disgruntled Brazilians. Wrapped in the national flag, wearing the canary-yellow jersey of Brazil's national soccer team, and sometimes accompanied by uniformed black nannies pushing their kids' strollers, these members (or wannabe members) of the Brazilian elites validated the simplistic and misguided narrative that the PT in general, and President Rousseff in particular, were the source of all that was wrong in/with Brazil; a narrative that ultimately materialized into the parliamentary coup d'état.

Although the coup government only started a little over a year ago—if we consider as day one April 17, 2016, when Rousseff's vice-president Michel Temer became interim president—many of the important achievements that Brazil obtained since 2003 are now under serious threat. A congress made up of a very high number of corrupt politicians, almost two thirds of whom are under corruption investigation, has worked quickly to approve a draconian labor reform that will dismantle workers' rights and sanction the precarity of labor and labor relations. A tyrannical pension reform, that significantly increases the minimum retirement age and increases the number of years that workers must pay for social security, is also about to be approved. In addition to that, as of December 2017, Brazil's unemployment rate is over 12 percent, and according to a World Bank forecast, by the end of 2017, 3.6 million Brazilians will be once again living under the poverty line.[1] Permeating this neoliberal process of austerity, privatization, and social cuts is a conservative narrative concerning race, gender, and sexual identities.

It seems impossible not to describe the dismantling of Brazil's welfare state and the overall attack on the accomplishments of the last administrations as a colossal *regression*. The overpowering sense that we are walking *backward*, that we are *receding* toward a *previous* and *less advanced* stage of the country's development has informed the leftist analyses of the recent turn of events.

Unsurprisingly, words like reversion, retreat, decline, degeneration, and regression have abounded in these assessments, which have such titles as: "Temer: In Ten Months, 100 years of retrogression!";[2] "The list of setbacks of Michel Temer's government";[3] and "A government tied to regression." The latter discusses Temer's close ties to fundamentalist neo-Pentecostals and the risks that this poses to the secular character of the Brazilian state, consequently threatening the survival of hard-won LGBTQ and women's rights.[4] Appalled by my country's sudden *regression*, I too have caught myself employing the same evolutionist language that I have been critical of in my study of the African American roots tourism discourse on Brazil and Afro-Brazilians. Refusing to accept this rupture and the shattering of so many hard-won gains, I cannot help but frame Brazil's new and depressing reality as a complete retrogression.

The shock and outrage, however, should not make us lose sight of the fact that evolutionist understandings are unproductive, even when they seem appealing. Because it relies on a linear understanding of history, evolutionism focuses on or prioritizes some actors, elements, and processes over others instead of providing more holistic and inclusive frameworks. This linearity is, in turn, conceived of as a continuous move toward progress, development, improvement, when in reality there are no guarantees that are we "evolving." Undoubtedly, evolutionism is an even more inadequate concept when applied to compare two different societies, or two groups inhabiting different societies, as in the example of the constant comparison between the "development stages" of Afro-Brazilians vis-à-vis African Americans. But even to analyze a single society or country, the evolutionist language that establishes that we are supposedly always moving forward is fraught with problems. History is better understood as a series of nodes, where multiple processes take place simultaneously, and, above all, where multiple and often times opposing actors dispute the very meaning of progress as well as to whom its gains should be extended.

On the one hand, there is no assurance that we are continuously moving toward a more improved future, as unforeseen historical events have often shown; on the other hand, it is not possible to return to a purer or better point in time either. It is thus necessary to deal with the messiness of the here and now while at the same time drawing from past experiences of pain and horror. And this is exactly what numerous resistance movements are doing, both in Brazil and elsewhere. One of the most inspiring forms of mobilization against the coup has taken the form of an intersectional, multicentered, multigenerational, race-aware, and gender-bending resistance movement that has sprung in Brazil's major cities since 2016. Occupying schools, public offices, and governmental buildings, and spearheaded by a coalition of high school and college students who were born after the end of the military dictatorship, this movement operates beyond a framework of "advances" versus "reversions."[5]

In common with other resistance mobilizations emerging across the world, these movements have made strategic use of the Internet and have established transnational links of solidarity. Women's groups, LGBTQ collectives, and black organizations have all sought out their counterparts abroad with the goals of mutually enlightening one another and building coalition. An important example was that in July 2016, as Brazil was getting ready to host the Olympic Games for the first time, a delegation of Black Lives Matter activists traveled to Rio de Janeiro to meet with Brazilian activists who are equally fighting police violence. Similar to previous black transnational movements, the members of this coalition are aware that racism must be fought both locally and globally, and that, notwithstanding local specificities, they can all learn from their shared struggles and forms of resistance. Furthermore, these activists are equally aware that, despite the commonality of antiblack racism across the globe, the power attached to their national identities also affects the visibility of their struggles. Evidence of this is the recognition that the U.S. Black Lives Matter movement has obtained, and which has led black activist organizations around the world to borrow their powerful name-cum-catchphrase, sometimes even to rebrand themselves. The awareness of the power of U.S. identities within global contexts, even for the members of U.S. racialized minorities, is thus a major component of this recently formed transnational link of black solidarity. This is candidly expressed in the words of Daunasia Yancey, the director of the Boston chapter of Black Lives Matter, and who spearheaded the visit to Brazil: "We have been invited here by local activists and we're here to lend our solidarity and our American-ness; to use United States privilege to bring media attention to the issues."[6]

This slowly growing but remarkable new trend of activist diaspora travel to Brazil is emerging at the same time when African American roots tourism to Cuba is increasing. Although African American intellectuals, activists, and religious revivalists have long sought to establish links with Afro-Cubans, often managing to bypass the U.S. embargo in order to travel to the island, the restoration of diplomatic relations between the United States and Cuba in 2015 has already shown signs of an upsurge of African American heritage tours to Cuba. Two of my key interviewees, both of whom have been organizing African American roots tours to Brazil—one since the late 1980s and the other since 2004—have now begun to organize trips to Cuba. These tours seem to follow a similar structure to the tours carried out in Brazil and, most important, they equally revolve around the search for the Africanness and cultural roots that abound in the Afro-Cuban religions, cuisine, music, and dance. Another similarity is that the members of the tours to Cuba, like the roots tourists who travel to Brazil, are also predominantly female and elderly.

Only time will tell if this budding roots tourism to Cuba will challenge the especial position of Brazil in the map of Africanness, where it has been represented as a closer Africa and the ideal place to find roots. Perhaps the younger generation of African Americans and Afro-Brazilians that have been mobilizing across national boundaries to fight the globalization of police brutality will gradually pave the way for a new trend of diaspora tourism, where searching for roots may be less vital than asserting, even now, the humanity of black lives. Some might argue that this is yet another sign of regression since this should no longer be necessary in a post–civil rights era. I prefer to see it as a shift of focus; a focus on a different set of actors, who are not only members of a different generation, but also whose racial identities are intersected with their membership to different social classes. As such, they are trailing different journeys, following different directions, and are possibly guided by an altogether different compass.

Notes

Introduction

1. Pinho, "African-American Roots Tourism in Brazil," and *Mama Africa*.

2. The *blocos afro* are black cultural organizations that emerged in Bahia in the 1970s seeking to defeat racism within the sphere of Carnival. They have since expanded beyond the boundaries of Carnival to develop social projects aimed at elevating the self-esteem of black youth. Although they have constructed an oppositional black identity that challenges Brazil's dominant myth of racial democracy, central elements of their cultural production, such as music and aesthetics for example, have been incorporated into the mainstream notion of Bahianness that is promoted by the state and the tourism industry. For more on this topic, see Pinho, *Mama Africa*.

3. This information is corroborated by the State of Bahia's Secretariat of Tourism in *African Heritage Tourism in Bahia*, 20.

4. Gilroy, *The Black Atlantic*; Clifford, "Diasporas"; among others.

5. Definitions of "detour" according to the *New Oxford American Dictionary*.

6. *New Oxford American Dictionary*.

7. Pinho, "African-American Roots Tourism in Brazil," 71.

8. For a discussion of tourism as a reenactment of colonialism, see Hiller, "Tourism: Development of Dependence?," and Crick, "Representations of International Tourism in the Social Sciences." For an analysis of tourism as a form of imperialism, see Nash, "Tourism as a Form of Imperialism."

9. For nuanced analyses of the intersections of tourism and identity, see Merrill, *Negotiating Paradise*; Babb, *The Tourism Encounter*; Little, *Mayas in the Marketplace*; and Freire-Medeiros, *Touring Poverty*, among others.

10. Merrill, *Negotiating Paradise*.

11. Babb, *The Tourism Encounter*.

12. Little, *Mayas in the Marketplace*.

13. Freire-Medeiros, *Touring Poverty*.

14. Selwyn, *The Tourist Image*, 9.

15. Quijano, "Coloniality of Power."

16. Ashchoft et al., *The Empire Writes Back*; Mignolo, *The Idea of Latin America*.

17. Stam and Shohat, *Race in Translation*.

18. Coles and Timothy, *Tourism, Diasporas and Space*; Leite, "Travels to an Ancestral Past"; Cohen, "A Phenomenology of Tourist Experiences."

19. Cohen, "A Phenomenology of Tourist Experiences," 191.

20. Pinho, *Mama Africa*.

21. Quijano, "Coloniality of Power."

22. Wallerstein, *World-Systems Analysis*.

23. According to market research on African American travelers, 81 percent of them "more significantly desire pampering as part of the travel experience versus 66% for total leisure travelers" (Mandala, *The African American Traveler*, 12).

24. Cohen, "A Phenomenology of Tourist Experiences," 192.

25. On the tourist bubble, see Cohen, "Toward a sociology of international tourism," and Graburn, "Tourism: The sacred journey," among others.

26. Despite the importance of the topic, not much research has been done on the connections between U.S.-based Yoruba revivalists and Candomblé temples in Bahia. Capone briefly touches on this theme as she describes the irony of the visit to Bahia by purist revivalists during the hybrid Festival of the Boa Morte, which is marked by the syncretism of Catholicism and Afro-Brazilian religions (*Os Yoruba do Novo Mundo*, 306).

27. Ferreira, "E se o Gringo for 'Negão'?"

28. Mitchell, *Tourist Attractions*, 184.

29. Pinho, "Comment Trouver l'Afrique a Bahia," "Viajando a la tierra de *Ashé*," and "African American Roots Tourism in Brazil."

30. MacCannell, *Empty Meeting Grounds*; Van Den Berghe, *The Quest for the Other*.

31. Coles and Timothy, *Tourism, Diasporas and Space*. See also Meethan, "To stand in the shoes of my ancestors," 138; Stephenson, "Travelling to the Ancestral Homelands."

32. Leite, "Travels to an Ancestral Past."

33. "Travels to an Ancestral Past," 276.

34. These and other examples of diaspora tourism practices are mentioned in Coles and Timothy, *Tourism, Diasporas and Space*.

35. Barbosa, "Mercado de Grupos Étnicos." The average income level of African Americans experienced an annual growth rate of approximately 16 percent between 1990 and 2000; a period in which they represented a market worth US$400 billion in disposable spending. "This means that the African-American market could be considered the fourteenth largest market in the world with more disposable and discretionary income than residents of Australia, Mexico or Russia" (Timothy and Teye, "American children of the African diaspora," 114).

36. Coles and Timothy, *Tourism, Diaspora and Space*, 13.

37. Coles and Timothy, 1.

38. Timothy, *Cultural Heritage and Tourism*.

39. Crick, "Representations of International Tourism in the Social Sciences," 312.

40. Del Sarto, "Foundations—Introduction," 157.

41. Del Sarto et al., *The Latin American Cultural Studies Reader*.

42. See, for example, Hollinshead, "Tourism, Hybridity, and Ambiguity"; Echtner and Prasad, "The Context of Third World Tourism Marketing"; Jaworski and Pritchard, *Discourse, Communication and Tourism*; among others.

43. Jaworski and Pritchard, *Discourse, Communication and Tourism*.

44. Cartier and Lew, *Seductions of Place*; Jamal and Robinson, *The Sage Handbook of Tourism Studies*; Berger and Wood, *Holiday in Mexico*.

45. Coleman and Crang, *Tourism: Between Place and Performance*; Hall and Tucker, *Tourism and Postcolonialism*; Coles and Timothy, *Tourism, Diasporas, and Space*; Jaworski and Pritchard, *Discourse, Communication and Tourism*.

46. Barker, *Cultural Studies*.

47. Willis's *Learning to Labor* is probably the most well known and influential example of a British cultural studies project that relied centrally on ethnographic methods.

48. Del Sarto, "Foundations—Introduction."

49. Clifford and Marcus, *Writing Culture.*

50. Geertz, *The Interpretation of Cultures.*

51. Ethnographic research among tourists has proved challenging, especially because their presence is, by definition, ephemeral, as argued by Graburn ("The Ethnographic Tourist") and Leite and Graburn ("Anthropological Interventions in Tourism Studies"). "Anthropologists have had to adapt their research methods to capture the transient tourist-as-native's point of view. Some researchers spend many months at a single tourist destination, slowly building up an understanding of visitor's motivation, behavior and experience by talking with and moving among them on a daily basis. . . . Others accompany package tours as full participants . . . even making the same journey repeatedly with a series of different groups. Adopting the role of translator . . . or even academic guide . . . during an international package tour offers additional complexity and insight to the participant-observer role" (Leite and Graburn, "Anthropological Interventions in Tourism Studies," 37).

52. Pinho, *Mama Africa.*

53. In chapter 5, I explain the reason why the official name of the office in English (Coordination of African Heritage Tourism) is different from its official name in Portuguese (Coordenação do Turismo Étnico Afro).

54. As Bruner argues, a tour group is a traveling social unit: they assemble in their area of origin, travel together, become a tight unit, and then disband at the end of the trip, which makes it difficult to penetrate the group at midpoint. Thus, the earlier a researcher can join the tour group, the more she can participate in this unit (*Culture on Tour*, 195).

55. Clifford, "Introduction: Partial Truths," 14.

56. Clifford, 17.

57. Clifford, "Introduction: Partial Truths," 6; Crapanzano, "Hermes' Dilemma."

58. Leite, "Travels to an Ancestral Past."

59. Osagie and Buzinde, "Culture and Postcolonial Resistance," 212.

60. Albers and James, "Travel Photography," 150.

61. Foucault, *Power/Knowledge*, and *The Order of Things*; Hall, *Representation.*

62. Renda, *Taking Haiti*, 24.

63. Bruner, *Culture on Tour*, 24.

64. Johnson, "Brazil: The Way We Were," 160.

65. Brockbank and Traves (1996), quoted in Aitchison, "Gender and Tourism Discourses," 633.

66. On governmental efforts to attract diaspora tourists, see Lew and Wong, "Sojourners, Guanxi and Clan Associations" on China; Hannam, "India and the ambivalences of diaspora tourism" on India; Holsey, *Routes of Remembrance* on Ghana; Forte, "Diaspora Homecoming" on Benin; and Karam, "The Politics of Anti-Zionism" on Syria and Lebanon.

67. "Brazil: The Awakening Giant," *Ebony*, 35.

68. PT's terms in the presidency include Luis Inácio Lula da Silva (2003–2006, 2007–2010), and Dilma Rousseff (2011–2014). Rousseff's second term in office, that started in 2015, was interrupted via a parliamentary coup in August 2016. PT's terms in the state of

Bahia governor's office include Jacques Wagner (2007–2010, 2011–2014), and Rui Costa (2015–2018).

69. Sheller, "Teorizações indisciplinadas," 124.

70. According to the UNWTO, tourism accounts for 235 million jobs worldwide, 5 percent of direct global GDP, and 30 percent of the world's exports of services. International tourism generated in 2011 US$1,032 billion in export earnings. Information available at UNWTO, "Why Tourism?"

71. Hollinshead, "Worldmaking and the Transformation of Place and Culture," 185.

Chapter One

1. Pinho, "African-American Roots Tourism in Brazil," and *Mama Africa*.

2. Hughes, *I Wonder as I Wander*.

3. Stinson (1920), in Hellwig, *African American Reflections*, 45.

4. Guridy, *Forging Diaspora*, 153.

5. Gill, *Beauty Shop Politics*, 89.

6. It was in the 1940s that important African American scholars, such as E. Franklin Frazier and Lorenzo Dow Turner, began to carry out research on Brazil's Africanisms.

7. On this topic, see Pereira, *"O Mundo Negro."* And for a thorough analysis of the representations of the United States in the Afro-Brazilian press and the exchanges between African American and Afro-Brazilian journalists and leaders during that time period, see Seigel, *Uneven Encounters*.

8. Emigration attempts of black Americans to the African continent started as early as 1787, according to Meade and Pirio, "In Search of the Afro-American 'Eldorado,'" 86.

9. See Sundiata, *Brothers and Strangers*, for a thorough analysis of the foundation of Liberia and the emigration projects of African Americans to this African nation.

10. Simmons, *Reconstructing Racial Identity*; Mann-Hamilton, "What Rises from the Ashes."

11. Article 5 of Federal Decree N. 4247 (January 6, 1921), specifically prohibited black immigrants from entering Brazil, according to Meade and Pirio, "In Search of the Afro-American 'Eldorado,'" 87.

12. Meade and Pirio, "In Search of the Afro-American 'Eldorado.'"

13. "The Truth about Brazil," *Ebony*, 36–37.

14. Hellwig, *African American Reflections*.

15. Hellwig, 170–171.

16. Calomee, in Hellwig, 252.

17. Hall, "Encoding, Decoding," 483.

18. Gill, oral presentation.

19. Clarke, *Mapping Yoruba Networks*.

20. The interview with William was carried out on the bus on the way from Salvador to Cachoeira in August 2000.

21. Clarke, *Mapping Yoruba Networks*; Jacobson, *Roots Too*.

22. According to Wright, *The World and a Very Small Place*, 225, Haley's *Roots* sold 1.5 million copies in the first year after its publication, and has been translated into several dozen languages.

23. Clarke, *Mapping Yoruba Networks.*

24. I interviewed the Bahiatursa employee and coorganizer of the festival in Salvador (2004, 2011), Lidia Matos in Salvador (1999), and Lionel Washington in Salvador (2003) and in Cachoeira (2013).

25. Interview via Skype, October 2014.

26. Interview via Skype, October 2014.

27. The information that the First New World Festival of the African Diaspora was modeled after FESTAC 77 was relayed by the festival organizer, and it is also included in the festival program, which begins with the following introduction: "The idea of a new world festival is not new. Many noble attempts have been made and the periodic CARIFESTA is now well established. While working as a member of the U.S. Zonal Committee for FESTAC, the Second World Black and African Festival of Arts and Cultures in Lagos, Nigeria, Professor Richard Long of Atlanta University conceived the idea of holding frequent Bi-National Festivals. . . . The First New World Festival is now scheduled to take place in Brasil [*sic*]."

28. Interview via Skype, October 2014.

29. Program, New World Festival of the African Diaspora, n.p.

30. Interview, Salvador, August 2004. In 2011, I interviewed him once again, and the information he shared with me was virtually the same as what he had shared with me in 2004.

31. Ron Harris, "U.S. Blacks Seek a Part of Their History."

32. One of the tour guides that I interviewed in Salvador in 2011, and who worked for the group led by *Essence*, told me that there were 200 women in total attending the gathering. However, Gail Harris, who participated in the retreat and wrote about it in her book, *A Woman's War*, states that eighty women were in attendance.

33. One hundred twenty-five conferees participated in the NABSW conference in Bahia. Although it usually takes place in July, the conference was pushed back to August in order to coincide with the Boa Morte celebration, according to Copeland, "Awaken in Brazil," a social worker who attended the conference.

34. Interview, August 2004.

35. Interview, August 2013.

36. Conference flyer, New World Festival of the African Diaspora, 1978.

37. Conference flyer, New World Festival of the African Diaspora, 1978.

38. Tate, "First New World Festival," 34.

39. Rohter, "Cultural Exchange and Controversy in Rio," n.p.

40. Tate, "First New World Festival," 32.

41. Quoted in Tate, 33. I was not able to locate the original pamphlet distributed by the MNU during the festival, but Rohter's newspaper article, "Cultural Exchange and Controversy in Rio," offers a very similar translation of the original Portuguese text provided in Tate's article. Although, the ending is a little different as it identifies African Americans as the beneficiaries of the festival as a commercial enterprise: "'The Festival of Black Culture now taking place would merit our full support if it were a real exchange between black Brazilians and Americans,' says a leaflet the protestors have been handing out at festival programs. 'But we have seen that its main focus is commercial, based on support from black American businessmen and tourist enterprises.'"

42. Interview via Skype, October 2014.

43. In Chapter 5, I analyze how the positions of the state and federal governments' vis-à-vis African American tourists have drastically changed over the last three and a half decades.

44. Rohter, "Cultural Exchange and Controversy in Rio," n.p.

45. Tate's article, "First New World Festival," also states that the Brazilian government opposed the event and even the presence of black Americans in the country.

46. When I asked him who were these activists, he refused to mention names, except for the names of those whom he defined as the "cosmopolitan" Brazilian revolutionaries, such as Lélia Gonzalez and Abdias do Nascimento. He said he wouldn't mention the names of the "community level" activists because some of them "have since established a platform and have become more sophisticated," but in the late 1970s "they were just learning and this (the festival) was their first access to information." Interview, October 2014.

47. The festival program depicted Salvador da Bahia as "the oldest African city of the western type, so pervasive is influence of African on its customs. The interweaving of African religions and Catholicism produced Bahian African religion, whose pantheon consists of Yoruba divinities. The cuisine of Bahia belongs to the New World spectrum of Creole cooking and is a distinctive element therein. The rhythms and pulsation of the city's markets again bespeak Africa."

48. Among the twenty members of the tour group that I accompanied in 2004, five were members of the ATA.

49. Although there are several slave sites and tours that commemorate the history of slavery in the United States, as discussed in the work of Buzinde and Santos, "Interpreting Slavery Tourism," and Lelo and Jamal, "African Americans at Sites of Darkness," among others, none of the tourists that I interviewed over the course of almost a decade and a half ever commented on having visited any of these sites.

50. Lidia Matos was the first person I interviewed for this research, in Salvador, August 1999.

51. Interview, Salvador, August 2004.

52. Informal conversation, Cachoeira, 2000.

53. Interview, Salvador, August 1999.

54. Interview, Salvador, August 2004.

55. Interview, Cachoeira, August 2000.

56. Interview with David, tour guide, Cachoeira, August 2004.

57. Interview with mixed/Afro-Brazilian female tour guide, Salvador, August 2011.

58. Ebron contends that conspicuous consumption habits marked the entire trip, even those moments when the tourists experienced the emotions of reconnecting with the brutality of the history of slavery, such as when they visited the Maison des Esclaves in Gorée Island, Senegal: "Yet even the most moving moments of deep immersion in the pilgrimage tour seemed to be followed by a break; moments of high emotion were tempered by opportunities to shop for souvenirs" (*Performing Africa*, 206).

59. Hernandez-Reguant, "Kwanzaa and the U.S. Ethnic Mosaic," 107.

60. Interview with the Bahiatursa employee who coorganized the 1978 festival, Salvador, August 2004.

61. Garcia Canclini, *Consumers and Citizens*, 39.

62. Interview, Salvador, August 2012.

63. Cohen, "A Phenomenology of Tourist Experiences"; Leite, "Travels to an Ancestral Past"; Lew and Wong, "Existential Tourism and the Homeland."

64. Cohen, "A Phenomenology of Tourist Experiences," 193.

65. MacCannell, *Empty Meeting Grounds*.

66. Stam and Shohat, *Race in Translation*, 46–48, explains why France was so alluring for African American artists and intellectuals at a time when Francophone Caribbean intellectuals such as Cesaire and Fanon found it so terribly racist. The different historical and geographical origins of both groups strongly informed their distinct perspectives on France. While African Americans were coming from a context marked by the horrors of racial segregation, Francophone Caribbean writers were moving from semicolonized yet black-majority islands where blackness was the norm. Besides, African Americans in France were seen also, and sometimes primarily, as Americans.

67. Gilroy, *The Black Atlantic*.

68. Interview carried out on the bus trip from Salvador to Cachoeira, August 2000.

69. Interview, Cachoeira, August 2000.

70. Bruner, "Tourism in Ghana." Elmina and Cape Coast castles were designated World Heritage Sites by UNESCO in 1979, according to Holsey, *Routes of Remembrance*, 160.

71. Leite, "Travels to an Ancestral Past," 281.

72. Seigel, *Uneven Encounters*, 237.

73. Holsey, *Routes of Remembrance*, 15.

74. Holsey, 237.

75. Bruner, "Tourism in Ghana"; Reed, *Pilgrimage Tourism*, 5.

76. Pierre, *The Predicament of Blackness*, 148.

77. Holsey, *Routes of Remembrance*; Reed, *Pilgrimage Tourism*.

78. Schramm, "Coming Home to the Motherland"; Holsey, *Routes of Remembrance*.

79. Schramm, "Coming Home to the Motherland."

80. Holsey, *Routes of Remembrance*, 237.

81. Tillet, "In the Shadow of the Castle," 137.

82. Sutherland, "In Memory of the Slaves," 196.

83. Forte, "Diaspora Homecoming," 184.

84. Forte, 187.

85. Capone, *Os Yoruba do Novo Mundo*, 306; Clarke, *Mapping Yoruba Networks*.

86. Apter, *The Pan-African Nation*, 3–6.

87. Wright, *The World and a Very Small Place*.

88. According to Wright, the accuracy of the most important facts in Haley's narrative was subsequently questioned, and several historians critiqued what they viewed as his misinterpretations, misappropriations, and outright invention of historical facts. See Wright, "Uprooting Kunta Kinte" and *The World and a Very Small Place*. "The book won a Pulitzer Prize in an entirely new category of literature, created for Roots, called 'Faction'—a story based on fact, but with fictionalized dialogue." Wright, *The World and a Very Small Place*, 226.

89. Rahier, "Roots/Heritage Tourism in Juffureh."

90. For a thorough analysis of the transformation of Gorée Island into an international tourism destination, see Araujo, "Welcome the Diaspora."

91. Holsey, *Routes of Remembrance*, 157.

92. Schenck and Candido, "Uncomfortable Pasts."

93. Forte, "Diaspora Homecoming."

94. Robben Island Museum, n.d.

95. Gupta and Ferguson, "Beyond 'Culture,'" 8.

96. Hall, *New Cultures for Old*, 176.

97. Ebron, *Performing Africa*, 200.

98. Timothy and Teye, "American Children of the African Diaspora," 117–121.

99. Timothy and Teye, 118.

100. On touring poverty, see Freire-Medeiros, *Touring Poverty*. On travels to sites marked by histories of revolutions see Babb, *The Tourism Encounter*.

101. Gates, *Wonders of the African World*.

102. Ioannides and Cohen Ioannides, "Jewish Past as a 'Foreign Country,'" 108.

103. "The European trips bring Jewish-Americans to the ghettos where their ancestors had once lived, such as the Old Jewish Quarter in Prague, the ancient ghetto in Venice, the Judenplatz in Vienna and Kazimierz, the ghetto in Krakow. Jews also visit Nazi extermination camps, such as Auschwitz in almost ritual-like 'nostalgic tours [that] allow the visitor a chance to see the "graves" of their forebears and perform, with others who have the same need, the required acts of public mourning for martyrs who are not necessarily family members'" (Ioannides and Cohen Ioannides, "Pilgrimages of Nostalgia," 19).

104. Schramm, "Coming Home to the Motherland," 148.

105. Interview, Salvador, August 2004.

106. Philipp, "Race and Tourism Choice," 484–485.

107. Stephenson, "Tourism, Racism and the UK Afro-Caribbean Diaspora," 70.

108. Urry, *The Tourist Gaze*.

109. Bruner, "Tourism in Ghana"; Finley, "The Door of (No) Return"; Reed, *Pilgrimage Tourism*.

110. Interview, Salvador, August 2004.

111. Interview with male tourist, Salvador, August 2004, my emphasis.

112. Hughes, *I Wonder as I Wander*, 7.

113. Randle, "Senegal," 82.

114. Cobb, "Blame it on Rio," 204.

115. Interview, Salvador, August 1999, my emphasis.

116. Interview, October 2014.

117. Interview, Rio de Janeiro, August 2012.

118. Tate, "First New World Festival," 37. Similar to Harris's documentary, Tate's article describes the local black children as being supposedly aware of their shared connection across national boundaries: "Little children flocked to the American visitors, drawn by a sense of kindred—an identification with our blackness that paralleled their own" (Tate, "First New World Festival," 32).

119. For analyses of the term *Oburoni* in Ghana, see Holsey, *Routes of Remembrance*, and Reed, *Pilgrimage Tourism*. About the term *Oyinbo* in Nigeria, see Clarke, *Mapping Yoruba Networks*, and Capone, *Os Yoruba do Novo Mundo*. On the term *Yovo* in Benin, see Forte, "Diaspora Homecoming," and on the term *Toubob* in Senegal, see Ebron, *Performing Africa*.

120. Rich, *Blood, Bread, and Poetry*, 212.

121. Hellwig, *African American Reflections*, 169.

Chapter Two

1. Interview, Salvador, August 2012.

2. Sylvia Marie often used the term "diasporic counterparts" to refer to Afro-Brazilians.

3. Examples include Haggins, *The African-American Travel Guide*; White and Quenum, *Roots Recovered*; and Freelon, *Kiratiana's Travel Guide to Black Paris*.

4. Urry and Larsen, *The Tourist Gaze 3.0*, 1.

5. Hall, *Representation*.

6. Urry, *The Tourist Gaze*, 1–2.

7. Crouch, "Surrounded by Place," 210.

8. Cartier, Introduction to *Seductions of Place*, 2.

9. Crouch, "Surrounded by Place," and "Flirting with Space."

10. Crouch, "Flirting with Space," 209.

11. Crouch, 23.

12. Hall, *Representation*.

13. Foucault, *Power/Knowledge*, and *The Order of Things*.

14. The first edition of *The Tourist Gaze* was published in 2002. The third and last edition of the book, published in 2011, and aptly titled *The Tourist Gaze 3.0*, also includes an important assessment of the most recent forms of communications technologies, including the Internet, social media, instant messaging, and the digitization of photography.

15. In a later article, Crouch recognizes Urry's growing awareness of the embodied nature of the gaze: "While Urry (2002) stays with an emphasis on the visual and its evolution through increasing mobility, easily related to aspects of tourism, he is increasingly nonetheless attuned to the incompleteness of vision alone." Crouch, "The Diverse Dynamics of Cultural Studies and Tourism," 88.

16. For critiques of the theory of the tourist gaze, see Veijola and Jokinen, "The Body in Tourism"; Crouch, "Surrounded by Place," and "Flirting with Space"; Cartier, Introduction to *Seductions of Place*; Leite, "Travels to an Ancestral Past"; among others.

17. Interview, Rio de Janeiro, August 2012.

18. Mandala's quantitative research about African American travelers also emphasized the importance of word of mouth in disseminating destinations: "Word of mouth (recommendations from friends and family) ranks highest (55%) among sources of information for leisure travel, slightly ahead of online activity" (Mandala, *The African American Traveler*, 12). On page 75 of Mandala's report, this information is reiterated: "Fifty-five percent of African American travelers seek the advice of family and friends to gather information about their possible leisure trips, and nearly as many go directly to the website of the destinations they are considering visiting."

19. Interview, Cachoeira, August 2004.

20. Interview, Cachoeira, August 2000.

21. Interview, New York, May 2013.

22. Interview, Salvador, August 1999.

23. For more on this issue, see Pinho, *Mama Africa*.

24. Interview with Afro-Brazilian tour guide, carried out on the trip from Cachoeira to Salvador, following the Boa Morte Festival, August 2012.

25. Ebron describes a similar purpose for the orientation session that preceded the visit of the African American roots tourists that she accompanied to Senegambia: to offer the tourists an initial tutoring session on the "shared meaning of Africa" and to provide them with the "proper way to approach Africa." Ebron, *Performing Africa*, 193.

26. Interview, Salvador, August 2004.

27. Chatfield-Taylor, "Dance of Life to Honor Death."

28. Interview, Salvador, August 2004.

29. Interview, Salvador, August 2004.

30. I analyzed closely the editions of *Ebony* and *Essence*, spanning from 1986 to 2007.

31. Mandala, *The African American Traveler*, 81.

32. Albers and James, "Travel Photography," 140.

33. Caton and Almeida Santos note that the academic literature on tourism representations has focused much more on the first half of this circle, that is, on how the tourism media represents tourist destinations. They argue that more attention must be given to the second half of the hermeneutic circle that is on how "tourists complete the hermeneutic circle by producing photographs that look very similar to those found in the brochures that target them." Caton and Almeida Santos, "Closing the Hermeneutic Circle?," 8.

34. Urry, *The Tourist Gaze*, 3.

35. Foucault, *The Order of Things*.

36. Said, *Orientalism*, 41.

37. Said, 42.

38. Hall, *Representation*.

39. Raiford and Raphael-Hernandez, *Migrating the Black Body*, 3–9.

40. Interview, New York, May 2013.

41. Interview, Salvador, August 2004.

42. Interview, Salvador, August 2011.

43. Interview, Salvador, October 2005.

44. Interview, Rio de Janeiro, August 2012.

45. Interview, Salvador, August 1999. Anastácia is represented in popular culture as a very beautiful enslaved African woman who, with her dark skin and inexplicably blue eyes, attracted the attention of her master who sexually abused her. Her master's wife, jealous of her beauty, further molested her by obliging her to wear a permanent, iron facemask. Although there is no evidence to corroborate Anastácia's material existence, she has become a powerful symbol of black women's struggles, and images and statues of her abound in Brazil. Some also worship her as a saint. See Burdick, *Blessed Anastacia*, for a fascinating analysis of Anastácia's representations in Rio de Janeiro.

46. Interview, Rio de Janeiro, August 2012.

47. Interview, Rio de Janeiro, August 2012.

48. Wasserman, *Brazil, a Celebration of Life*. Although promoted by a Brazilian airline company, it was an African American writer, Jessica Harris, who wrote the script for VARIG's video. At that time, Harris regularly wrote a travel column for *Essence*, and she is also the author of several books on food, including *Tasting Brazil: Regional Recipes and Reminiscences*.

49. Wasserman, *Brazil, a Celebration of Life*, my emphasis.

50. Wasserman.

51. Strickland-Abuwi, "Bahia," 89.

52. Interview, Cachoeira, August 2013.

53. Interview, Salvador, August 1999.

54. Interview, Salvador, August 1999.

55. Arthur, "Romantic Imaginings."

56. Mintz and Price, *The Birth of African-American Culture.*

57. Peterson, "Where Africa Also Lives."

58. "Where Africa Also Lives," 66.

59. This painting by Augustus Earle, "Negroes Fighting, Brazil" (1821–1824), can be seen in Hackforth-Jones, *Augustus Earle: Travel Artist,* 66.

60. Peterson, "Where Africa Also Lives," 76, my emphasis.

61. Brewer, *Bahia: Africa in the Americas.*

62. When the transatlantic slavery began, the Yoruba were not an "ethnic group." The term Yoruba originally referred to groups that spoke the Yoruba language, and which inhabited areas of what is today Nigeria, Togo, and Benin. Although speakers of a same language might have shared roughly similar religious and cultural traditions, they did not see themselves as sharing a common identity. Yoruba, in this case, is thus an identity that emerged in the New World and as a result of the processes of colonialism and slavery. See Matory, *Black Atlantic Religion;* Capone, *Searching for Africa in Brazil, Os Yoruba do Novo Mundo;* Pinho, "Nurturing Bantu Africanness in Brazil."

63. Wasserman, *Brazil, a Celebration of Life.* These are several other quotes from the documentary that illustrate the idea that there was a transplantation of a fully formed African culture to Brazil. For example: "The Candomblé religion practiced in Salvador and throughout the State of Bahia is still one of the purest expressions of the African religion that was brought to Brazil in the wretched holds of slave ships." The documentary also defines capoeira as "an Afro-Brazilian dance/martial art [that] came to Brazil in the 16th century with Bantu people from Angola."

64. Wasserman, *Brazil, a Celebration of Life.*

65. Araujo, *Public Memory of Slavery,* 259–260.

66. ICOMOS, World Heritage List number 308, December 28, 1983, quoted in Araujo, *Public Memory of Slavery,* 260.

67. Araujo argues that one of the reasons why the Mercado Modelo became erroneously represented as a site where the enslaved were disembarked and kept for sale is the lack of official markers of slavery in Bahia, which has led to a process of memory replacement. Araujo, *Shadows of the Slave Past.*

68. Holsey, *Routes of Remembrance,* 189.

69. Pinho, *Mama Africa.* The idea of black cultures as "infectious" is Browning's, *Infectious Rhythm.*

70. Herskovits, *The New World Negro,* among other titles.

71. Romo, *Brazil's Living Museum,* 114.

72. For a thorough overview of the development of the tourism industry in Bahia, rich in quantitative data, see Queiroz, *Turismo na Bahia.*

73. Ickes, *African Brazilian Culture and Regional Identity in Bahia, Brazil.* On the "staging of capoeira" for "folkloric shows" for tourists, see Hofling, "Staging Capoeira, Samba, Maculelê and Candomblé."

74. Romo, *Brazil's Living Museum.*

75. Santos, *O Poder da Cultura.*

76. Interview, Salvador, August 2006, my emphasis.

77. Interview, Salvador, August 2004.

78. MacCannell, *Empty Meeting Grounds.*

79. Interview, Salvador, August 2006.

80. Strickland-Abuwi, "Bahia," 90.

81. Female tourist, age described as "late sixties," questionnaire 2004. The "villages" referred to by the tourist are Cachoeira and Maragogipe, towns located in the Recôncavo area of Bahia.

82. Female tourist, age described as "mid-sixties," questionnaire 2004.

83. Female tourist, no age indicated, questionnaire 2004.

84. Christmas, "The African Flavor of Bahia."

85. Christmas, "In Harmony with Brazil's African Pulse."

86. Arie, Interview with Neal Conan, 2006.

87. Arie, "There's Hope."

88. Interview with Afro-Brazilian tour guide, carried out on the trip from Cachoeira to Salvador, following the Boa Morte Festival, August 2012.

89. Interview with tour guide, Salvador, August 2012.

90. White, "Black Pride, Brazilian Style," 64.

91. "Afro-Americanos procuram suas origens," *A Tarde.*

92. Chatfield-Taylor, "Dance of Life to Honor Death," 8.

93. Wasserman (1992).

94. Vianna, *The Mystery of Samba.*

95. On the importance of Carmen Miranda's role in shaping an alluring and exotic image of Brazil in the United States in the 1940s, see Bishop-Sanchez, *Creating Carmen Miranda,* and Balieiro, "Consuming Carmen Miranda."

96. Stam, *Tropical Multiculturalism.*

97. Stam, 176.

98. In one of his memoirs, President Barack Obama describes the effect of *Black Orpheus* on his mother, and how the image of the movie's "childlike" Brazilian blacks fed the fantasy of white Americans: "Her face, lit by the blue glow of the screen, was set in a wistful gaze. At that moment, I felt as if I were being given a window into her heart, the unreflective heart of her youth. I suddenly realized that the depiction of *childlike blacks* I was now seeing on the screen, the reverse image of Conrad's dark savages, was what my mother had carried with her to Hawaii all those years before, a reflection of the simple fantasies that had been forbidden to a white middle-class girl from Kansas, the promise of another life: warm, sensual, exotic, different" (Obama, *Dreams from My Father,* 124, my emphasis).

99. Interview, Albany, May 2004.

100. Freire-Medeiros, *Gringo na Laje,* 98.

101. Cantú, "*De Ambiente.*"

102. O'Rourke, *Cannibal Tours.*

103. Whitaker, "Blacks in Brazil," my emphasis.

104. Whitaker, 60.

105. Whitaker, 62, my emphasis.

106. Interview, Cachoeira, August 2000.

107. Christmas, "In Harmony with Brazil's African Pulse."

108. Pinho, "Decentering the United States in the Studies of Blackness in Brazil."

109. Walker, "Africanity vs Blackness."

110. "Brazil: The Awakening Giant," *Ebony*.

111. "Brazil: The Awakening Giant," my emphasis.

112. Davis, "Brazil, the Sleeping Giant," 20, my emphasis.

113. Interview, Salvador, August 2006, my emphasis.

114. Interview, Cachoeira, August 2000, my emphasis.

115. Interview, New York City, May 2013.

116. Reis, "A falta de negros na mídia."

117. E-mail exchange on February 9, 2012.

118. Said, *Orientalism*, 41.

119. Fairclough, *Critical Discourse Analysis*.

120. Fabian, *Time and the Other*, 15–16.

121. Johnson, "Brazil: The Way We Were," 160–161, my emphasis.

122. Lew and Wong, "Existential Tourism and the Homeland," 294.

123. Basu, *Highland Homecomings*, 153.

124. Hall and Tucker, *Tourism and Postcolonialism*, 6.

125. Dussel, *The Invention of the Americas*, 10.

Chapter Three

1. The seminar was part of the conference organized by the International Brazilian Institute of Criminal Sciences.

2. Redação iBahia, "Professor americano negro é barrado em hotel," *Exame*.

3. Redação iBahia.

4. Hart, Interview.

5. Hart, "O Viral e o Crônico."

6. Representative Afonso Arinos wrote the project for the new law within a weekend's time. Within a month, the project was presented, voted on, and sanctioned. It became law # 1.390/1951 in July 1951, according to Campos, "Discriminação racial e imprensa." It is important to mention that this law has rarely been employed to penalize racists.

7. Babb, *The Tourism Encounter*.

8. Bruner, *Culture on Tour*.

9. Matory, *Black Atlantic Religion*; Guridy, *Forging Diaspora*.

10. Renda, *Taking Haiti*, 187.

11. Von Eschen, *Race Against Empire*. "In the last years of his life Martin Luther King Jr. developed a critique of the American capitalist economy and embraced antiimperialist policies, challenging the United States to address its gross disparities in wealth and condemning its intervention in Vietnam as immoral. But as King attempted to reconnect the international and domestic politics that had been so thoroughly severed during the Cold War, he was increasingly isolated and chastised, abandoned by both white liberal and black establishment allies." Von Eschen, *Race Against Empire*, 188.

12. Guridy, *Forging Diaspora*, 11–12.

13. Gordon, *Disparate Diasporas.*

14. Ebron, *Performing Africa.*

15. Ebron, 190.

16. Ebron, 206–207.

17. Ebron, ix.

18. Ebron, 208.

19. Guridy, *Forging Diaspora.*

20. Interview, Albany, May 2004.

21. Clarke, *Mapping Yoruba Networks,* xxiv.

22. SENAC, *Serviço Nacional de Aprendizagem Comercial* (National Service for Commercial Education), is a private nonprofit institution created in 1946 to provide professional qualification for adults and vocational training for young apprentices. "Through Decree 8621, of 10 January 1946, the Brazilian federal government authorized the National Federation of Commerce to organize and administrate commercial training centers throughout Brazil for people seeking work or already employed in the area of commerce. Senac thus came into being. Under a decentralization program, Senac established branches throughout the country, forming regional administrations, with the Regional Board as the deliberative body, and the Regional Department as the executive body." SENAC, n.d.

23. Interview via Skype, October 2014.

24. Cited in Hellwig, *African American Reflections,* 45.

25. Hellwig, 108.

26. Interview via Skype, October 2014.

27. Pratt, *Imperial Eyes,* 217.

28. Pratt, 205.

29. Pratt, 213. Wright traveled to Ghana in 1957 and wrote about the newly independent country from the point of view of his multiple identities, as American *and* black. According to Pratt, while describing Accra, Wright's "perception gets fragmented, but (Western) consciousness and selfhood do not" (Pratt, 222).

30. Mitchell, "TurboConsumers™ in Paradise."

31. Mitchell, 674.

32. Puar, "Circuits of Queer Mobility," 124.

33. Alexander, "Imperial Desire/Sexual Utopias."

34. Thayer, *Making Transnational Feminism,* 39.

35. Thayer, 13.

36. Mahrouse, *Conflicted Commitments.*

37. Woods and Hunter, *Don't Blame It on Rio,* 200.

38. Woods and Hunter.

39. Woods and Hunter, 207.

40. Guridy, *Forging Diaspora,* 12.

41. Gilroy, "British Cultural Studies and the Pitfalls of Identity," 41.

42. Massey, *Space, Place and Gender.*

43. See Gada Mahrouse, *Conflicted Commitments,* for an insightful analysis of how this form of transnational solidarity can unwittingly reproduce racialized power asymmetries that are embedded in imperial and colonial legacies.

44. Interview, Salvador, August 2003.

45. Interview, Salvador, August 2012.

46. Interview, Salvador, August 2012.

47. Thornton, *Africa and Africans in the Making of the Atlantic World.*

48. Interview, Salvador, August 2012.

49. Interview, Salvador, October 2005.

50. Interview, Salvador, August 2003.

51. Interview, Salvador, August 2011.

52. Interview, Salvador, August 2003.

53. Ferreira, "E se o Gringo for 'Negão'?," 11.

54. Interview, Salvador, August 1999.

55. Ferreira, "E se o Gringo for 'Negão'?," 88.

56. Castro, *Irmãs de Fé*, 110.

57. Amado, "Tomo da Cuia de Esmoler."

58. Amado.

59. The newspaper article "Irmandade da Boa Morte visita terreiros da capital," published by *A Tarde* on October 8, 1994, contains a photograph of the building with this banner hanging in the front wall. The photograph is not dated, so it is not possible to know when the photograph was taken.

60. Amado, "Tomo da Cuia de Esmoler."

61. Selka, "Cityscapes and contact zones," 414.

62. Interview, Cachoeira, August 2013.

63. Interview, Cachoeira, August 2013.

64. Interview, Cachoeira, August 2013.

65. Interview, Cachoeira, August 2013.

66. Selka, "Cityscapes and contact zones," 418.

67. Lew and Wong, "Sojourners, Guanxi and Clan Associations," 202.

68. Hannam, "India and the Ambivalences of Diaspora Tourism."

69. Robin Kelley, in the Introduction to C. L. R. James's *A History of Pan-African Revolt*, 21, uses this expression in reference to C. L. R. James's analyses of Marcus Garvey: "In a world where the very humanity of dark-skinned people was perpetually assaulted and questioned, Garvey gave his followers a sense of history and personhood. By linking the entire black world to Africa and to each other, he turned a national minority into an international majority."

70. Interview, Rio de Janeiro, August 2012.

71. Interview, Salvador, August 2003.

72. Interview via Skype, January 2016.

73. The institute's curriculum includes a course called "Cidadania e Consciência Negra" (Citizenship and Black Consciousness), which seeks to increase among the students their knowledge of the history of the black communities in Brazil and the Africa diaspora.

74. Interview via Skype, January 2016.

75. Interview, Salvador, July 2011.

76. Interview, Salvador, July 2011.

77. Informal conversation with Afro-Bahian activist, Cachoeira, August 2011.

78. Gilroy, "British Cultural Studies and the Pitfalls of Identity," 40.

79. Interview, Salvador, August 2003, my emphasis.

80. Interview, Salvador, August 2004.

81. Other examples of the African American awareness of the stigma attached to their American identity can be found in other time periods and locations. While visiting Haiti in the late 1930s to research vodun dance and religion, Katherine Dunham commented on how her American identity could potentially shatter the commonalities she sought to emphasize with black Haitians: "When the stigma of being an American had worn off, there was great and protective interest in the recognition of 'Guinean' blood ties and great concern for my ancestors, who had not received the proper ritual attention because that group of slaves taken farther north had been cut off from their brothers in the Caribbean and had forgotten these practices." Dunham, *Dances of Haiti*, xxiv.

82. Interview, female tourist, sixty-five years old, August 2006.

83. Interview, Salvador, August 2004.

84. Interview, Salvador, August 2004.

85. Pierre, *The Predicament of Blackness*, 171. According to Pierre and also to Reed, *Pilgrimage Tourism*, the Joseph Project, launched in 2007 in celebration of the 200th anniversary of the abolition of the slave trade and to coincide with the celebration of the fiftieth anniversary of Ghana's independence, is one of the major initiatives of the Ghanaian government to attract diaspora tourists. The Joseph Project is based on the biblical story of Joseph, the eleventh son of Jacob, who had been sold into slavery by his jealous brothers, but later became a very powerful man in Egypt and used his power to protect the very family that had betrayed him. Conceived as a healing ceremony aimed at reconnecting diaspora blacks with Africans, the Joseph Project problematically represents Ghanaians as the disloyal brothers that sold Joseph into slavery, and African Americans as the noble and forgiving Joseph.

86. Holsey, *Routes of Remembrance*, 214–215.

87. Kincaid, *A Small Place*.

88. Ebron, *Performing Africa*, 205.

89. Interview, Salvador, August 2011.

90. Interview, Albany, NY, male tourist, fifty-five years old, 2004. Ebron makes a similar critique to the African American tourists that she accompanied in the Senegambia: "Many of the travelers experienced an overwhelming sense of dissatisfaction when things did not go as expected. . . . The tour guides quickly grew agitated by the rumblings of what appeared to them to be a group of privileged Americans." Ebron, *Performing Africa*, 207.

91. Interview, Salvador, August 2012.

92. Forte, "Diaspora Homecoming."

93. Holsey, *Routes of Remembrance*, 220. Ann Reed, *Pilgrimage Tourism*, 153–54, explains that the term *oburoni* and its many modifiers in the Akan language are used to refer to each foreigner's place of origin. Although these modifiers are not commonly used in everyday speech, they are, she argues, "important to consider because they suggest that there is some variability in how Akans perceive different segments of foreigners."

94. Ebron, *Performing Africa*, 205.

95. Capone, *Os Yoruba do Novo Mundo*; Clarke, *Mapping Yoruba Networks*.

96. Capone, *Os Yoruba do Novo Mundo*.

97. Hartman, *Lose Your Mother*.

98. Nelson, *A Finger in the Wound*, 62.

99. Featherstone, *Solidarity*, 17.

100. Nascimento and Nascimento, "Reflexões sobre o Movimento Negro no Brasil, 1938–1997," 212.

101. Obama, interview on CNN's Anderson Cooper, my emphasis.

102. Goldberg, *The Racial State*.

103. Kaplan, *Questions of Travel*.

104. Gilroy, "British Cultural Studies and the Pitfalls of Identity"; Gilmore, *Golden Gulag*; Featherstone, *Solidarity*.

105. Featherstone, *Solidarity*.

Chapter Four

1. MacCannell, *The Tourist*, xvii.

2. There are some interesting exceptions that have focused on female sex tourists, such as Ebron's *Performing Africa*, Kempadoo's *Sexing the Caribbean*, among others. The volume edited by Kinnaird and Hall, *Tourism: A Gender Analysis*, also has a section on women travelers.

3. Kinnaird and Hall make a similar critique in *Tourism*, 188.

4. Blake, "A Woman's Trek."

5. Blake.

6. Kinnaird and Hall, *Tourism*, 193.

7. Massey, *Space, Place and Gender*, 180.

8. Enloe, *Bananas, Beaches and Bases*.

9. Enloe, 55.

10. Julius, *Os Destinos das Comissárias de Voo*.

11. Acosta, "Yesterday They Killed Me."

12. Hasan, "Let's Face the Truth."

13. Enloe, *Bananas, Beaches and Bases*, 58.

14. International Women's Travel Center, 2016.

15. Jordan, *Some of Us Did Not Die*, 213.

16. Williams, *Sex Tourism in Bahia*.

17. Interview, Salvador, August 2012.

18. Female tourist, sixty-five years old, questionnaire 2006.

19. Female tourist, fifty-three years old, questionnaire 2006.

20. Female tourist, fifty-one years old, questionnaire 2004.

21. Female tourist, thirty-eight years old, questionnaire 2012. She was the youngest member of Sylvia Marie's group, and she had already visited nineteen countries before visiting Brazil.

22. Thomas Allen Harris, interviewed by Wilson Morales.

23. Harris, *That's My Face*.

24. Interview, Salvador, August 2012, emphasis in the original.

25. Interview, Cachoeira, August 2000.

26. Interview, Cachoeira, August 2000.

27. Tillet, "In the Shadow of the Castle," and *Sites of Slavery*.

28. Ferreira, "E se o Gringo for 'Negão'?"

29. When an African American group travels exclusively to Bahia it is usually to attend a professional conference, such as the symposium of the Association of Black Cardiologists, held in Salvador from December 27, 2005 to January 3, 2006.

30. Ebron, *Performing Africa*.

31. Examples include Holsey, *Routes of Remembrance*; Reed, *Pilgrimage Tourism*; Powers, "Reimaging the Imagined Community."

32. "There is some evidence to suggest that more women than men are involved in heritage tourism" in the United States and abroad, according to Timothy, *Cultural Heritage and Tourism*, 28.

33. See Mottiar and Quinn, "Couple Dynamics in Household Tourism Decision Making" on women as the gatekeepers within households to the tourism product. Pearce, *Tourist Development*, 12, states that women play the lead role in the choice of family vacations.

34. Informal conversation, Salvador, August 2004.

35. Smith, "Women: The Tastemakers in Tourism"; Pearce, *Tourist Development*; Mottiar and Quinn, "Couple Dynamics in Household Tourism Decision Making"; among others.

36. Interview, Salvador, August 2012.

37. Fish, *Black and White Women's Travel Narratives*.

38. Gómez-Barris and Gray, *Toward a Sociology of the Trace*, xv.

39. Williams, *The Long Revolution*.

40. Nixon, *Resisting Paradise*, 64.

41. Raiford, "The Here and Now of Eslanda Robeson's *African Journey*."

42. McKittrick, *Demonic Grounds*, xxiv.

43. Jordan, *Some of Us Did Not Die*.

44. Jordan, 213.

45. Blake, "A Woman's Trek," 354.

46. Kaplan, *Questions of Travel*, 25.

47. Interview, Cachoeira, August 2000.

48. McKittrick, *Demonic Grounds*, xxiii–xxiv.

49. Statement made in Salvador, August 2012, my emphasis.

50. Interview with two female African American tourists in Cachoeira, August 2000, my emphasis.

51. Nelson, *The Social Life of DNA*, 4.

52. Nelson.

53. Nelson, 6.

54. Nelson, 71.

55. Rosenthal, "Kinkeeping in the Familial Division of Labor."

56. Massey, *Space, Place and Gender*, 179.

57. Massey, 257.

58. Massey, "The Conceptualization of Place," 65.

59. Massey.

60. Interview, Salvador, October 2011.

61. Babb, *The Tourism Encounter*; Little, *Mayas in the Marketplace*.

62. Little, *Mayas in the Marketplace*.

63. Babb, *The Tourism Encounter*, 167.

64. De la Cadena, "Women Are More Indian."

65. Interview, Salvador, August 2004.

66. MacCannell, *Empty Meeting Grounds.*

67. Kaplan, *Questions of Travel.*

68. Interview, Salvador, August 2004.

69. Informal conversation, Salvador, August 2013.

70. Williams, *Sex Tourism in Bahia*; Mitchell, *Tourist Attractions.*

71. Cobb, "Blame It on Rio."

72. The topic of African American sex tourism in Brazil has also been discussed in Woods and Hunter's *Don't Blame It on Rio* and in Sharpley-Whiting's *Pimps Up, Ho's Down: Hip Hop's Hold on Young Black Women.* The YouTube video is called *Frustrated: Black American Men in Brazil.* When I watched it on February 20, 2014, it had hit over 516,000 views.

73. Cobb, "Blame It on Rio"; Woods and Hunter, *Don't Blame It on Rio.* Another important sex tourism destination for African American men is the Dominican Republic. Describing the country as a more affordable destination where paid sex is cheaper than in Brazil, the African American sex tourists interviewed for an *Essence* article defined the DR as "the poor man's Brazil," according to Murphy and Dean, "Fool's Paradise." The men explained that in the DR they pay a whole lot less to fulfill the same desires that are sought out in Brazil, that is, women who "throw themselves" at them, make themselves sexually available, cook for them and make them "feel like kings."

74. Campt and Thomas, "Gendering Diaspora."

75. Clifford, "Diasporas."

76. Gilroy, *The Black Atlantic*; Stephens, *Black Empire*; Brown, *Dropping Anchor*; Campt and Thomas, "Gendering Diaspora."

77. McKittrick, *Demonic Grounds*, xxiv.

Chapter Five

1. There are two articles written by African American travelers to Brazil that refer to the country as a giant. The first is an article published in *Ebony* magazine in February 1997 and titled: "Brazil: The Awakening Giant," and which has no author listed. The second is an article published in 2007 by a longtime African American tour agent, titled: "Brazil, The Sleeping Giant: Land of Heritage, History, Hospitality and Hope."

2. PT's terms in the state of Bahia governor's office include: Jacques Wagner (2007–2010; 2011–2014), and Rui Costa (2015–2018).

3. Pinho, "African-American Roots Tourism in Brazil."

4. "Bahia: Jaques e Marta assinam convênios em Cachoeira."

5. These funds were part of the PRODETUR/NE II (Programa de Desenvolvimento to Turismo no Nordeste). "Bahia: Jaques e Marta assinam convênios em Cachoeira."

6. Liderança do PT, "Governo e Ministério assinam convênio para intensificar turismo étnico afro."

7. Mohammed, "Rice Dances in Brazil's Historic Slave Port of Salvador"; Flaherty, "Rice Plays Tourist on Trip to Brazil"; Pacheco, "Condoleezza cai no samba."

8. "Secretária de estado americana se empolga com o Centro Histórico."

9. U.S. Department of State, "Remarks with President of Neoenergia Marcelo Correa and Governor of da Bahia Jacques Wagner."

10. For more on the critique of *baianidade*, see Araújo Pinho, "A Bahia no Fundamental"; Pinho, *Mama Africa*; Romo, *Brazil's Living Museum*; among others.

11. For insightful analyses of the restoration of Pelourinho, see Araújo Pinho, "A Bahia no Fundamental," and Collins, *Revolt of the Saints*.

12. This split was established via the State Law # 10.549.

13. Siquini, *Bahia Life*, 10.

14. Definition of ethnic tourism according to MTUR, cited in Brasil, Ministério do Turismo, *Segmentação do Turismo*, 17–18.

15. Siquini, *Bahia Life*; Bahia, Secretaria de Turismo, *African Heritage Tourism in Bahia*; and *Estratégia Turística da Bahia*.

16. Câmara dos Deputados, Bahia 2008.

17. Bahia, Secretaria de Turismo, *African Heritage Tourism in Bahia*, 119.

18. Bahia, Secretaria de Turismo, *Estratégia Turística da Bahia*, 53.

19. Siquini, *Bahia Life*, 38.

20. Interview, Salvador, August 2011.

21. Bahia, Secretaria de Turismo, *African Heritage Tourism in Bahia*, 4.

22. Bahia, Secretaria de Turismo, preface by Governor Jacques Wagner, n.p.

23. Bahia, Secretaria de Turismo, 21.

24. SECOM, Bahia, "Turismo Étnico Afro."

25. In Portuguese, "Coordenação Especial de Promoção da Igualdade Racial."

26. "São Paulo segue exemplo do Turismo Étnico baiano," http://bahia.com.br /noticias/sao-paulo-segue-exemplo-do-turismo-etnico-baiano/.

27. Bahia, Secretaria de Turismo, *African Heritage Tourism in Bahia*.

28. Ministry of Tourism/WTO/UNDP 1996, 78, cited in Timothy and Teye, "American Children of the African Diaspora," 116.

29. Pierre, *The Predicament of Blackness*, 131.

30. Basu, *Highland Homecomings*, 2.

31. See Karam, *Another Arabesque*, especially chapter 6, "Air Turbulence in Homeland Tourism."

32. Cohen, "Preparation, Simulation and the Creation of Community," 128.

33. Boxer and Saxe, "The Birthright Israel Generation," 289. For a detailed discussion of Birthright Israel, see Kelner, *Tours That Bind*.

34. Hannam, "India and the Ambivalences of Diaspora Tourism."

35. Hannam, 246.

36. Jenkins 1975, 151, cited in Holsey, *Routes of Remembrance*, 154.

37. For a critique of the idea of African Americans as the "lucky" progeny of enslaved Africans, see Hartman, *Lose Your Mother*, and Pierre, *The Predicament of Blackness*.

38. Morgan and Pritchard, "Mae'n Bryd I ddod Adref," 238.

39. Coles, "Diaspora, Cultural Capital and the Production of Tourism."

40. Coles, 228.

41. Bahia, Secretaria de Turismo, *African Heritage Tourism in Bahia*, 19.

42. Interview, Salvador, August 2013.

43. Carvalho e Avila, "O Turismo Étnico e seus Reflexos," 70.

44. Statements made during presentation of my research in Salvador, August 2013.

45. Bahia, Secretaria de Turismo, *African Heritage Tourism in Bahia*, 107.

46. Interview, Salvador, August 2013, my emphasis.

47. Interview, Salvador, August 2013, my emphasis.

48. Santos, *O Poder da Cultura*, 89.

49. Santos.

50. Dunn, *Contracultura*, 134.

51. The letter from the editors reads: "The magazine *Viver Bahia* is back. It resumes its purpose of publishing, disseminating, prizing and helping to preserve the historical, tourist, artistic, cultural and environmental heritage of Bahia." *Viver Bahia*, "Carta dos Editores."

52. According to Marcelino in "Análise do processo tradutório," *Viver Bahia* is distributed for free in Bahia (in hotels, international events, etc.) as well as abroad, where Bahiatursa makes the magazine available in Brazilian embassies and consulates in the United States and European countries.

53. "Herança Viva da Escravidão," *Viver Bahia*.

54. "O Pai do Prazer, Filho da Dor," *Viver Bahia*.

55. "Salvador Cidade da Bahia," *Viver Bahia*.

56. "Rainhas Negras nas Ruas de Cachoeira," *Viver Bahia*.

57. Postcard/flyer produced by Your World Consultant Group, 2006.

58. See Cicalo, "From Public Amnesia to Public Memory," for an analysis of the process of memorialization of slavery revolving around the Valongo Wharf.

59. Commenting on the dissociation between the public celebration of Brazil's African roots from references to the country's significant involvement in the Atlantic slave trade, historian Ana Lucia Araujo describes as evidence of this erasure the scarcity of monuments, memorials, or museums that represent Brazil's slave past. Araujo, *Public Memory of Slavery*.

60. Meade and Pirio, "In Search of the Afro-American 'Eldorado,'" 98.

61. Meade and Pirio, 102.

62. Lesser, "Are African-Americans African or American?"

63. Informação para o senhor presidente da república, "Festival de Arte e Cultura Afro-Americana no Brasil," June 19, 1978, CPDOC/FGV, Arquivo Geisel, pasta: 1975/EG pr 1974.03.00/2.

64. Historian Jerry Dávila briefly discusses the polemic that the festival generated among the federal government when Embratur, viewing this as an opportunity to attract black American tourists, sought the support of Brazil's Ministry of Foreign Relations, which viewed the idea of an "African diaspora" a threat to Brazil's ideology of racial integration (*Hotel Trópico*, 249).

65. Bourdieu, *Acts of Resistance*; Wacquant, *Punishing the Poor*.

Epilogue

1. UOL, "Crise pode levar 3,6 milhões de brasileiros de volta à pobreza."

2. Auler, "Temer: Em dez meses."

3. Castro, "A lista de retrocessos."

4. Gumieri, "Um governo de braços dados com o retrocesso."

5. See the fabulous documentary #*Resistência*, directed by Eliza Capai, 2017.

6. Townes, "Black Brazilians and Americans in Rio."

Bibliography

Books, Articles, and Monographs

A Tarde. "Afro-Americanos procuram suas origens na Festa da Boa Morte." August 28, 1994.
———. "Irmandade da Boa Morte visita terreiros da capital." October 8, 1994.
Acosta, Guadalupe. "Yesterday They Killed Me." Telesurtv, March 5, 2016. http://www
.telesurtv.net/english/news/Yesterday-They-Killed-Me-Goes-Viral-20160305-0037.html.
Aitchison, Cara. "Gender and Tourism Discourses: Advancing the Gender Project in
Tourism Studies." In *The Sage Handbook of Tourism Studies*, edited by Tazim Jamal and
Mike Robinson, 631–644. London: Sage, 2009.
Albers, Patricia, and William James. "Travel Photography: A Methodological Approach."
Annals of Tourism Research 15 (1988): 134–158.
Alexander, M. Jacqui. "Imperial Desire/Sexual Utopias: White Gay Capital and
Transnational Tourism." In *Talking Visions: Multicultural Feminism in a Transnational
Age*, edited by Ella Shohat, 281–305. Cambridge: MIT Press, 1998.
Amado, Jorge. "Tomo da Cuia de Esmoler." *Folha de S. Paulo*, January 27, 1995.
Angelou, Maya. *All God's Children Need Traveling Shoes*. New York: Vintage Books, 1991.
Apter, Andrew. *The Pan-African Nation: Oil and the Spectacle of Culture in Nigeria*.
Chicago: University of Chicago Press, 2005.
Araujo, Ana Lucia. *Shadows of the Slave Past: Memory, Heritage, and Slavery*. London:
Routledge, 2014.
———. *Public Memory of Slavery: Victims and Perpetrators in the South Atlantic*. Amherst,
NY: Cambria, 2010.
———. "Welcome the Diaspora: Slave Trade Heritage Tourism and the Public Memory
of Slavery." *Ethnologies* 32, no. 2 (2010): 145–178.
Araújo Pinho, Osmundo de. "A Bahia no Fundamental: Notas para uma Interpretação do
discurso Ideológico de Baianidade." *Revista Brasileira de Ciências Sociais* 13, no. 36
(1998): 109–120.
Arie, India. Interview with Neal Conan. National Public Radio. July 20, 2006. https://
www.npr.org/templates/transcript/transcript.php?storyId=5565789&ft=nprml&f
=5565789.
Arthur, Tori. "Romantic Imaginings: African American Tourists, Transatlantic Double
Consciousness, and Racial Identity in the Journey to Africa." Paper presented at the
conference Roots/Heritage Tourism in Africa and the African Diaspora: Case Studies
for a Comparative Approach, Miami, Florida, February 12–14, 2015.
Ashcroft, Bill, Garreth Griffiths, and Helen Tiffin. *The Empire Writes Back: Theory and
Practice in Post-Colonial Literatures*. London: Routledge, 2002.
Auler, Marcelo. "Temer: Em dez meses, retrocesso de 100 anos!" March 22, 2017. http://
marceloauler.com.br/temer-em-dez-meses-retrocesso-de-100-anos.

Bahia, Secretaria de Turismo. *Estratégia Turística da Bahia: O Terceiro Salto, 2007–2016.* Salvador, Bahia: Secretaria de Turismo, 2011.

———. *African Heritage Tourism in Bahia.* Salvador, Brazil: Fundação Pedro Calmon, 2009.

Babb, Florence. *The Tourism Encounter: Fashioning Latin American Nations and Histories.* Stanford: Stanford University Press, 2010.

Barbosa, Rubens. "Mercado de Grupos Étnicos." *O Globo,* September 14, 2004.

Barker, Chris. *Cultural Studies: Theory and Practice.* London: Sage, 2004.

Basu, Paul. *Highland Homecomings: Genealogy and Heritage Tourism in the Scottish Diaspora.* London: Routledge, 2006.

Belausteguigoitia, Marisa. "Border." In *Dictionary of Latin American Cultural Studies,* edited by Robert MKee and Monica Szurmuk, 38–45. Gainesville: University Press of Florida, 2012.

Berger, Dina, and Andrew Grant Wood. *Holiday in Mexico: Critical Reflections on Tourism and Tourist Encounters.* Durham, NC: Duke University Press, 2010.

Berry, Bertice. *Essence* 34, no. 4 (2003): 114.

Bishop-Sanchez, Kathryn. *Creating Carmen Miranda: Race, Camp, and Transnational Stardom.* Nashville: Vanderbilt University Press, 2016.

Blake, Susan. "A Woman's Trek: What Difference Does Gender Make?" *Women's Studies International Forum* 13, no. 4 (1990): 347–355.

Bourdieu, Pierre. *Acts of Resistance: Against the New Myths of Our Time.* Cambridge: Polity Press, 1998.

Boxer, Matthew, and Leonard Saxe. "The Birthright Israel Generation: Being a Jewish Young Adult in Contemporary America." In *Who Is A Jew?: Reflections on History, Religion, and Culture,* edited by Leonard J. Greenspoon, 285–298. West Lafayette, IN: Purdue University Press, 2015.

Brasil, Ministério do Turismo. *Segmentação do Turismo: Marcos Conceituais.* Brasília: Ministério do Turismo, 2006. Accessed March 16, 2016. http://www.turismo.gov.br/sites/default/turismo/o_ministerio/publicacoes/downloads_publicacoes/Marcos_Conceituais.pdf.

Briggs, Cyril. "Brazil." In *African-American Reflections on Brazil's Racial Paradise,* edited by David J. Hellwig, 37–39. Philadelphia: Temple University Press, [1920] 1992.

Brown, Jacqueline Nassy. *Dropping Anchor, Setting Sail: Geographies of Race in Black Liverpool.* Princeton: Princeton University Press, 2005.

Browning, Barbara. *Infectious Rhythm: Metaphors of Contagion and the Spread of African Culture.* New York: Routledge, 1998.

Bruner, Edward. *Culture on Tour: Ethnographies of Travel.* Chicago: University of Chicago Press, 2005.

———. "Tourism in Ghana. The Representation of Slavery and the Return of the Black Diaspora." *American Anthropologist* 98, no. 2 (1996): 290–304.

———. "Of Cannibals, Tourists, and Ethnographers." *Cultural Anthropology* 4, no. 4 (1989): 438–445.

Burdick, John. *Blessed Anastácia: Women, Race and Popular Christianity in Brazil.* London: Routledge, 1998.

Buzinde, Christine, and Carla Almeida Santos. "Interpreting Slavery Tourism." *Annals of Tourism Research* 36, no. 3 (2009): 439–458.

Calomee, Gloria. "Brazil and the Blacks of South America." In *African-American Reflections on Brazil's Racial Paradise*, edited by David J. Hellwig, 249–252. Philadelphia: Temple University Press, [1986] 1992.

Campos, Walter de Oliveira. "Discriminação racial e imprensa no início dos anos 1950: um retrato da Lei Afonso Arinos em sua concepção e nascimento." *Patrimônio e Memória* 11, no. 1 (2015): 283–304.

Campt, Tina, and Deborah Thomas. "Gendering Diaspora: Transnational Feminism, Diaspora and Its Hegemonies." *Feminist Review* 90 (2008): 1–8.

Cantú, Lionel. "*De Ambiente*: Queer Tourism and the Shifting Boundaries of Mexican Male Sexualities." *GLQ: A Journal of Lesbian and Gay Studies* 8, nos. 1–6 (2002): 141–168.

Capone, Stefania. *Os Yoruba do Novo Mundo. Religião, Etnicidade e Nacionalismo Negro nos Estados Unidos*. Rio de Janeiro: Pallas, 2011.

———. *Searching for Africa in Brazil: Power and Tradition in Candomblé*. Durham, NC: Duke University Press, 2010.

Cartier, Carolyn. "Introduction." In *Seductions of Place: Geographical Perspectives on Globalization and Touristed Landscapes*, edited by Carolyn Cartier and Alan A. Lew, 1–20. London: Routledge, 2005.

Cartier, Carolyn, and Alan Lew, eds. *Seductions of Place: Geographical Perspectives on Globalization and Touristed Landscapes*. London and New York: Routledge, 2005.

Carvalho, Renata Coppieters Oliveira, and Marco Aurélio Avila. "O Turismo Étnico e seus reflexos nos Terreiros de Candomblé Angola em Salvador—Bahia." *Políticas Culturais em Revista* 1, no. 5 (2012): 58–90.

Castro, Armando. *Irmãs de Fé: Tradição e Turismo no Recôncavo Baiano*. Rio de Janeiro: E-Papers, 2006.

Castro, Kika. "A lista de retrocessos do governo de Michel Temer." May 25, 2016. https://kikacastro.com.br/2016/05/25/retrocessos-governo-michel-temer/.

Caton, Kellee, and Carla Almeida Santos. "Closing the Hermeneutic Circle? Photographic Encounters with the Other." *Annals of Tourism Research* 35, no. 1 (2008): 7–26.

Chatfield-Taylor, Joan. "Dance of Life to Honor Death." *New York Times*, 2004, Travel Section, 1, 8, 10.

Christmas, Rachel J. "The African Flavor of Bahia." *Washington Post*, September 11, 1988.

———. "In Harmony with Brazil's African Pulse." *New York Times*, November 20, 1988, xx, 43.

Cicalo, Andre. "From Public Amnesia to Public Memory." In *African Heritage and Memories of Slavery in Brazil and the South Atlantic World*, edited by Ana Lucia Araujo, 179–211. Amherst, NY: Cambria Press, 2015.

Clarke, Kamari M. *Mapping Yoruba Networks: Power and Agency in the Making of Transnational Communities*. Durham, NC: Duke University Press, 2004.

Clifford, James. "Introduction: Partial Truths." In *Writing Culture: The Poetics and Politics of Ethnography*, edited by James Clifford and George E. Marcus, 1–26. Berkeley: University of California Press, 2010.

———. "Diasporas." In *Routes: Travel and Translation in the Late Twentieth Century*, 244–277. Cambridge: Harvard University Press, 1997.

Clifford, James, and George E. Marcus. *Writing Culture: The Poetics and Politics of Ethnography*. Berkeley: University of California Press, 2010.

Cobb, William Jelani. "Blame It on Rio." *Essence* 37, no. 5 (2006): 204, 206–208, 258.

Cohen, Erik. "Preparation, Simulation and the Creation of Community: Exodus and the Case of Diaspora Education Tourism." In *Tourism, Diasporas and Space*, edited by Tim Coles and Dallen J. Timothy, 124–138. London: Routledge, 2004.

———. "A Phenomenology of Tourist Experiences." *Sociology* 13 (1979): 179–201.

———. "Toward a Sociology of International Tourism." *Social Research* 39, no. 1 (1972): 64–82.

Coleman, Simon, and Mike Crang. *Tourism: Between Place and Performance*. New York: Berghahn Books, 2002.

Coles, Tim. "Diaspora, Cultural Capital and the Production of Tourism: Lessons from Enticing Jewish-Americans to Germany." In *Tourism, Diasporas and Space*, edited by Tim Coles and Dallen J. Timothy, 217–232. London: Routledge, 2004.

Coles, Tim, and Dallen J. Timothy. "'My Field Is the World': Conceptualizing Diasporas, Travel and Tourism." In *Tourism, Diasporas and Space*, edited by Tim Coles and Dallen J. Timothy, 1–29. London: Routledge, 2004.

Collins, John. *Revolt of the Saints: Memory and Redemption in the Twilight of Brazilian Racial Democracy*. Durham, NC: Duke University Press, 2015.

Copeland, Sam. "Awaken in Brazil: The Experience Begins in Bahia." *National Association of Black Social Workers Newsletter*, 2006, 6–11.

Correio da Bahia. "Secretária de estado americana se empolga com o Centro Histórico." March 3, 2008. http://www.correiodabahia.com.br/aquisalvador/noticia.asp?codigo =149640.

Crapanzano, Vicent. "Hermes' Dilemma: The Masking of Subversion in Ehtnographic Description." In *Writing Culture: The Poetics and Politics of Ethnography*, edited by James Clifford and George E. Marcus, 51–76. Berkeley: University of California Press, 2010.

Crick, Malcolm. "Representations of International Tourism in the Social Sciences: Sun, Sex, Sights, Savings, and Servility." *Annual Review of Anthropology* 18 (1989): 307–344.

Crouch, David. "The Diverse Dynamics of Cultural Studies and Tourism." In *The Sage Handbook of Tourism Studies*, edited by Tazim Jamal and Mike Robinson, 82–97. London: Sage, 2009.

———. "Flirting with Space: Tourism Geographies as Sensuous/Expressive Practice." In *Seductions of Place: Geographical Perspectives on Globalization and Touristed Landscapes*, edited by Carolyn Cartier and Alan A. Lew, 23–35. London: Routledge, 2005.

———. "Surrounded by Place: Embodied Encounters." In *Tourism: Between Place and Performance*, edited by Simon Coleman and Mike Crang, 207–218. New York: Berghahn Books, 2002.

Dann, Graham. "Limitations in the Use of 'Nationality' and 'Country of Residency' Variables." In *Tourism Research: Critiques and Challenges*, edited by Douglas Pearce and Richard Butler, 88–112. London: Routledge, 1993.

Dávila, Jerry. *Hotel Trópico: Brazil and the Challenge of African Decolonization, 1950–1980*. Durham, NC: Duke University Press, 2010.

Davis, Earl. "Brazil, the Sleeping Giant: Land of Heritage, History, Hospitality and Hope." *Calabar Magazine*, May/June (2007): 18–20.

De la Cadena, Marisol. "Women are More Indian." In *Ethnicity and Gender in a Community Near Cuzco. Ethnicity, Markets, and Migration in the Andes: At the Crossroads of History and Anthropology*, edited by Olivia Harris, Brooke Larson, and Enrique Tandeter, 329–348. Durham, NC: Duke University Press, 1995.

Del Sarto, Ana. "Foundations—Introduction." In *The Latin American Cultural Studies Reader*, edited by Ana Del Sarto, Alicia Ríos, and Abril Trigo, 153–181. Durham, NC: Duke University Press, 2004.

Del Sarto, Ana, Alicia Ríos, and Abril Trigo, eds. *The Latin American Cultural Studies Reader*. Durham, NC: Duke University Press, 2004.

Dunham, Katherine. *Dances of Haiti*. Los Angeles: Center for Afro-American Studies, University of California, 1983.

Dunn, Christopher. *Contracultura: Alternative Arts and Social Transformation in Authoritarian Brazil*. Chapel Hill: University of North Carolina Press, 2017.

Dussel, Enrique. *The Invention of the Americas: Eclipse of "the Other" and the Myth of Modernity*. New York: Continuum, 1995.

Ebony. "The Truth about Brazil." November 1945, 36–37.

———. "Brazil: The Awakening Giant." February 1997, 35–36, 170L–170N.

Ebron, Paulla. *Performing Africa*. Princeton: Princeton University Press, 2002.

Echtner, Charlotte, and Pushkala Prasad. "The Context of Third World Tourism Marketing." *Annals of Tourism Research* 30, no. 3 (2003): 660–682.

Enloe, Cynthia. *Bananas, Beaches and Bases: Making Feminist Sense of International Politics*. 2nd edition. Berkeley: University of California Press, 2014.

Exame. "Professor negro é alvo de seguranças em hotel de São Paulo." Accessed September 21, 2015. http://exame.abril.com.br/brasil/noticias/negro-e-com -dreadlocks-professor-da-universidade-de-columbi/.

Fabian, Johannes. *Time and the Other: How Anthropology Makes Its Object*. New York: Columbia University Press, 2014.

Fairclough, Norman. *Critical Discourse Analysis: The Critical Study of Language*. London: Longman, 1995.

Featherstone, David. *Solidarity: Hidden Histories and Geographies of Internationalism*. London: Zed Books, 2012.

Ferreira, Marcelo Henrique. "E se o Gringo for 'Negão'? Raça, gênero e sexualidade no Rio de Janeiro—A experiência dos turistas 'negros' norteamericanos." MA thesis, Saúde Coletiva, Instituto de Medicina Social da Universidade do Estado do Rio de Janeiro, 2005.

Finley, Cheryl. "The Door of (No) Return." www.common-place.org 1, no. 4 (July 2001).

Fish, Cheryl J. *Black and White Women's Travel Narratives: Antebellum Explorations*. Gainesville: University Press of Florida, 2004.

Flaherty, Anne. "Rice Plays Tourist on Trip to Brazil." *USA Today*, March 14, 2008. http:// usatoday30.usatoday.com/news/washington/2008-03-14-2946966665_x.htm.

Forte, Jung Ran. "Diaspora Homecoming, Vodun Ancestry, and the Ambiguities of Transnational Belongings in the Republic of Benin." In *Global Circuits of Blackness: Interrogating the African Diaspora*, edited by Jean Rahier, Percy Hintzen, and Felipe Smith, 174–200. Champaign: University of Illinois Press, 2010.

Foucault, Michel. *The Order of Things: An Archaeology of the Human Sciences*. New York: Vintage Books, 1994.

———. *Power/Knowledge: Selected Interviews and Other Writings, 1972–1977*. New York: Pantheon Books, 1980.

Frazier, E. Franklin. "The Negro Family in Bahia, Brazil." *American Sociological Review* 4, no. 7 (1942): 465–478.

Freelon, Kiratiana. *Kiratiana's Travel Guide to Black Paris: Get Lost and Get Found.* Chicago: Eunique, 2010.

Freire-Medeiros, Bianca. *Touring Poverty.* London: Routledge, 2014.

———. *Gringo na Laje: Produção, Circulação e Consumo da Favela Turística.* Rio de Janeiro: Editora FGV, 2009.

García Canclini, Néstor. *Consumers and Citizens: Globalization and Multicultural Conflicts.* Minneapolis: University of Minnesota Press, 2001.

Geertz, Clifford. *The Interpretation of Cultures: Selected Essays.* New York: Basic Books, 1973.

Gill, Tiffany. "Africa Must Be Seen to be Believed: African Americans and the Roots of Heritage Tourism in the Age of Decolonization." Oral presentation delivered at the conference Roots/Heritage Tourism in Africa and the African Diaspora: Case Studies for a Comparative Approach, Miami, February 2015.

———. *Beauty Shop Politics: African American Women's Activism in the Beauty Industry.* Urbana: University of Illinois Press, 2010.

Gilliam, Angela. "From Roxbury to Rio-and Back in a Hurry." In *African-American Reflections on Brazil's Racial Paradise,* edited by David J. Hellwig, 173–181. Philadelphia: Temple University Press, [1970] 1992.

Gilmore, Ruth Wilson. *Golden Gulag: Prisons, Surplus, Crisis, and Opposition in Globalizing California.* Berkeley: University of California Press, 2007.

Gilroy, Paul. "British Cultural Studies and the Pitfalls of Identity." In *Cultural Studies and Communications,* edited by James Curran, David Morley, and Valerie Walderdine, 35–49. London: Arnold, 1996.

———. *The Black Atlantic: Modernity and Double Consciousness.* Cambridge, MA: Harvard University Press, 1993.

Goldberg, David Theo. *The Racial State.* Malden, MA: Blackwell, 2001.

Gómez-Barris, Macarena, and Herman Gray, eds. *Toward a Sociology of the Trace.* Minneapolis: University of Minnesota Press, 2010.

Gordon, Edmund T. *Disparate Diasporas: Identity and Politics in an African-Nicaraguan Community.* Austin: University of Texas Press, 1998.

Graburn, Nelson. "The Ethnographic Tourist." In *The Tourist as Metaphor of the Social World,* edited by Graham Dann, 19–39. Wallingford, UK: CABI, 2002.

———. "Tourism: The Sacred Journey." In *Hosts and Guests: The Anthropology of Tourism,* edited by Valene Smith, 2nd ed., 21–36. Philadelphia: University of Pennsylvania Press, 1989.

Gumieri, Sinara. "Um governo de braços dados com o retrocesso." May 17 2016. http://justificando.cartacapital.com.br/2016/05/17/um-governo-de-bracos-dados-com-o-retrocesso/.

Gupta, Akhil, and James Ferguson. "Beyond 'Culture': Space, Identity, and the Politics of Difference." *Cultural Anthropology* 7, no. 1 (1992): 6–23.

Guridy, Andre Frank. *Forging Diaspora: Afro-Cubans and African-Americans in a World of Empire and Jim Crow.* Chapel Hill: University of North Carolina Press, 2010.

Hackforth-Jones, Jocelyn. *Augustus Earle: Travel Artist: Paintings and Drawings in the Rex Nan Kivell Collection, National Library of Australia.* London: Scholar Press, 1980.

Haggins, Jon. *The African-American Travel Guide: To Hot, Exotic, and Fun-Filled Places.* New York: Amber Communications Group, 2002.

Haley, Alex. *Roots: The Saga of an American Family.* Garden City, NY: Doubleday, 1976.

Hall, C. Michael, and Hazel Tucker, eds. *Tourism and Postcolonialism: Contested Discourses, Identities and Representation.* London: Routledge, 2004.

Hall, Stuart. "Encoding, Decoding." In *The Cultural Studies Reader,* edited by Simon During, 3rd ed., 477–487. London: Routledge, 2007.

———. *Representation: Cultural Representations and Signifying Practices.* London: Sage, 1997.

———. "New Cultures for Old." In *A Place in the World? Places, Cultures, and Globalization,* edited by Doreen Massey and Pat Jess, 175–213. Oxford: Oxford University Press, 1995.

Hannam, Kevin. "India and the Ambivalences of Diaspora Tourism." In *Tourism, Diasporas and Space,* edited by Tim Coles and Dallen J. Timothy, 246–260. London: Routledge, 2004.

Harris, Gail. *A Woman's War: The Professional and Personal Journey of the Navy's First African American Female Intelligence Officer.* Lanham, MD: Scarecrow Press.

Harris, Jessica. *Tasting Brazil. Regional Recipes and Reminiscences.* New York: Macmillan, 1992.

Harris, Ron. "U.S. Blacks Seek a Part of Their History in Brazil." *Los Angeles Times,* September 5, 1994.

Harris, Thomas Allen. Interview by Wilson Morales for blackfilm.com. Accessed June 10, 2014. http://www.blackfilm.com/20030523/features/thomasallenharris.shtml.

Hart, Carl. Interview with Carl Hart. Accessed September 21, 2015. http://justificando .com/2015/08/28/carl-hart-e-barrado-na-portaria-de-hotel-cinco-estrelas-onde-ocorre -seminario-criminal-/.

———. "O Viral e o Crônico." *Folha de S. Paulo.* September 9, 2015.

Hartman, Saidiya. *Lose Your Mother: A Journey Along the Atlantic Slave Route.* New York: Farrar, Straus and Giroux, 2007.

Hasan, Uzair. "Let's Face the Truth: India IS Unsafe for Women." *Huffington Post,* April 22, 2015. http://www.huffingtonpost.in/uzair-hasan-rizvi/women-insecurity-plagues-_b _6953956.html.

Hellwig, David, ed. *African American Reflections on Brazil's Racial Paradise.* Philadelphia: Temple University Press, 1992.

Hernandez-Reguant, Ariana. "Kwanzaa and the U.S. Ethnic Mosaic." In *Representations of Blackness and the Performance of Identities,* edited by Jean Muteba Rahier, 101–122. Westport, CT: Bergin & Garvey, 1999.

Herskovits, Melville. *The New World Negro: Selected Papers in Afroamerican Studies.* Bloomington: Indiana University Press, 1966.

Hiller, H. L. "Tourism: Development or Dependence?" In *The Restless Caribbean: Changing Patterns of International Relations,* edited by R. Miller and W. M. Will, 51–61. New York: Praeger, 1979.

Hofling, Ana Paula. "Staging Capoeira, Samba, Maculelê and Candomblé." In *Performing Brazil: Essays on Culture, Identity, and the Performing Arts,* edited by Severino Albuquerque and Kathryn Bishop-Sanchez, 98–125. Madison: University of Wisconsin Press, 2015.

Hollinshead, Keith. "Worldmaking and the Transformation of Place and Culture: The Enlargement of Meethan's Analysis of Tourism and Global Change." In *The Critical Turn in Tourism Studies,* edited by Irena Ateljevic, Nigel Morgan, and Annette Pritchard, 165–196. Oxford: Elsevier, 2007.

———. "Tourism, Hybridity, and Ambiguity: The Relevance of Bhabha's 'Third Space' Cultures." *Journal of Leisure Research* 30, no. 1 (1998):121–156.

Holsey, Bayo. *Routes of Remembrance: Refashioning the Slave Trade in Ghana*. Chicago: University of Chicago Press, 2008.

Hughes, Langston. *I Wonder as I Wander: An Autobiographical Journey*. New York: Hill and Wang, 1993.

Hurston, Zora Neale. *Tell My Horse: Voodoo and Life in Haiti and Jamaica*. New York: Harper & Row, 1990.

Ickes, Scott. *African Brazilian Culture and Regional Identity in Bahia, Brazil*. Gainesville: University Press of Florida, 2015.

International Women's Travel Center. "Brazil." April 6, 2016. http://www .internationalwomenstravelcenter.com/brazil/.

Ioannides, Dimitri, and Mara Cohen Ioannides. "Jewish Past as a 'Foreign Country': The Travel Experiences of American Jews." In *Tourism, Diasporas and Space*, edited by Tim Coles and Dallen J. Timothy, 95–110. London; New York: Routledge, 2004.

———. "Pilgrimages of Nostalgia: Patterns of Jewish Travel in the United States." *Tourism Recreation Research* 27, no. 2 (2002): 17–25.

Jacobson, Michael Frye. *Roots Too: White Ethnic Revival in Post-Civil Rights America*. Cambridge: Harvard University Press, 2008.

Jamal, Tazim, and Mike Robinson. *The Sage Handbook of Tourism Studies*. London: Sage, 2009.

Jaworski, Adam, and Annette Pritchard. "Introduction." In *Discourse, Communication and Tourism*, edited by Adam Jaworski and Annette Pritchard, 1–16. Clevedon, UK: Channel View, 2005.

Johnson, Pamela. "Brazil: The Way We Were." *Essence* 32, no. 2 (2001): 160, 162, 164, 193.

Jordan, June. *Some of Us Did Not Die: New and Selected Essays of June Jordan*. New York: Basic Civitas Books, 2003.

Julius, Flávia. *Os Destinos das Comissárias de Voo: Guia com 50 Viagens Só para Mulheres*. Gettysburg, PA: Panda Books, 2015.

Kaplan, Caren. *Questions of Travel: Postmodern Discourses of Displacement*. Durham, NC: Duke University Press, 1996.

———. "The Politics of Location and Transnational Feminist Practice." In *Scattered Hegemonies: Postmodernity and Transnational Feminist Practices*, edited by Inderpal Grewal and Caren Kaplan, 137–152. Minneapolis: University of Minnesota Press, 1994.

Karam, John Tofik. "The Politics of Anti-Zionism and Racial Democracy in Homeland Tourism." In *The Middle East and Brazil: Perspectives on the New Global South*, edited by Paul Amar, 215–227. Bloomington: Indiana University Press, 2014.

———. *Another Arabesque. Syrian-Lebanese Ethnicity in Neoliberal Brazil*. Philadelphia: Temple University Press, 2007.

Kehr, Dave. "Film in Review: 'É Minha Cara/That's My Face.'" *New York Times*, May 23, 2003.

Kelley, Robin D. G. "Introduction." In *A History of Pan-African Revolt*, edited by C. L. R. James, 1–33. Oakland, CA: P.M. Press, 2012.

Kelner, Shaul. *Tours That Bind: Diaspora, Pilgrimage, and Israeli Birthright Tourism*. New York: New York University Press, 2010.

Kempadoo, Kamala. *Sexing the Caribbean: Gender, Race, and Sexual Labor*. New York: Routledge, 2004.

Kincaid, Jamaica. *A Small Place*. New York: Farrar, Straus and Giroux, 2000.

Kinnaird, Vivian, and Derek Hall, eds. *Tourism: A Gender Analysis*. London: Belhaven Press, 1994.

Leite, Naomi. "Travels to an Ancestral Past: On Diasporic Tourism, Embodied Memory, and Identity." *Antropológicas* 9 (2005): 273–302.

Leite, Naomi, and Nelson Graburn. "Anthropological Interventions in Tourism Studies." In *The Sage Handbook of Tourism Studies*, edited by Tazim Jamal and Mike Robinson, 35–64. London: Sage, 2009.

Lelo, Linda, and Tazim Jamal. "African Americans at Sites of Darkness: Roots—Seeking, Diasporic Identities and Place Making." In *Dark Tourism and Place Identity: Managing and Interpreting Dark Places*, edited by Leanne White and Elspeth Frew, 28–45. London: Routledge, 2013.

Leonelli, Domingos. "Preface." *African Heritage Tourism in Bahia*. Salvador, Brazil: Fundação Pedro Calmon, 2009. https://issuu.com/setur/docs/namef345c4/27?e=0.

Lesser, Jeffrey. "Are African-Americans African or American? Brazilian Immigration Policy in the 1920s." *Review of Latin American Studies* 4, no. 1 (1991): 115–137.

Lew, Alan A., and Alan Wong. "Existential Tourism and the Homeland: The Overseas Chinese Experience." In *Seductions of Place: Geographical Perspectives on Globalization and Touristed Landscapes*, edited by Carolyn Cartier and Alan A. Lew, 286–300. London: Routledge, 2005.

Lew, Alan A., and Alan Wong. "Sojourners, Guanxi and Clan Associations: Social Capital and Overseas Chinese Tourism to China." In *Tourism, Diasporas and Space*, edited by Tim Coles and Dallen J. Timothy, 202–214. London: Routledge, 2004.

Liderança do PT. "Governo e Ministério assinam convênio para intensificar turismo étnico afro." August 8, 2007. http://liderancadoptbahia.com.br/novo/noticias.php?id_noticia=7576.

Little, Walter. *Mayas in the Marketplace: Tourism, Globalization, and Cultural Identity*. Austin: University of Texas Press, 2004.

MacCannell, Dean. *Empty Meeting Grounds: The Tourist Papers*. London: Routledge, 1992.

———. *The Tourist: A New Theory of the Leisure Class*. New York: Schocken Books, 1989.

Mahrouse, Gada. *Conflicted Commitments: Race, Privilege, and Power in Solidarity Activism*. Montreal: McGill-Queen's University Press, 2014.

Mandala Research, LLC. *The African American Traveler*. Alexandria, VA: Author, 2011.

Mann-Hamilton, Ryan. "What Rises from the Ashes: Nation and Race in the African American Wnclave of Samaná." In *Migrant Marginality: A Transnational Perspective*, edited by Philip Kretsedemas, Jorge Capetillo-Ponce, and Glenn Jacobs, 222–238. London: Routledge, 2013.

Marcelino, Jacqueline Laranja Leal. "Análise do processo tradutório sob a perspectiva Discursiva: Reportagens turísticas bílingues da Revista Viver Bahia." *Anais do SILEL* 2, no. 2 (2011): 1–15.

Marshall, Paule. *Praisesong for the Widow*. New York: Dutton, 1984.

Massey, Doreen. "The Conceptualization of Place." In *A Place in the World? Places, Cultures, and Globalization*, edited by Doreen Massey and Pat Jess, 45–85. Oxford: Oxford University Press, 2002.

———. *Space, Place and Gender*. Cambridge: Polity Press, 1994.

Matory, James Lorand. *Black Atlantic Religion: Tradition, Transnationalism, and Matriarchy in the Afro-Brazilian Candomblé*. Princeton: Princeton University Press, 2005.

McDowell, Akkida. "The 360°." *Essence* 43, no. 12 (2013): 10.

McKittrick, Katherine. *Demonic Grounds: Black Women and the Cartographies of Struggle*. Minneapolis: University of Minnesota Press, 2006.

Meade, Teresa, and Gregory Alonso Pirio. "In Search of the Afro-American 'Eldorado': Attempts by North American Blacks to Enter Brazil in the 1920s." *Luso-Brazilian Review* 25, no. 1 (1988): 85–110.

Meethan, Kevin. "'To Stand in the Shoes of My Ancestors': Tourism and Genealogy." In *Tourism, Diasporas and Space*, edited by Tim Coles and Dallen J. Timothy, 139–150. London: Routledge, 2004.

Merrill, Dennis. *Negotiating Paradise: U. S. Tourism and Empire in Twentieth-Century Latin America*. Chapel Hill: University of North Carolina Press, 2009.

Mignolo, Walter D. *The Idea of Latin America*. Malden, MA: Blackwell, 2005.

Mitchell, Gregory. *Tourist Attractions: Performing Race and Masculinity in Brazil's Sexual Economy*. Chicago: University of Chicago Press, 2016.

———. "TurboConsumers™ in Paradise: Tourism, Civil Rights, and Brazil's Gay Sex Industry." *American Ethnologist* 38, no. 4 (2011): 666–682.

Mintz, Sidney, and Richard Price. *The Birth of African-American Culture: An Anthropological Perspective*. Boston: Beacon Press, 1992.

Mohammed, Arshad. "Rice Dances in Brazil's Historic Slave Port of Salvador." Reuters, March 14, 2008. http://www.reuters.com/article/us-brazil-rice -idUSN1335307820080314.

Morgan, Nigel, and Annette Pritchard. "Mae'n Bryd I ddod Adref—It's Time to Come Home: Exploring the Contested Emotional Geographies of Wales." In *Tourism, Diasporas and Space*, edited by Tim Coles and Dallen J. Timothy, 233–245. London: Routledge, 2004.

Mottiar, Ziene, and Deirdre Quinn. "Couple Dynamics in Household Tourism Decision Making: Women as the Gatekeepers?" *Journal of Vacation Marketing* 10, no. 2 (2004): 149–160.

Murphy, Keith, and Terrance Dean. "Fool's Paradise." *Essence* 40(10) (2010): 131–135, 158.

Nascimento, Abdias do. "Katherine Dunham and Us." *Kaiso! Writings by and about Katherine Dunham*, edited by Veve A. Clark and Sara E. Johnson, 317–319. Madison: University of Wisconsin Press, 2005.

Nascimento, Abdias do, and Elisa Larkin Nascimento. "Reflexões sobre o Movimento Negro no Brasil, 1938–1997." In *Tirando a Máscara: Ensaios sobre o Racismo no Brasil*, edited by Antonio Sergio Alfredo Guimarães and Lynn Huntley, 203–235. São Paulo: Paz e Terra, 2000.

———. *Africans in Brazil: A Pan-African Perspective*. Trenton, NJ: Africa World Press, 1992.

Nash, Dennison. "Tourism as a Form of Imperialism." In *Hosts and Guests: The Anthropology of Tourism*, edited by Valene Smith, 2nd ed., 37–52. Philadelphia: University of Pennsylvania Press, 1989.

Nelson, Alondra. *The Social Life of DNA*. Boston: Beacon Press, 2016.

Nelson, Diane. *A Finger in the Wound: Body Politics in Quincentennial Guatemala*. Berkeley: University of California Press, 1999.

New Oxford American Dictionary. Online edition, edited by Angus Stevenson and Christine A. Lindberg. Oxford: Oxford University Press, 2011. http://www .oxfordreference.com/search?source=%2F10.1093%2Facref%2F9780195392883.001 .0001%2Facref-9780195392883&q= detour.

Nixon, Angelique. *Resisting Paradise: Tourism, Diaspora, and Sexuality in Caribbean Culture*. Jackson: University Press of Mississippi, 2015.

Obama, Barack. *Dreams from My Father: A Story of Race and Inheritance*. New York: Crown, 2004.

Osagie, Iyunolu, and Christine Buzindie. "Culture and Postcolonial Resistance: Antigua in Kincaid's *A Small Place*." *Annals of Tourism Research* 38, no. 1 (2011): 210–230.

Pacheco, Lenilde. "Condoleezza cai no samba." *A Tarde*, March 14, 2008. http://atarde.uol .com.br/bahia/salvador/noticias/1253020-condoleezza-cai-no-samba.

Pearce, Douglas. *Tourist Development*. London: Longman. 1989.

Pereira, Amilcar Araujo. "'O Mundo Negro': A Constituição do Movimento Negro Contemporâneo no Brasil (1970–1995)." PhD diss., Universidade Federal Fluminense, Instituto de Ciências Humanas e Filosofia, 2010.

Peterson, Audrey. "Where Africa also Lives." In *American Legacy: The Magazine of African-American History and Culture*, 66–84. New York: Forbes Magazine Group, 2006.

Philipp, Steven. "Race and Tourism Choice: A Legacy of Discrimination?" *Annals of Tourism Research* 21, no. 3 (1994): 479–488.

Pierre, Jemima. *The Predicament of Blackness: Postcolonial Ghana and the Politics of Race*. Chicago: University of Chicago Press, 2013.

Pinho, Patricia de Santana. "Bahia Is a Closer Africa." In *African Heritage and Memories of Slavery in Brazil and the South Atlantic World*, edited by Ana Lucia Araujo, 253–284. Amherst, NY: Cambria Press, 2015.

———. "Nurturing Bantu Africanness in Brazil." In *Comparative Perspectives on Afro-Latin America*, edited by Kwame Dixon and John Burdick, 21–41. Gainesville: University Press of Florida, 2012.

———. *Mama Africa: Reinventing Blackness in Bahia*. Durham, NC: Duke University Press, 2010.

———. "African-American Roots Tourism in Brazil." *Latin American Perspectives* 35, no. 3 (May 2008): 70–86.

———. "Decentering the United States in the Studies of Blackness in Brazil." *Revista Brasileira de Ciências Sociais* [online], vol. 2, Special Edition, 2006.

———. "Viajando a la tierra de *Ashé*: Turismo Etnico Afro-Americano na Bahia, Brasil." *Revista del Caribe* 41 (2003): 76–82.

———. "Comment Trouver l'Afrique à Bahia en suivant les ethno-touristes Afro-Americains." *Cahiers du Brésil Contemporain* (2002): 49–50.

Política Real. "Bahia: Jaques e Marta assinam convênios em Cachoeira." August 15, 2007. http://www.politicareal.com.br/noticias/nordestinas/3508/bahia-jaques-e-marta -assinam-convenios-em-cachoeira-.

Powers, Jillian L. "Reimaging the Imagined Community: Homeland Tourism and the Role of Place." *American Behavioral Scientist* 55, no. 10 (2011): 1362–1378.

Pratt, Mary Louise. *Imperial Eyes: Travel Writing and Transculturation*. London: Routledge, 1992.

Puar, Jasbir K. "Circuits of Queer Mobility: Tourism, Travel, and Globalization." *GLQ: A Journal of Lesbian and Gay Studies* 8, nos. 1–2 (2002): 101–137.

Queiroz, Lúcia Aquino de. *Turismo na Bahia: Estratégias para o desenvolvimento*. Salvador: Secretaria da Cultura e Turismo, 2002.

Quijano, Aníbal. "Coloniality of Power, Eurocentrism, and Latin America." *Nepantla: Views from the South* 1, no. 3 (2000): 533–579.

Quilombo. "Prossegue a Cruzada para a Segunda Abolição." 2, no. 10 (1950): 8–9.

Rahier, Jean Muteba. "Roots/Heritage Tourism in Juffureh and Kunta Kinteh Island, the Gambia: Experiences of U.S.-Based Study Abroad Students." Paper presented at the conference Roots/Heritage Tourism in Africa and the African Diaspora: Case Studies for a Comparative Approach, Miami, Florida, February 12–4, 2015.

Raiford, Leigh. "The Here and Now of Eslanda Robeson's *African Journey.*" In *Migrating the Black Body: The African Diaspora and Visual Culture*, edited by Leigh Raiford and Heike Raphael-Hernandez, 134–152. Seattle: University of Washington Press, 2017.

Raiford, Leigh, and Heike Raphael-Hernandez. *Migrating the Black Body: The African Diaspora and Visual Culture*. Seattle: University of Washington Press, 2017.

Randle, Wilma Jean Emanuel. "Senegal: Goree and Beyond." *Savoy*, June/July 2005: 82–90.

Redação iBahia. "Professor americano negro é barrado em hotel onde iria ministrar palestra." Accessed September 21, 2015. http://www.ibahia.com/detalhe/noticia/ professor-americano-negro-e-barrado-em-hotel-onde-iria-ministrar-palestra/?cHash= 58685e6eb1a8e3e32af1cb686fb7c632.

Reed, Ann. *Pilgrimage Tourism of Diaspora Africans to Ghana*. New York: Routledge, 2015.

Reis, Luis Felipe. "A falta de negros na mídia o deixou inquieto: A sociedade brasileira segundo Spike Lee." Accessed May 21, 2012. http://mamapress.wordpress.com/2012/05/ 02/a-falta-de-negros-na-midia-o-deixou-inquieto-a-sociedade-brasileira-segundo -spike-lee/.

Renda, Mary A. *Taking Haiti: Military Occupation & the Culture of U.S. Imperialism*. Chapel Hill: University of North Carolina Press, 2001.

Rice, Condoleezza. *No Higher Honor: A Memoir of My Years in Washington*. New York: Crown, 2011.

Rich, Adrienne. *Blood, Bread, and Poetry: Selected Prose, 1979–1985*. New York: W. W. Norton, 1986.

Robben Island Museum. "Robber Island Tours and Times." Accessed January 12, 2016. http://www.robben-island.org.za/tours#tourtypes.

Rohter, Larry. "Cultural Exchange and Controversy in Rio." *Washington Post*, August 21, 1978.

Romo, Anadelia. *Brazil's Living Museum: Race, Reform, and Tradition in Bahia*. Chapel Hill: University of North Carolina Press, 2010.

Rose, Gillian. "Place and Identity: A Sense of Place." In *A Place in the World? Places, Cultures, and Globalization*, edited by Doreen Massey and Pat Jess, 87–132. Oxford: Oxford University Press. 1995.

Rosenthal, Carolyn. "Kinkeeping in the Familial Division of Labor." *Journal of Marriage and the Family* 47 (1985): 965–974.

Said, Edward. *Orientalism*. New York: Vintage Books, 1994.

Santos, Jocelio Telles dos. *O Poder da Cultura e a Cultura no Poder. A Disputa Simbólica da Herança Cultural Negra no Brasil*. Salvador: Edufba, 2005.

Schenck, Marcia, and Mariana P. Candido. "Uncomfortable Pasts." In *African Heritage and Memories of Slavery in Brazil and the South Atlantic World,* edited by Ana Lucia Araujo, 213–252. Amherst, NY: Cambria Press, 2015.

Schramm, Katharina. "Coming Home to the Motherland. Pilgrimage Tourism in Ghana." In *Reframing Pilgrimage: Cultures in Motion,* edited by Simon Coleman and John Eade, 133–149. London: Routledge, 2004.

Seigel, Micol. *Uneven Encounters: Making Race and Nation in Brazil and the United States.* Durham, NC: Duke University Press, 2009.

Selka, Stephen. "Cityscapes and Contact Zones: Christianity, Candomblé, and African Heritage Tourism in Brazil." *Religion* 43, no. 3 (2013): 403–420.

Selwyn, Tom. "Introduction." In *The Tourist Image. Myths and Myth Making in Tourism,* edited by Tom Selwyn, 1–32. West Sussex: Wiley, 1996.

SENAC. Accessed January 24, 2016. https://www.sp.senac.br/jsp/default.jsp?newsID=a13164.htm&testeira=1063.

Sharpley-Whiting, T. Denean. *Pimps Up, Ho's Down: Hip Hop's Hold on Young Black Women.* New York: New York University Press, 2008.

Sheller, Mimi. "Teorizações indisciplinadas: (i)mobilidade como metáfora, conceito e método—Entrevista com Mimi Sheller realizada por Patricia de Santana Pinho and Bianca Freire-Medeiros." *PLURAL, Revista do Programa de Pós-Graduação em Sociologia da USP* 23, no. 2 (2016): 118–125.

Simmons, Beverley Ann. "Saying the Same Old Things: A Contemporary Travel Discourse and the Popular Magazine Text." In *Tourism and Postcolonialism: Contested Discourses, Identities and Representation,* edited by C. Michael Hall and Hazel Tucker, 43–56. London: Routledge, 2004.

Simmons, Kimberly. *Reconstructing Racial Identity and the African Past in the Dominican Republic.* Gainesville: University Press of Florida, 2009.

Siquini, Claudemir. *Bahia Life: State of Bahia Guide Golden Book.* Nova Iguaçu, RJ: Editora Siquini, 2008.

Smith, Valene. "Women: The Tastemakers in Tourism." *Annals of Tourism Research* 6 (1979): 49–60.

Stam, Robert. *Tropical Multiculturalism: A Comparative History of Race in Brazilian Cinema and Culture.* Durham, NC: Duke University Press, 1997.

Stam, Robert, and Ella Shohat. *Race in Translation: Culture Wars around the Postcolonial Atlantic.* New York: New York University Press, 2012.

Stephens, Michelle. *Black Empire: The Masculine Global Imaginary of Caribbean Intellectuals in the United States, 1914–1962.* Durham, NC: Duke University Press, 2005.

Stephenson, Marcus L. "Tourism, Racism and the UK Afro-Caribbean Diaspora." In *Tourism, Diasporas and Space,* edited by Tim Coles and Dallen J. Timothy, 62–77. London: Routledge, 2004.

———. "Travelling to the Ancestral Homelands: The Aspirations and Experiences of a UK Caribbean Community." *Current Issues in Tourism* 5, no. 5 (2002): 378–425.

Stewart, Ollie. "The Color Line in South America's Largest Republic." In *African-American Reflections on Brazil's Racial Paradise,* edited by David J. Hellwig, 91–108. Philadelphia: Temple University Press, [1940] 1992.

Stinson, L. H. "South America and Its Prospects in 1920." In *African-American Reflections on Brazil's Racial Paradise*, edited by David J. Hellwig, 44–46. Philadelphia: Temple University Press, [1920] 1992.

Strickland-Abuwi, Lula. "Bahia." *Essence* 22, no. 12 (1992): 89–90.

Sundiata, Ibrahim. *Brothers and Strangers: Black Zion, Black Slavery, 1914–1940*. Durham, NC: Duke University Press, 2003.

Sutherland, Peter. "In Memory of the Slaves: An African View of the Diaspora in the Americas." In *Representations of Blackness and the Performance of Identities*, edited by Jean Muteba Rahier, 195–211. Westport, CT: Bergin & Garvey, 1999.

Tate, Mae. "First New World Festival of the African Diaspora: A Cultural Celebration." *Black Art: An International Quartely* 2, no. 4 (1978): 32–37.

Taylor, Mikki. "Beauty Director Mikki Taylor Observes the Girl from Ipanema." *Essence* 32, no. 2 (2011): 46.

Taylor, Mikki, and Pamela Macklin. "Blame It on Rio." *Essence* 32, no. 2 (2001): 42–44.

Taylor, Susan. "The Everyday Sacred." *Essence* 30, no. 5 (1999): 93.

Thayer, Millie. *Making Transnational Feminism: Rural Women, NGO Activists, and Northern Donors in Brazil*. New York: Routledge, 2010.

Thornton, John. *Africa and Africans in the Making of the Atlantic World, 1400–1800*. Cambridge: Cambridge University Press, 1998.

Tillet, Salamishah. *Sites of Slavery: Citizenship and Racial Democracy in the Post-Civil Rights Imagination*. Durham, NC: Duke University Press, 2012.

———. "In the Shadow of the Castle: (Trans)Nationalism, African American Tourism, and Gorée Island." *Research in African Literatures* 40 no. 4 (2009): 122–141.

Timothy, Dallen J. *Cultural Heritage and Tourism: An Introduction*. Bristol: Channel View, 2011.

Timothy, Dallen J., and Tim Coles. "Tourism and Diasporas: Current Issues and Future Opportunities." In *Tourism, Diasporas and Space*, edited by Tim Coles and Dallen J. Timothy, 291–297. London: Routledge, 2004.

Timothy, Dallen J., and Victor B. Teye. "American Children of the African Diaspora: Journeys to the Motherland." In *Tourism, Diasporas, and Space*, edited by Tim Coles and Dallen J. Timothy, 111–123. London: Routledge, 2004.

Townes, Carimah. "Black Brazilians and Americans in Rio Made the Fight for Their Lives a Global One." Accessed June 14, 2017.

https://thinkprogress.org/black-brazilians-and-americans-in-rio-made-the-fight-for-their -lives-a-global-one-bcb61522edee.

Turner, Lorenzo. "The Negro in Brazil." In *African-American Reflections on Brazil's Racial Paradise*, edited by David J. Hellwig, 159–165. Philadelphia: Temple University Press, [1957] 1992.

Turner, Renée D. "Summer Fun across the Land and on the Islands." *Ebony*, May 1990, 134–144.

UNTWO. "Why Tourism?" Accessed July 2, 2013. http://www2.unwto.org/en/content/ why-tourism.

UOL. "Crise pode levar 3,6 milhões de brasileiros de volta à pobreza, diz estudo." February 2, 2017. https://economia.uol.com.br/noticias/redacao/2017/02/13/crise -pode-levar-36-milhoes-de-brasileiros-de-volta-a-pobreza-diz-estudo.htm.

Urry, John. *The Tourist Gaze*. 2nd ed. London: Sage, 2002.

Urry, John, and Jonas Larsen. *The Tourist Gaze 3.0*. London: Sage, 2011.

Van Den Berghe, Pierre. *The Quest for the Other: Ethnic Tourism in San Cristobal, Mexico*. Seattle: University of Washington Press, 1994.

Veijola, Soile, and Eeva Jokinen. "The Body in Tourism." *Theory, Culture & Society* 11 (1994): 125–151.

Vianna, Hermano. *The Mystery of Samba: Popular Music and National Identity in Brazil*. Chapel Hill: University of North Carolina Press, 1999.

Viver Bahia. "Carta dos Editores." 1, no. 1 (2007).

———. "Herança Viva da Escravidão." 1, no. 4 (2007): 35.

———. "O Pai do Prazer, Filho da Dor." 1, no. 4 (2007): 48–50.

———. "Rainhas Negras nas Ruas de Cachoeira. Irmandade de Nossa Senhora da Boa Morte." 1, no. 1 (2007): 18–22.

———. "Salvador Cidade da Bahia. Aqui Tudo é Diferente." 1, no. 1 (2007): 26–27.

Von Eschen, Penny M. *Race against Empire: Black Americans and Anticolonialism, 1937–1957*. Ithaca, NY: Cornell University Press, 1997.

Wacquant, Loic. *Punishing the Poor: The Neoliberal Government of Social Insecurity*. Durham, NC: Duke University Press, 2009.

Walker, Sheila. "Africanity vs Blackness: Race, Class and Culture in Brazil." *NACLA, Report on the Americas*, vol. 35, pt. 3, May–June 2002.

Wallerstein, Immanuel. *World-Systems Analysis: An Introduction*. Durham, NC: Duke University Press, 2004.

Whitaker, Charles. "Blacks in Brazil: The Myth and the Reality." *Ebony*, February 1991, 60–64.

White, Evelyn. "Black Pride, Brazilian Style." *Essence* 28, no. 10 (1998): 160–161.

White, James E., and Jean-Gontram Quenum. *Roots Recovered!: The How to Guide for Tracing African-American and West Indian Roots Back to Africa and Going There for Free or on a Shoestring Budget*. Booklocker.com, 2004.

Wilkerson, Isabel, and Nicole Saun. "God Is Working on Me." *Essence* 34, no. 3 (2003): 120–129.

Williams, Erica L. *Sex Tourism in Bahia: Ambiguous Entanglements*. Urbana: University of Illinois Press, 2013.

Williams, Raymond. *The Long Revolution*. New York: Columbia University Press, 1961.

Willis, Paul. *Learning to Labor: How Working Class Kids Get Working Class Jobs*. New York: Columbia University Press, 1981.

Woods, Jewel, and Karen Hunter. *Don't Blame It on Rio: The Real Deal Behind Why Men Go to Brazil for Sex*. New York: Grand Central Publishing, 2008.

World Tourism Organization. *Annual Report 2011*. Madrid: UNWTO, 2012.

Wright, Donald R. *The World and a Very Small Place in Africa: A History of Globalization in Niumi, the Gambia*. Armonk, NY: M. E. Sharpe, 2004.

———. "Uprooting Kunta Kinte: On the Perils of Relying on Encyclopedic Informants." *History in Africa* 8 (1981): 205–217.

Wright, Richard. *Black Power. A Record of Reactions in a Land of Pathos*. Westport, CT: Greenwood Press, [1954] 1974.

Brochures, Flyers, and Documents

Bahia, Secretaria de Turismo. "Bahia: A Maior Expressão da Cultura Afro no Brasil./The Deepest Expression of African Culture in Brazil."

Câmara dos Deputados, Bahia. "Aposta no turismo étnico com mais investimento." August 25, 2008. http://www2.camara.leg.br/atividade-legislativa/comissoes/comissoes-permanentes/ctur/noticias/aposta-no-turismo-etnico-com-mais-investimento.

Conference flyer, New World Festival of the African Diaspora, 1978.

Informação para o senhor presidente da república. "Festival de Arte e Cultura Afro-Americana no Brasil." June 19, 1978, CPDOC/FGV, Arquivo Geisel, pasta: 1975/EG pr 1974.03.00/2.

SECOM, Bahia. "Turismo Étnico Afro." July 27, 2009. http://www.secom.ba.gov.br/2009/07/90540/Assinatura-de-Ordem-de-Servico-para-Implantacao-de-Sinalizacao-Turistica-no-Litoral-Sul-Baiano.html.

U.S. Department of State, Archive. "Remarks with President of Neoenergia Marcelo Correa and Governor of da Bahia Jacques Wagner." Secretary Condoleezza Rice, Salvador da Bahia, Brazil, March 14, 2008. https://20012009.state.gov/secretary/rm/2008/03/102280.htm.

Videos

Brewer, Michael. *Bahia: Africa in the Americas*. Los Angeles: Brewer Media Associates, 2006.

Capai, Eliza. *#Resistência*. 2017.

Frustrated: Black American Men in Brazil. Accessed February 20, 2014. http://www.youtube.com/watch?v= BOjvPOBvd9A.

Gates Jr., Henry Louis. *Black in Latin America–Brazil: A Racial Paradise*. PBS, 2011.

———. *Wonders of the African World*. Produced by Wall to Wall Television for BBC and PBS, 2003.

Harris, Thomas Allen. *That's My Face/É Minha Cara*. Brooklyn, NY: Chimpanzee Productions, 2001.

Obama, Barack. Interview with CNN's Anderson Cooper on July 15, 2009. http://www.youtube.com/watch?v= bRMEr-J6hXY.

O'Rourke, Dennis. *Cannibal Tours*. Santa Monica, CA: Direct Cinema Ltd., 1987.

Varig Airlines. *Brazil, a Celebration of Life*. Directed by Bernard Wasserman, 1992.

Index